AUTOMATION AND CONTROL TRENDS

Edited by **Pedro Ponce, Arturo Molina Gutiérrez** and **Luis M. Ibarra**

Automation and Control Trends
http://dx.doi.org/10.5772/61646
Edited by Pedro Ponce, Arturo Molina Gutiérrez and Luis M. Ibarra

Contributors

Romulus Lungu, Saul Tovar-Arriaga, Jose Emilio Vargas-Soto, Efren Gorrostieta-Hurtado, Jesus Carlos Pedraza-Ortega, Juan-Manuel Ramos-Arreguin, Jonathan Marcello Pinto, Ian Gomes, Pedro Luiz da C. Saldanha, Eustério Furieri, Paulo Frutuoso e Melo, Mitja Košir, Enrique Del Sol Acero, Takahito Osawa, David Balderas Silva, Mario Rojas, Edgar Omar Lopez-Caudana, César Daniel González Gutiérrez

CBS, Edition **2018**

Published by InTech

Janeza Trdine 9, 51000 Rijeka, Croatia

Publishing Process Manager Iva Simčić

Technical Editor SPi Global

Cover Designer InTech Design Team

Additional hard copies can be obtained from orders@intechopen.com

Automation and Control Trends , Edited by Pedro Ponce, Arturo Molina Gutiérrez and Luis M. Ibarra
p. cm.
Print ISBN 978-953-51-2670-6
Online ISBN 978-953-51-2671-3

INTECH

open science | open minds

Contents

Preface

Engineering, on its most general sense, points to the continuous improvement of processes from very simple to complex ones. Any engineering branch will follow specific scientific methodologies, enabling in this way, the attainment of reliable results. Briefly, one can say engineering is a purposeful use of science, focusing directly on the betterment of life quality.

In the same spirit, control engineers must bring forward all kinds of solutions to subject the physical magnitudes involved in our daily lives: energy generation and consumption, precise manufacturing, water supply, etc. As the adequacy of the medium becomes more evident, the control objectives grow in ambition so the controlled systems are then required to be, namely, robust, optimal, adaptable, and dependable, among others.

A more modern perspective incorporates artificial intelligence to control and automation systems, trying to enhance more subjective (or difficult) processes. In this way, the variables to control are not direct anymore and the desired reference signals to follow come from large sets of data or almost indecipherable brain signals. These new control objectives require the integration of traditional basis together with modern techniques in order to fulfill the required specifications.

In addition to the increased complexity of the systems to face, the environmental, economical, and innovative current areas of opportunity have led to new proposals and obstacles, so forcing the control and automation engineering horizon to diversify. This makes the theoretical approaches, specific applications, normative analysis, and novel ideas to coexist under a common label. This book exhibits an intent to bring such different perspectives into a single volume, providing brief examples of aforementioned areas, which could not be normally grouped under a traditional point of view.

A broader perspective could help control engineers propose the required solutions to those demanding issues. Current problems can be tackled through inclusive techniques or having each problem isolated and solved in particular. On the other hand, being aware of those different paths that converge to a common complex problem could facilitate the formulation of a comprehensive solution, which could be later expanded or incorporated by new research.

The diversity around a common issue will forcefully help each individual to understand, improve, analyze, or fully tackle a problem. The interaction between individual paths has only one outcome, which is to move faster toward a complete result. In the light of a new era of control and automation engineering, isolated problems should be placed within their full context, enhancing the separate technical potentials of collaborative, not competing, diverse endeavors.

Pedro Ponce, Arturo Molina Gutiérrez and Luis M. Ibarra
Escuela de Posgrado en Ingeniería
Tecnológico de Monterrey,
Campus Ciudad de México, RZMCM,
Mexico

Chapter 1

New Strategy to Approach the Inverse Kinematics Model for Manipulators with Rotational Joints

José-Emilio Vargas-Soto, Efren Gorrostieta-Hurtado,
Saúl Tovar-Arriaga,
Jesús-Carlos Pedraza-Ortega and
Juan-Manuel Ramos-Arreguín

Additional information is available at the end of the chapter

http://dx.doi.org/10.5772/63541

Abstract

The chapter describes a new strategy to approach the solution of the inverse kinematics problem for robot manipulators. A method to determine a polynomial model approximation for the joints positions is described by applying the divided differences with a new point of view for lineal path in the end-effector of the robot manipulator. Results of the mathematical approach are analysed by obtaining the kinematics inverse model and the approximate model for lineal trajectories of a manipulator for three degrees of freedom. Finally, future research approaches are commented.

Keywords: inverse kinematics approach

1. Introduction

The modeling of robot manipulators with rotational joints has been extensively studied for decades. A robot manipulator is formed from the mechanical point of view by a kinematic chain of rigid bodies (links) which are joined together by linear or rotational joints. The modeling of the kinematics for a robot manipulator allows us to analyze the movements of the end-effector in order to perform a specific task.

To determine the kinematics model for a robot manipulator, conventionally there are two types of analysis, the first is called "Direct Kinematics Problem" and the second analysis is "Inverse Kinematics Problem." Depending on what is required for a specific task in the manipulator, different mathematical models can be used to control the behavior of a wide variety of robot manipulators [1–3]. The Direct Kinematics Problem determines the position of the end-effector of the robot manipulator as a function of the degrees of freedom (joint), wherein each degree of freedom is an independent movement in the mechanical structure of the robot manipulator. In contrast, the Inverse Kinematics Problem is oriented to determine the variation of the degrees of freedom of the manipulator according to the kinematics of the end-effector of the robot manipulator. This last situation is usually more complex from the point of view of mathematical modeling and its solution, given the high nonlinearity of behavior of the robot manipulators. A further disadvantage of conventional models of the Inverse Kinematics Problem is called redundancy. This happens when more than one solution is obtained by the mathematical model of the robot manipulator, causing theoretical configurations that do not occur in practical movements of an industrial manipulator. Additionally, another problem that occurs in the analysis of manipulators is when matrices for translations and rotations are used in the modeling. There is the possibility that this inverse matrix shows singular points, causing undefined mathematical solutions. Translations and rotations are essentials to solve the Kinematics Inverse Problem, to do that, auxiliary reference systems are used to refer the kinematics of the end-effector in the reference inertial system. In this regard, this chapter shows a new strategy to solve the Inverse Kinematics Problem for manipulators with rotational joints by approximating with cubic polynomial functions that define the positions of the joints.

2. Solutions for the Inverse Kinematics Problem

One of the first methods developed to solve the inverse kinematics for manipulator is by "Algebraic Method". In general, the algebraic methods are obtained by vector equations that respond to the links geometry of the manipulator. By this way, trigonometric relationships and algebraic equations are obtained to get mathematical functions that determine the behavior of the degrees of freedom in the manipulator [4–6]. It might be supposed that this method is the most effective however; it presents mathematical uncertainties, inconsistencies, and considerable complexity.

Another method developed to determine inverse kinematics is by spatial geometry. This method is based on the decomposition of the spatial geometry of the manipulator in planar geometric systems. For many serial or parallel manipulators, this decomposition is simple when the axes of consecutive degrees of freedom present changes as 0°, 90°, and 270°. However, it is not always the case, so this method cannot always be applied. The inverse kinematics of each degree of freedom usually has more than one solution. Also, given the trigonometric relationships of mathematical models obtained, they cannot always be solved because it is more complex to obtain an exact solution for a greater number of degrees of freedom [7, 8].

One of the most used alternative to solve the inverse kinematics of robot manipulators is based on Newton methods. These algorithms seek target configurations which posed as solutions to minimization problem [9]. Due to extreme complexity, these methods are known to be less practical. There are also methods based on statistical filtering [10] and sequential iterative approaches [11]. However, these statistical methods suffer high computational cost.

Research about the use of polynomial functions with some relationships with the inverse kinematics problem for manipulators is not new. However, some of the applications are oriented to trajectory planning [12], and also to solve the inverse kinematics problem by polynomial of n-degrees by using genetic algorithms [13, 14].

This work presents a novel approach to the inverse kinematic problem by cubic polynomial functions which are built under the definition of new parameters and the divided differences recursive method. The present approach is different to other strategies to get a solution for inverse kinematics problem. The benefits of the proposed method are essentially the simplicity to obtain a polynomial function for rotational joints that solve the inverse kinematics problem (position, speed, and acceleration), and the warranty to get a unique solution with no singularities. However, as many of the mathematical models that attempt to describe a real physical phenomenon, the method has several restrictions: bi-dimensional work space, the end-effector paths are straight lines, two joints are free and a third joint have fixed orientation, and four points of the path trajectory are needed.

3. The method of divided differences

From the mathematics point of view, the divided differences is a recursive division process of increments. The method can be used to calculate the coefficients in the interpolation polynomial in the Newton form when data points (x_i, y_i) are known, where i is an integer ranging from 0 to (n−1) and n is the number of points.

By definition, it is called divided difference of f in the points (x_i, y_i) to the value $f[x_0, x_1, x_2, .., x_k]$ which is calculated recursively by these equations [15]:

$$f[x_i] = f(x_i) = y_i \quad (1)$$

$$f[x_i, x_{i+1}] = \frac{f[x_{i+1}] - f[x_i]}{x_{i+1} - x_i} \quad (2)$$

$$f[x_i, x_{i+1}, \ldots, x_{i+k}] = \frac{f[x_{i+1}, x_{i+2}, .., x_{i+k}] - f[x_i, x_{i+1}, .., x_{i+k-1}]}{x_{i+k} - x_i} \quad (3)$$

To properly apply the method, it is essential to order in a table the values corresponding to the points (x_i, y_i), so that the x_i column is sorted from the highest to lowest number, or vice versa. Considering an approach with four known points, the divided differences are defined as shown in **Figure 1**:

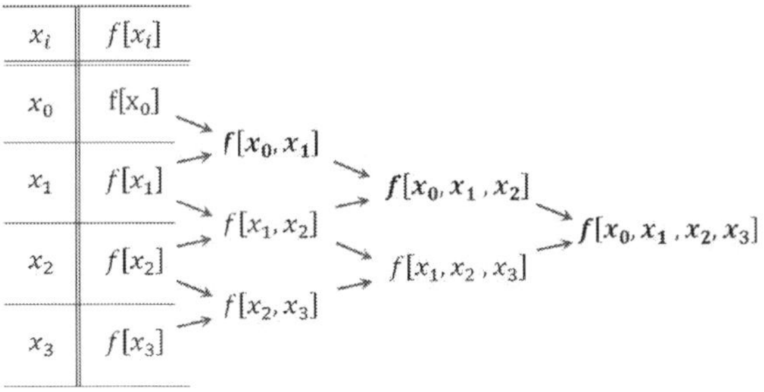

Figure 1. Sequence of Divided Differences to four points.

Such polynomial function f(x) is determined as:

$$
\begin{aligned}
f(x) = {} & f[x_0] + f[x_0, x_1](x - x_0) + f[x_0, x_1, x_2](x - x_0)(x - x_1) \\
& + f[x_0, x_1, x_2, x_3](x - x_0)(x - x_1)(x - x_2)
\end{aligned}
\tag{4}
$$

or expressed in the reduced form:

$$
f(x) = f[x_0] + \sum_{i=1}^{n-1} \left(f[x_0,, x_i] * \prod_{j}^{i-1} (x - x_j) \right) \tag{5}
$$

4. Polynomial approach strategy

A new feature in the mathematical development shown in this work is to adapt the method of divided differences to approximate the functions that define the changes of the rotational joints θ_{1i} y θ_{2i}. For the approximation by polynomials, a table of four points known of the manipulator robot is formed; then the polynomial approach strategy can be applied. It is important to mention that for the analysis developed in this work, it is considered a robot manipulator with three rotational joints.

Point *i*	x_i	y_i	θ_{1i}	θ_{2i}	θ_{3i}
1	x_1	y_1	θ_{11}	θ_{21}	θ_{31}
2	x_2	y_2	θ_{12}	θ_{22}	θ_{32}
3	x_3	y_3	θ_{13}	θ_{23}	θ_{33}
4	x_4	y_4	θ_{14}	θ_{24}	θ_{34}

Table 1. Known values of the four positions of the manipulator.

Before showing how to construct polynomials, it is relevant to note that the movement of the end-effector of the robot manipulator performs a linear motion by keeping constant the orientation of the end-effector (θ_3). In the case of analysis shown in the X-Y coordinate plane, the positions changes occur in both coordinates. In this case, proportionality of change of θ_1 and θ_2 will be done considering the changes of x with respect to y. This is because both coordinates participate proportionally varying θ_1 and θ_2. To this end, we have defined two new indices denominated: incidence factor of x, and incidence factor of y. Both indices respond to the model of linear proportionality by the following equations:

$$\theta_1 = (\textit{Incidence factor of } x)\theta_1 + (\textit{incidence factor of } y)\theta_1 \tag{6}$$

$$\theta_2 = (\textit{incidence factor of } x)\theta_2 + (\textit{incidence factor of } y)\theta_2 \tag{7}$$

Taking into account that the sum of the percentages of both coordinates is 100%, the incidence factor of y in θ (in percentage) is determined as:

$$\%\ of\ y = 100\% - \%\ of\ x \tag{8}$$

For example, for the line defined by the equation y = x, the proportionality of the change is the same for both coordinates, so the variation of the x coordinate has a 50% incidence in the changes of θ_1 and θ_2. Similarly, the variation of the y-coordinate has a 50% incidence in the changes of θ_1 and θ_2.

The determination % of x is obtained by the value of the slope of the straight line m, the incidence factor of x in θ (percentage) is calculated using the following equation:

$$\%of\ x = \frac{100}{1+|m|} \tag{9}$$

The absolute value of m is obtained because it is only of our interest to obtain the proportionality of the changes of the angles θ_1 and θ_2 as a function of lineal movements. So that,

$$\theta_1 = \theta_1(x,y) = \left(\frac{\%of\ x}{100\%}\right)\theta_1 + \left(\frac{\%of\ y}{100\%}\right)\theta_1 \tag{10}$$

similarly,

$$\theta_2 = \theta_2(x,y) = \left(\frac{\%of\ x}{100\%}\right)\theta_2 + \left(\frac{\%of\ y}{100\%}\right)\theta_2 \tag{11}$$

The tables to determine the polynomials that approximate the behavior of the angle θ_1 are built based on the new approach strategy presented here, remaining as:

i	$\mathbf{X}_i$	$\left(\frac{\%\ of\ x_i}{100\%}\right)\theta_{1i}$
1	x_1	$\left(\frac{\%\ of\ x_1}{100\%}\right)\theta_{11}$
2	x_2	$\left(\frac{\%\ of\ x_2}{100\%}\right)\theta_{12}$
3	x_3	$\left(\frac{\%\ of\ x_3}{100\%}\right)\theta_{13}$
4	x_4	$\left(\frac{\%\ of\ x_4}{100\%}\right)\theta_{14}$

Table 2. x vs. influence of x in θ_1.

i	$\mathbf{Y}_i$	$\left(\frac{\%\ of\ y_i}{100\%}\right)\theta_{1i}$
1	y_1	$\left(\frac{\%\ of\ y_1}{100\%}\right)\theta_{11}$
2	y_2	$\left(\frac{\%\ of\ y_2}{100\%}\right)\theta_{12}$
3	y_3	$\left(\frac{\%\ of\ y_3}{100\%}\right)\theta_{13}$
4	y_4	$\left(\frac{\%\ of\ y_4}{100\%}\right)\theta_{14}$

Table 3. y vs. influence of y in θ_1.

In a similar way,

http://dx.doi.org/10.5772/63541

I	X_i	$\left(\frac{\%\ of\ x_i}{100\%}\right)\theta_{2i}$
1	x_1	$\left(\frac{\%\ of\ x_1}{100\%}\right)\theta_{21}$
2	x_2	$\left(\frac{\%\ of\ x_2}{100\%}\right)\theta_{22}$
3	x_3	$\left(\frac{\%\ of\ x_3}{100\%}\right)\theta_{23}$
4	x_4	$\left(\frac{\%\ of\ x_4}{100\%}\right)\theta_{24}$

Table 4. x vs. influence of x in θ_2.

i	Y_i	$\left(\frac{\%\ of\ y_i}{100\%}\right)\theta_{2i}$
1	y_1	$\left(\frac{\%\ of\ y_1}{100\%}\right)\theta_{21}$
2	y_2	$\left(\frac{\%\ of\ y_2}{100\%}\right)\theta_{22}$
3	y_3	$\left(\frac{\%\ of\ y_3}{100\%}\right)\theta_{23}$
4	y_4	$\left(\frac{\%\ of\ y_4}{100\%}\right)\theta_{24}$

Table 5. y vs. influence of y in θ_2.

One of the contributions of the strategy presented here is the composition of polynomial functions of the joints of the robot manipulator θ_1 and θ_2, both as independent functions of "x" and "y". These compositions are defined as the following equations:

$$\theta_1(x,y) = \left(a_0 + a_1x + a_2x^2 + a_3x^3\right) + \left(b_0 + b_1y + b_2y^2 + b_3y^3\right) \tag{12}$$

$$\theta_2(x,y) = \left(c_0 + c_1x + c_2x^2 + c_3x^3\right) + \left(d_0 + d_1y + d_2y^2 + d_3y^3\right) \tag{13}$$

where a_i, b_i are coefficients obtained from **Tables 2** and **3**, and the coefficients c_i, d_i are obtained by **Table 4** respectively. Thus, divided differences are shown in **Figure 2**.

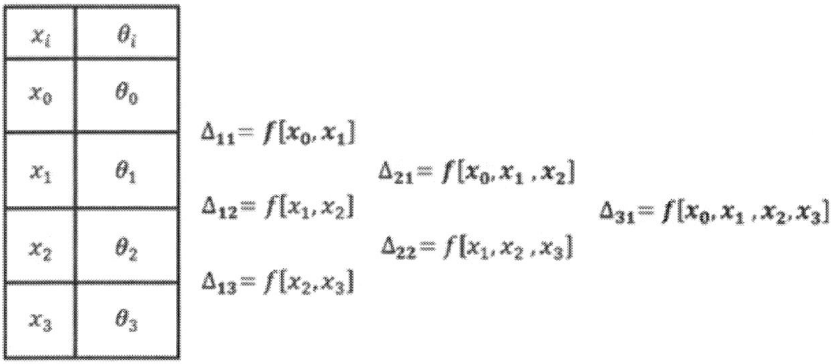

Figure 2. The Divided Differences of x vs. θ_i for four points.

where,

$$\Delta_{11} = \frac{\theta_1 - \theta_0}{x_1 - x_0} \tag{14}$$

$$\Delta_{12} = \frac{\theta_2 - \theta_1}{x_2 - x_1} \tag{15}$$

$$\Delta_{13} = \frac{\theta_3 - \theta_2}{x_3 - x_2} \tag{16}$$

$$\Delta_{21} = \frac{\Delta_{12} - \Delta_{11}}{x_2 - x_0} \tag{17}$$

$$\Delta_{22} = \frac{\Delta_{13} - \Delta_{12}}{x_3 - x_1} \tag{18}$$

$$\Delta_{31} = \frac{\Delta_{22} - \Delta_{21}}{x_3 - x_0} \tag{19}$$

developing the general equation,

$$\vartheta(x) = \vartheta[x_0] + \sum_{i=1}^{n-1}\left(\vartheta[x_0,,x_i] \times \prod_{j}^{i-1}(x - x_j)\right) \tag{20}$$

This equation allows us to obtain the model of the polynomial that approximates the angular position θ with respect to the variable x.

$$\vartheta(x) = f[x_0] + \Delta_{11}(x - x_0) + \Delta_{21}(x - x_0)(x - x_1) + \Delta_{31}(x - x_0)(x - x_1)(x - x_2) \tag{21}$$

In developing this equation and simplifying results,

$$\begin{aligned}\theta(x) = &(\theta_0 - \Delta_{11} + \Delta_{21}x_0x_1 - \Delta_{31}x_0x_1x_2) + \\ &\left[\Delta_{11} + \Delta_{21}(-x_1 - x_0) + \Delta_{31}(x_0x_1 + x_2(x_1 + x_0))\right]\boldsymbol{x} \\ &+\left[\Delta_{21} + \Delta_{21}(-x_2 - x_1 - x_0)\right]\boldsymbol{x}^2 + \Delta_{31}\boldsymbol{x}^3\end{aligned} \tag{22}$$

Similarly, the polynomial θ(y) is obtained, which has the following form:

$$\begin{aligned}\theta(y) = &(\theta_0 - \Delta_{11} + \Delta_{21}y_0y_1 - \Delta_{31}y_0y_1y_2) + \\ &\left[\Delta_{11} + \Delta_{21}(-y_1 - y_0) + \Delta_{31}(y_0y_1 + y_2(y_1 + y_0))\right]\boldsymbol{y} \\ &+\left[\Delta_{21} + \Delta_{21}(-y_2 - y_1 - y_0)\right]\boldsymbol{y}^2 + \Delta_{31}\boldsymbol{y}^3\end{aligned} \tag{23}$$

Clearly, the differences divided for this equation refers to the rate of change of the θ with respect to y, being defined by the polynomial approximation model of joint θ_1 and θ_2 of the robot manipulator, which in simplified form are expressed as:

$$\theta_1(x, y) = \theta_1(x) + \theta_1(y) \tag{24}$$

$$\theta_2(x, y) = \theta_2(x) + \theta_2(y) \tag{25}$$

5. Development of the approach by polynomials

In this section, the strategy proposed to approach the Kinematics Inverse Problem by polynomial functions of the rotational joints of a robot manipulator is shown. The procedures to three different cases of lineal path in the end-effector are analysed: a) slope of a straight line, m = 1, b) slope of a straight line, m < 1 and c) slope of a straight line, m > 1. To show the procedures, it is important to describe the mechanical configuration of the robot manipulator that is shown in **Figure 3**.

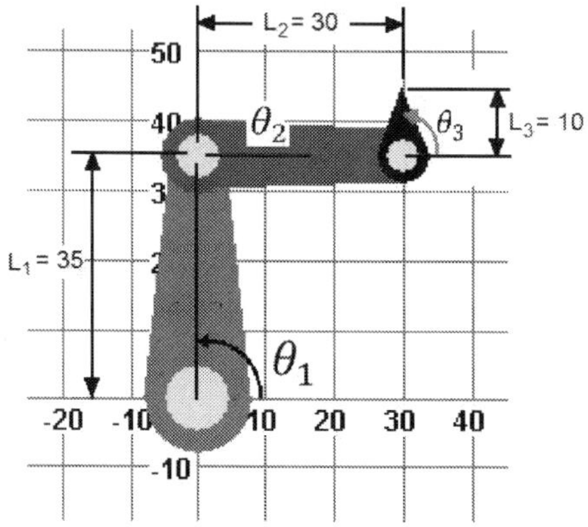

Figure 3. Configuration of the robot manipulator, Θ_1=90°, Θ_2=0°, Θ_3=90°.

The three degrees of freedom that are considered known in the plane of the robot manipulator moves are (x, y, θ_3). The link in the base of the robot manipulator is 35 units of effective length, the second link is 30 units of length, and third link is 10 units of length. The orientation of the end-effector is considered constant during the lineal movements.

Remembering that the procedure exposes that four positions of the configuration robot are known, the approach by polynomial function are described in the next lines:

a) Case 1. Slope of a straight line, m = 1.

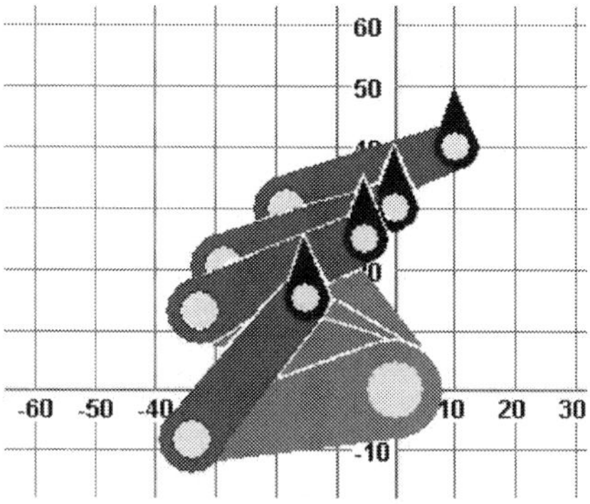

Figure 4. The four Robot positions, slope = 1.

In order to show the effectiveness of the developed strategy, the movement of the end-effector of the robot manipulator was selected by considering that the maximum length of the lineal trajectory is close to the effective length of link 1. For this case, the orientation of the end-effector is 90° and is keeping constant during its moves. Under these considerations, **Figure 4** shows the selected lineal trajectory.

The values of the four known positions of the robot manipulator are shown in **Table 6**.

x	y	Θ_1 [°]	Θ_2 [°]	Θ_3 [°]
−15	25	193.51°	50.58°	90°
−5	35	158.15°	23.53°	90°
0	40	144.28°	18.59°	90°
10	50	121.37°	19.71°	90°

Table 6. The four known positions of the lineal trajectory.

The incidence factor of x in θ, according to Eq. (9) and the value of the slope of a straight line is calculated as:

$$\%of\ x = \frac{100}{1+|m|} = \frac{100}{1+|1|}\frac{100}{2} = 50 \tag{26}$$

Then, from Eq. (8) the incidence factor of y in θ takes the next value:

$$\%of\ y = 100\% - \%ofx = 100 - 50 = 50 \tag{27}$$

Considering both factors, the tables to obtain the polynomial functions for the joint θ_1 are defined as:

i	X_i	θ_{1i} (x)
1	*−15*	96.755
2	−5	79.075
3	*0*	72.14
4	*10*	60.685

Table 7. x vs. incidence of x in θ_1.

i	Y_i	θ_{1i} (y)
1	25	96.755
2	35	79.075
3	40	72.14
4	50	60.685

Table 8. y vs. incidence of y in θ_1.

The polynomial approach of **Table 7** is determined by the divided differences according to Eqs. (14) to (19). In this way, next table shows the values obtained:

X_i	θ_{1i} (x)	Δ_{1i}	Δ_{2i}	Δ_{3i}
−15	**96.755**	**−1.768**	**0.0254**	**−0.000372**
−5	79.075	−1.387	0.0161	
0	72.14	−1.1455		
10	60.685			

Table 9. Values of the divided differences for $\theta_1(x)$.

Applying Eq. (22) and simplifying results:

$$\theta_1(x) = 72.14 - 1.2879\ x + 0.0179x^2 - 0.000372\ x^3 \tag{28}$$

This polynomial function represents the incidence of x in joint of θ_1. To complete the approach, it is also necessary to add the incidence of y in the same joint of θ_1. So the polynomial approach from **Table 8** is obtained by applying Eqs. (14) to (19).

Y_i	θ_{1i} (y)	Δ_{1i}	Δ_{2i}	Δ_{3i}
25	**96.755**	**−1.768**	**0.0254**	**−0.000372**
35	79.075	−1.387	0.0161	
40	72.14	−1.1455		
50	60.685			

Table 10. Values of the divided differences for $\theta_1(y)$.

Applying Eq. (23) and simplifying it gives:

$$\theta_1(y) = 176.2 - 4.5103y + 0.0626y^2 - 0.000372y^3 \quad (29)$$

According to Eq. (24) the complete function approximation of θ_1 becomes:

$$\theta_1(x, y) = 248.34 - 1.2879\ x + 0.0179\ x^2 - 0.000372\ x^3 - 4.5103\ y + 0.0626\ y^2 - 0.000372\ y^3 \quad (30)$$

The next step is to obtain the function approximation of $\theta_2(x)$. According to the above procedure, the differences divided for **Table 8** to get the polynomial approximation with respect of x takes the form:

X_i	θ_{2i} (x)	Δ_{1i}	Δ_{2i}	Δ_{3i}
−15	**25.29**	**−1.3525**	**0.05723**	**−0.0008267**
−15	11.765	−0.494	0.0366	
0	9.295	0.056		
10	9.855			

Table 11. Values of the divided differences for $\theta_2(x)$.

Applying Eq. (22) and simplifying it gives:

$$\theta_2(x) = 9.295 - 0.26953\ x + 0.04078\ x^2 - 0.00082267\ x^3 \quad (31)$$

Similarly, the divided differences of **Table 8** to get the polynomial approximation for $\theta_2(y)$ takes the form:

Y_i	θ_{2i} (y)	Δ_{1i}	Δ_{2i}	Δ_{3i}
25	**25.29**	**−1.3525**	**0.05723**	**−0.0008267**
35	11.765	−0.494	0.0366	
40	9.295	0.056		
50	9.855			

Table 12. The divided differences values for $\theta_2(y)$.

Applying Eq. (23) and simplifying it gives:

$$\theta_2(y) = 137.975 - 7.48073\ y + 0.1395\ y^2 - 0.00082267\ y^3 \quad (32)$$

According to Eq. (25) the complete function approximation of θ_2 becomes:

$$\begin{aligned}\theta_2(x,y) = 147.27 - 0.26953x + 0.04078x^2 - 0.00082267x^3 \\ -7.48073y + 0.1395y^2 - 0.00082267y^3\end{aligned} \tag{33}$$

Obtaining result from the complete approximation by polynomials θ_1 and θ_2:

$$\begin{aligned}\theta_1(x,y) = 248.34 - 1.2879x + 0.0179x^2 - 0.000372x^3 \\ -4.5103y + 0.0626y^2 - 0.000372y^3\end{aligned} \tag{34}$$

$$\begin{aligned}\theta_2(x,y) = 147.27 - 0.26953x + 0.04078x^2 - 0.00082267x^3 \\ -7.48073y + 0.1395y^2 - 0.00082267y^3\end{aligned} \tag{35}$$

$$\forall x \in (-15,10); \forall y \in (25,50)$$

After obtaining the desired approach, the next step is to check the positions of the end-effector of the robot manipulator in order to verify that a lineal trajectory is made. According to the Direct Kinematics Model of the robot manipulator, the approximate position of the end-effector is determined by:

$$\begin{bmatrix} x_{aprox} \\ y_{aprox} \end{bmatrix} = \begin{bmatrix} L_1 \cos\theta_1(X,Y) + L_2 \cos\theta_2(X,Y) + L_3 \cos\theta_3 \\ L_1 \sin\theta_1(X,Y) + L_2 \sin\theta_2(X,Y) + L_3 \sin\theta_3 \end{bmatrix} \tag{36}$$

Remembering that $L_1 = 35$, $L_2 = 30$, $L_3 = 10$ y $\theta_3 = 90°$, the Eq. (36) is evaluated in the range $x \in (-15, 50)$ where $y(x) = x + 40$. Considering an increment $\Delta x = 2.5$, the following table is obtained:

x	y	$\Theta_1(x,y)$ [°]	$\Theta_2(x,y)$ [°]	x_{approx}	y_{approx}
−15	25	193.497	50.580	−14.983	25.007
−12.5	27.5	183.534	41.286	−12.391	27.637
−10	30	174.368	33.782	-9.896	30.116
-7.5	32.5	165.930	27.915	-7.441	32.554
-5	35	158.149	23.530	-4.980	35.004
-2.5	37.5	150.955	20.473	-2.493	37.485
0	40	144.280	18.590	0.019	39.998

x	y	$\Theta_1(x,y)$ [°]	$\Theta_2(x,y)$ [°]	x_{approx}	y_{approx}
2.5	42.5	138.053	17.726	2.544	42.530
5	45	132.205	17.728	5.063	45.061
7.5	47.5	126.665	18.440	7.560	47.565
10	50	121.364	19.710	10.026	50.003

Table 13. Values of θ_1, θ_2, x_{approx} and y_{approx}.

In order to ensure the validity of the polynomial function, the Error of x, Error of y, and Error(x, y) are calculated by the next equations:

$$Error\ of\ x = x - x_{aprox} \tag{37}$$

$$Error\ of\ y = y - y_{aprox} \tag{38}$$

$$Error(x,y) = \sqrt{(x - x_{aprox})^2 + (y - y_{aprox})^2} \tag{39}$$

Getting the following table for the values of **Table 13**:

x	y	Error of x	Error of y	Error (x, y)
−15	25	−0.017	−0.007	0.0179
−12.5	**27.5**	**−0.109**	**−0.137**	**0.1754**
−10	30	−0.104	−0.116	0.1555
−7.5	32.5	−0.059	−0.054	0.0801
−5	35	−0.020	−0.004	0.0206
−2.5	37.5	−0.007	0.015	0.0161
0	40	−0.019	0.002	0.0190
2.5	42.5	−0.044	−0.030	0.0529
5	45	−0.063	−0.061	0.0879
7.5	47.5	−0.060	−0.065	0.0881

Table 14. Errors of the polynomial approach.

The error of interest is the maximum error, in this case the maximum error is 0.1754 units and occurs in the point (−12.5, 27.5). The percentage of maximum error is determined by the following equation:

$$\% \; Maximum \, error = \frac{|Maximum \, error(x,y)|}{\sqrt{(x_f - x_i)^2 + (y_f - y_i)^2}} \times 100 \tag{40}$$

where (x_i, y_i) are the coordinates of the starting point and (x_f, y_f) are the coordinates of the endpoint. That is, for an error rate, the maximum error is compared with the path length. Substituting values in Eq. (40), it gives:

$$\% \; Maximum \; error = \frac{|0.1754|}{\sqrt{(10-(-15))^2 + (50-25)^2}} \times 100 = \mathbf{0.496\%} \tag{41}$$

Considering that this value is acceptable, Eqs. (34) and (35) can be used to do a lineal trajectory in the end-effector of the robot manipulator.

b) Case 2. Slope of a straight line, m < 1.

Similarly, as in the previous case, the end-effector of the robot manipulator makes a lineal path, which is shown in **Figure 5**. In this case it is considered θ_3 as a constant, with the value of 45°.

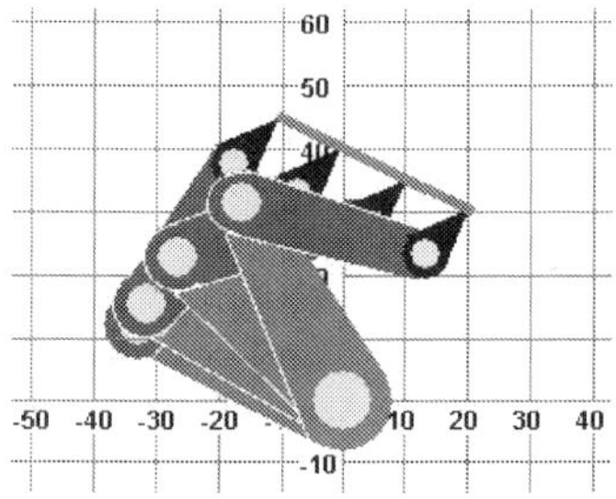

Figure 5. The four Robot positions, negative slope.

For this case, the values of four known positions of the manipulator robot are shown in the following table.

x	y	Θ_1[°]	Θ_2[°]	Θ_3[°]
−10	45	159.34	58.46	45
0	40	153.87	35.69	45
10	35	139.48	9.94	45
20	30	117.01	-15.99	45

Table 15. Four known positions of the manipulator, negative slope.

http://dx.doi.org/10.5772/63541

The four known positions correspond to the linear relationship y = −0.5 x + 40. Considering that slope: m = −0.5, the incidence factors can be calculated by the (8) and (9) equations, like this:

$$\% \, of \, x = \frac{100}{1+|m|} = \frac{100}{1+|-0.5|} = \frac{100}{1.5} = 66.66 \tag{42}$$

$$\% \, of \, y = 100\% - \%dex = 100 - 66.66 = 33.34 \tag{43}$$

According to the presented strategy, the incidence table to approximate polynomial functions θ_1 takes the next form:

i	x_i	$\theta_{1i}(x)$ [°]
1	−10	106.216
2	0	102.569
3	10	92.977
4	20	77.998

Table 16. x vs. incidence of x in θ_1.

i	y_i	θ_{1i} (y) [°]
1	45	53.108
2	40	51.284
3	35	46.488
4	30	38.999

Table 17. y vs. incidence of y in θ_1.

Calculating the polynomial approximation to $\theta_1(x)$, the next table is obtained:

X_i	θ_{1i} (x)	Δ_{1i}	Δ_{2i}	Δ_{3i}
−10	**106.2165**	**−0.3647**	**−0.029725**	**9.3×10^{-5}**
0	102.569	−0.9592	−0.026935	
10	92.977	−1.4979		
20	77.998			

Table 18. Divided differences values for $\theta_1(x)$.

Applying Eq. (22) and simplifying it gives:

$$\theta_1(x) = 102.569 - 0.67125x - 0.029725x^2 + 9.3\times10^{-5}x^3 \tag{44}$$

Likewise,

Y_i	θ_{1i} (y)	Δ_{1i}	Δ_{2i}	Δ_{3i}
45	53.108	**−0.3648**	**−0.05944**	**−0.000372**
40	51.284	0.9592	−0.05386	
35	46.488	1.4978		
30	38.999			

Table 19. Divided differences values for $\theta_1(y)$.

Applying Eq. (23) and simplifying it gives:

$$\theta_1(y) = -46.864 + 3.6409y - 0.0148y^2 - 0.000372y^3 \tag{45}$$

The complete function approximation of θ_1 becomes:

$$\begin{aligned}\theta_1(x,y) = 55.705 - 0.67125x - 0.029725x^2 + 9.3\times10^{-5}x^3 \\ + 3.6409y - 0.0148y^2 - 0.000372y^3\end{aligned} \tag{46}$$

Also, the tables to approximate polynomial functions θ_2 are:

i	X_i	θ_{2i} (x)
1	−10	38.969
2	0	23.790
3	10	6.626
4	20	−10.658

Table 20. x vs. Incidence of x in θ_2.

i	Y_i	θ_{2i} (y)
1	45	19.484
2	40	11.895
3	35	3.313
4	30	−5.329

Table 21. y vs. incidence of y in θ_2.

Calculating the polynomial approximation for the **Tables 20** and **21**, we obtain:

$$\theta_2(x) = 23.79 - 1.64823x - 0.009925x^2 + 0.00031083x^3 \quad (47)$$

$$\theta_2(y) = -6.193 - 2.7342y + 0.12942y^2 - 0.001244y^3 \quad (48)$$

According to Eq. (25) the function approximation of θ_2 becomes:

$$\begin{aligned}\theta_2(x,y) = {} & 17.597 - 1.64823x - 0.009925x^2 + 0.00031083x^3 \\ & - 2.7342y + 0.12942y^2 - 0.001244y^3\end{aligned} \quad (47)$$

Determining the complete polynomial approximation of θ_1 and θ_2 by Eqs. (46) and (47) respectively, it results to:

$$\begin{aligned}\theta_1(x,y) = {} & 55.705 - 0.67125x - 0.29725x^2 \\ & + 9.3\times10^{-5}x^3 + 3.6409y - 0.0148y^2 - 0.000372y^3\end{aligned} \quad (48)$$

$$\begin{aligned}\theta_2(x,y) = {} & 17.597 - 1.64823x - 0.009925x^2 + 0.00031083x^3 \\ & - 2.7342y + 0.12942y^2 - 0.001244y^3\end{aligned} \quad (49)$$

$$\forall x \in (-10,20); \forall y \in (45,30)$$

Applying the direct kinematic model of the robot manipulator defined by Eq. (36), it proceeds to verify polynomials approach θ_1 and θ_2. In this case, θ_3 is a constant with the value of 45°, where y = −0.5 x + 40, with x ∈ (−10.20). Considering an increase Δx = 3 units, the following table is obtained:

x	y	$\Theta_1(x,y)$ [°]	$\Theta_2(x,y)$ [°]	x_{approx}	y_{approx}
−10	45	159.324	58.453	−9.979	44.995
−7	43.5	158.669	52.102	−7.103	43.476
−4	42	157.158	45.306	−4.085	41.984
−1	40.5	154.815	38.142	−1.007	40.493
2	39	151.662	30.685	2.065	38.994
5	37.5	147.721	23.009	5.093	37.489
8	36	143.016	15.192	8.065	35.989
11	34.5	137.568	7.308	10.995	34.502
14	33	131.401	−0.566	13.923	33.028

x	y	$\Theta_1(x,y)$ [°]	$\Theta_2(x,y)$ [°]	x_{approx}	y_{approx}
17	31.5	124.536	−8.357	16.910	31.543
20	30	116.997	−15.987	20.023	29.995

Table 22. Values θ_1, θ_2, x_{approx} and y_{approx}.

Applying Eqs. (37), (38), and (39) the table of the errors become:

X	y	Error of x	Error of y	Error(x, y)
−10	45	−0.021	0.005	0.0218
-7	**43.5**	**0.103**	**0.024**	**0.1062**
−4	42	0.085	0.016	0.0863
-1	40.5	0.007	0.007	0.0099
2	39	−0.065	0.006	0.0654
5	37.5	−0.093	0.011	0.0938
8	36	−0.065	0.011	0.0656
11	34.5	0.005	−0.002	0.0059
14	33	0.077	−0.028	0.0816
17	31.5	0.090	−0.043	0.0995

Table 23. Errors of the polynomial approach.

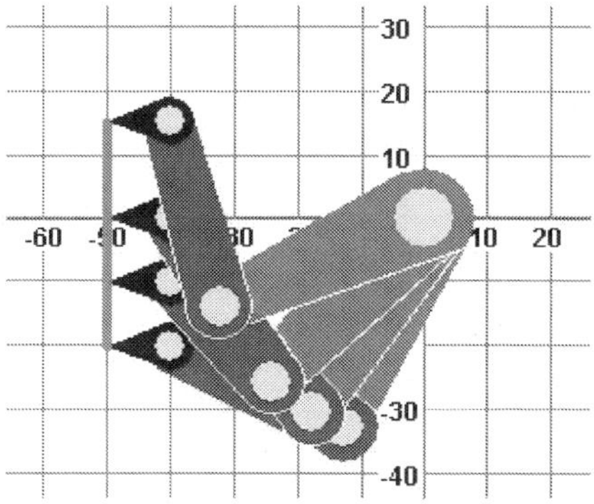

Figure 6. The four Robot positions, infinite slope.

The maximum error occurs at (−7, 43.5). From Eq. (40) the maximum percentage of error becomes:

$$\%\ Maximun\,error = \frac{|0.1062|}{\sqrt{(20-(-10))^2+(30-45)^2}} \times 100 = \mathbf{0.316\%} \tag{50}$$

Similarly as in the previous case, this value is reasonably acceptable. So for this case, Eqs. (48) and (49) can be used to do the lineal trajectory in the end-effector of the robot manipulator.

c) Case 3. Slope of a straight line, m > 1.

As in the two previous cases, the end-effector of the robot performs a linear path. In this case, the geometric robot positions were made considering an infinite slope (x = constant). **Figure 6** shows these positions, and the angle of the end-effector is considered constant with a value of 180°.

The values of the known positions are shown in the **Table 24**:

X	y	Θ_1 [°]	Θ_2 [°]	Θ_3 [°]
–50	–20	248.6	155.16	180
–50	–10	239.46	137.78	180
–50	0	226.55	122.06	180
–50	15	203.45	105.24	180

Table 24. Four know positions of the manipulator, infinite slope.

Considering that slope: m = ∞, the incidence factors can be calculated by the (8) and (9) equations like this:

$$\%\ of\ x = \frac{100}{1+|m|} = \frac{100}{1+|\infty|} = \frac{100}{\infty} = 0 \tag{51}$$

$$\%\ of\ y = 100\% - \%\ de\ x = 100 \tag{52}$$

As expected, the change in x has no any incidence on changes in θ_1 and θ_2, it is in this case that the change of y causes the change in both degrees of freedom of the robot manipulator.

The incidence tables to approximate polynomial functions θ_1 and θ_2 take the next form:

I	y_i	θ_{1i} (X) [°]
1	-20	248.6
2	-10	239.46
3	0	226.55
4	15	203.45

Table 25. y vs. incidence of y in θ_1.

I	y_i	θ_{2i} (X) [°]
1	-20	155.16
2	-10	137.78
3	0	122.06
4	15	105.24

Table 26. y vs. incidence of y in θ_2.

Performing the same procedure as in the previous cases, the desired functions of polynomial approximation are obtained for both **Tables 25** and **26**:

$$\theta_1(y) = 226.55 - 1.4287y - 0.01123y^2 + 0.000254y^3 \tag{53}$$

$$\theta_2(y) = 122.06 - 1.4334y + 0.01663y^2 + 0.0002779y^3 \tag{54}$$

In this case $\theta_3 = 180°$, with $y \in (-20, 15)$ and x = 50. Considering an increase $\Delta x = 3.5$ units, the following **Table 27** is obtained:

y	$\Theta_1(X, Y)$ [°]	$\Theta_2(X, Y)$ [°]	y_{aprox}	*Error of y*
-20	248.600	155.16	−19.983	−19.983
−16.5	245.925	148.990	−16.500	0.000
−13	242.667	142.894	−12.994	−0.006
-9.5	238.891	136.940	-9.484	−0.016
−6	234.663	131.199	-5.979	−0.021
−2.5	230.048	125.743	-2.481	−0.019
1	225.110	120.644	1.014	−0.014
4.5	219.917	115.972	4.512	−0.012
8	214.532	111.799	8.015	−0.015
11.5	209.021	108.198	11.520	−0.020
15	203.450	105.239	15.017	−0.017

Table 27. Values θ_1, θ_2, y_{aprox}, and Error of y.

The maximum error in this case is in y =−6. From Eq. (40) the maximum percentage of error becomes:

$$\%\, error\, máximo = \frac{|-0.021|}{\sqrt{(50-50)^2 + (15-(-20))^2}} \times 100 = \mathbf{0.06\%} \tag{55}$$

http://dx.doi.org/10.5772/63541

This value is so small that it can provide security to use the approximation obtained by Eqs. (53) and (54).

Until now, there have been three different cases that demonstrate an acceptable approximation in the position of θ_1 and θ_2 by polynomial functions. Given that the position of the end-effector of the robot is known, it is considered in this work that the speed and acceleration of the end-effector are well-known. Considering that the polynomial approximation for any degree of freedom has the following form:

$$\theta(x,y) = c_0 + c_1x + c_2x^2 + c_3x^3 + c_1y + c_2y^2 + c_3y^3 \tag{56}$$

Deriving this equation, the speed for any degree of freedom is defined as:

$$\dot{\theta}(x,y) = \frac{d}{dt}(\theta(x,y)) = \frac{\theta(x,y)}{dx} * \frac{dx}{dt} + \frac{\theta(x,y)}{dy} * \frac{dy}{dt} \tag{57}$$

Deriving newly, the acceleration for any degree of freedom becomes:

$$\begin{aligned}\ddot{\theta}(x,y) = &\frac{d}{dt}\left(\frac{\theta(x,y)}{dx}\right) * \frac{dx}{dt} + \frac{\theta(x,y)}{dx} * \frac{d}{dt}\left(\frac{dx}{dt}\right) + \\ &\frac{d}{dt}\left(\frac{\theta(x,y)}{dy}\right) * \frac{dy}{dt} + \frac{\theta(x,y)}{dy} * \frac{d}{dt}\left(\frac{dy}{dt}\right)\end{aligned} \tag{58}$$

By applying Eqs. (57) and (58), speed and acceleration for any degrees of freedom of the manipulator can be obtained respectively.

6. Conclusions

One of the basic activities related to the movement of industrial robots is the solution of the Inverse Kinematics Problem. This chapter has presented a new strategy that allows for an approximate solution without the use of conventional methods. However, the approach method has several restrictions. Thus, it is possible to achieve an alternative solution to the Inverse Kinematics Problem by polynomial functions that define the behaviour of the rotational joints. An advantage of this strategy is that it is easy to implement, and after getting the polynomial function for the position of the joints, the speed and acceleration can be obtained by conventional derivation.

Moreover, because this approach is made from four known configurations of the robot, it can be considered that the methodology described is a way of discretizing the continuous kinematics of the robot, which is an interpolation technique to the inverse kinematic problem.

Given the restrictions described in the analysed cases, further research is needed to determine if this strategy could be used for nonlinear paths; or for a kind of paths that require changes in the orientation of the end-effector, and also explore the possibility to extend the method for manipulator with more degrees of freedom.

Author details

José-Emilio Vargas-Soto, Efren Gorrostieta-Hurtado, Saúl Tovar-Arriaga*, Jesús-Carlos Pedraza-Ortega and Juan-Manuel Ramos-Arreguín

*Address all correspondence to: saul.tovar@uaq.mx

Autonomous University of Queretaro, Engineering School, Las Campanas, Querétaro, Mexico

References

[1] R. Paul. Robot manipulators: mathematics, programming and control: the computer control of robot manipulators. MIT Press; 1981.

[2] L. Sciavicco, B. Siciliano. Modeling and Control of Robot Manipulators. 2nd ed. London: Springer Verlag; 2000.

[3] E. Dombre, W. Khalil. Robot Manipulators: Modeling, Performance Analysis and Control. USA: Wiley-ISTE; 2007.

[4] J. Craig. Geometric Algorithms in AdeptRAPID. In: P. Agarwal, L. Kavraki y M. Mason, editors. Robotics: The algorithmic Perspective: 1998. Massachusetts: AK Peters, Natick; 1988.

[5] H. Durrant_White. Uncertain Geometry in Robotics. IEEE Conference on Robotics and Automation; Raleigh, NC., IEEE; 1987.

[6] G. A. Kramer. Solving geometric constraint systems: a case study in kinematics. Cambridge, MA, USA: MIT Press; 1992.

[7] C. G. Lee, M. Ziegler. Geometric approach in solving inverse kinematics of PUMA robots. IEEE Transactions on Aerospace and Electronic Systems. 1984;6:695-706.

[8] D. Chablat, P. Wenger, I. Bonev. Kinematic analysis of the 3-RPR parallel manipulator. In: 10th International Symposium on Advances in Robot Kinematics; June 2006; Ljubljana, Slovenia. Kluwer Academic Publishers; 2006. pp. 221-228.

[9] A. Aristidou, J. Lasenby. Inverse Kinematics: a review of existing techniques and introduction of a new fast interactive solver. CUED/F-INFENG/TR-632 ed. Cambridge: University of Cambridge; 2009.

[10] N. Courty, E. Arnaud. Inverse kinematics using sequential monte carlo methods. In: Proceedings of the V Conference on Articulated Motion and Deformable Objects; Mallorca, Spain. 2008. pp. 1-10.

[11] L. Unzueta, M. Peinado, R. Boulic, A. Suescum. Full-body performance animation with sequential inverse kinematics. Journal of Graphical Models. 2008;70(5) pp. 87-104.

[12] H. R. E. Haghighi, M. A. Nekoui. Inverse kinematic for an 8 degrees of freedom biped robot based on cubic polynomial trajectory generation. In: International Conference on Control, Instrumentation and Automation (ICCIA 2011); Shiraz, Iran. 2011. pp. 935-940. DOI: 10.1109/ICCIAutom.2011.6356787.

[13] A. Machmudah, S. Parman, A. Zainuddin. nth degree polynomials joint angle path by approximation of inverse kinematics data using Genetic Algorithm. In: 2010 International Conference on Intelligent and Advanced Systems (ICIAS); Kuala Lumpur, Malaysia. 2010. p. 1-6. DOI: 10.1109/ICIAS.2010.5716213.

[14] F. Chapelle, P. Bidaud. A closed form for inverse kinematics approximation of general 6R manipulators using genetic programming. In: IEEE, editor. IEEE International Conference on Robotics and Automation (ICRA 2001); Seoul, Korea. 2001. p. 3364-3369. DOI: 10.1109/ROBOT.2001.933137.

[15] L. M. Milne-Thomson. The Calculus of Finite Differences. American Mathematical Society; Providence, RI, USA. 2000.

Chapter 2

Models for the Reliability Analysis of Digital Instrumentation and Control Systems for Nuclear Power Plants

Jonathan M. O. Pinto, Ian B. Gomes,
Pedro L. C. Saldanha, Eustério B. Furieri and
Paulo F. F. e Melo

Additional information is available at the end of the chapter

http://dx.doi.org/10.5772/64649

Abstract

The objective of this chapter is to discuss two approaches for reliability analysis of digital instrumentation and control systems in nuclear power plants taking into account the regulatory side. Dynamic Flowgraph Methodology (DFM) and Markov/Cell-to-Cell Mapping Technique (CCMT) are discussed and case studies developed are presented. These case studies involve simplified control systems for a steam generator and a pressurizer of a Pressurized Water Reactor (PWR) plant for the purpose of evaluating each method. Advantages and limitations of each approach are addressed. For the DFM approach, three concerns in the literature are addressed: modeling of the system itself, incorporation of the methodology results into existing Probabilistic Safety Assessments (PSA), and identification of software failures. The Markov/CCMT, which has been used in dynamic probabilistic safety assessments, is approached by means of a simplified digitally controlled water volume control system. The Markov/CCMT methodology results in detailed data of the system reliability behavior in relation to time. However, it demands a higher computational effort than usual as the complexity (i.e., number of components and failure states) of the system increases. As a regulatory research conclusion, the methodologies presented can be used on PSA risk informed assessment, contributing to the regulatory side.

Keywords: DFM, MARKOV/CCMT, digital I&C systems, reliability

1. Introduction

Instrumentation and Control Systems (I&C) are an essential element in the normal, abnormal, and emergency operation of nuclear power plants [1]. These systems measure thousands of variables and activate several devices to control and protect the plant [2].

The I&C are designed to keep the process variables within plant design limits. I&C ensure plants' safety and efficient production by reacting appropriately to failures and abnormal events [2, 3].

Given the increasing incorporation of digital systems in nuclear power plants, due to their numerous advantages over analog systems, a specific approach to reliability and risk analysis has been required [4]. These systems reflect many interactions between their components (process variables, hardware, software, and human actions). Besides, physical system components have a well-defined reliability approach. The same is not true in terms of software component [5, 6].

On digital systems, software promotes flexibility, cost reduction, and reliability through its high capacity of modification without the need of replacements. If one can complete debugs software, it will continue working indefinitely, and therefore, there is no possibility of aging [5].

However, there is no perfect software. Its development process presumes human failures besides documentation and cognitive errors. Therefore, a reliability approach that models the behavior of these elements is necessary.

The construction of new reactors and the I&C modernization in the operating ones are demanding licensing and safety evaluation activities by the regulatory bodies, particularly, regulatory preparedness concerning computer-based I&C systems licensing.

The safety of nuclear power reactors is centered on deterministic concepts like defense-in-depth and diversity to minimize risks from internal or external events, which may lead to common cause failures of passive and active systems. Risk studies and lessons learned of operating reactors have contributed to improve the reliability of the new digital I&C design, but the benefits of digital technology could be impaired by the growing complexity of the components and I&C architecture due to difficulties during the regulatory review [7].

The combination of deterministic and probabilistic approaches, system architecture designed with Defense-in-Depth and diversity (D-in-D concept), the use of the best-estimate methodology for beyond design base events, like Software Common Cause Failure (SCCF), have been accepted to demonstrate the adequacy of digital I&C architectures and their functionality to meet the acceptance criteria.

In this context, the quantification of probabilistic risk analysis to demonstrate the quality and reliability attributes has been arisen many different interpretations from the industries and regulators, even considering the very low probability of the combination of some design-based accidents [like Large Break Loss of Coolant Accident (LBLOCA), in conjunction with Software Common Cause Failure].

To some extent, difficulties of regulatory decision making have been arisen because of different positions and interpretations from industry and regulators in explaining and applying some numbers of failure rate probabilities on digital instrumentation technologies.

The use of operational experience in case of safety qualification of digital instrumentation should be processed with relative care because of different approaches in processing operational experience data and the lack of sufficient statistical data related to safety instrumentation.

The application of traditional safety concepts and design philosophy of nuclear reactors, in the case of the new digital I&C systems, have been shown different interpretations and evaluations for the reliability and qualification of functions, and components of digital I&C systems and architectures.

Each country has its own legislation and a particular licensing process to implement the review and assessment of safety analyses. As the safety functions could be impaired by the failure of digital I&C systems redundancies (through potential software Common Cause Failure [CCF]), the currently approach know as Quantitative Software Reliability Analysis (QSRA) have been shown difficulties for regulatory decision making. The application of the D-in-D concept conservative approach (with diversity of both software and hardware) from the NRC (Nuclear Regulatory Commission) [7] has been strengthened by some regulators of countries involved with new reactor licensing (i.e., European Pressurizer Reactors, EPR design).

The industries claim that the reliability figures of new digital I&C systems have been shown equal or better failure rates than hardware and human failures. More information on recent regulatory positions and studies of quantitative software reliability analysis can be found in reference [7]. There are examples of international regulatory research to improve the bases and tools on using quantitative risk analysis for regulatory review of digital I&C technologies with more complex architecture, which include digital displays and human-factor analysis of highly integrated digital control rooms.

There are dynamic interactions present in the systems that are not treated by the traditional approaches (fault trees methodology). In addition, there are existing requirements in reliability and safety analysis (e.g., the availability of relevant information to users (as cut sets and failure probabilities) and the possibility of incorporating the results into Probabilistic Safety Assessment (PSA)) that must be met in conjunction with the dynamic interactions [4, 5, 8].

Appropriate methods for assessing safety and reliability are the key to establishing the acceptability of digital I&C systems in safety and control systems of nuclear power plants (hardware and software).

Reliability models suitable for digital I&C systems are in development process or in validation process.

Reference [8] presents the desirable characteristics a PSA methodology of a digital system must have to be applied satisfactorily. The methodologies that fulfilled the most the requirements were the Dynamic Flowgraph Methodology (DFM) and the Markov/CCMT (Cell-to-Cell Mapping Technique).

The objective of this chapter is to present two different approaches for reliability analysis of digital I&C systems applying the methodologies cited above in different case studies [5, 9–11]. Consequently, these approaches are analyzed in terms of acceptability in the regulatory context.

This chapter is organized as follows: the discussion of Dynamic Flowgraph Methodology and Markov/CCMT (Cell to Cell Mapping Technique) is presented in the following two sections. Conclusions are presented at the last section.

2. Dynamic flowgraph methodology

DFM discretizes the most relevant variables of the analyzed system in states that reflect their behavior, sets the logic that connects them through decision tables, and finally performs a system analysis, aiming, for example, the root causes (prime implicants) of a given failure top event of a fault tree.

The experience accumulated and reported in the literature indicates the DFM [4, 8] as the one that meets the most the requirements mentioned on the previous section regarding digital systems.

DFM describes interactions among the control system and other subsystems, as well as process variables. It models a system as a whole. There are examples of applications concerning failures of control systems in nuclear power plants and failures in spatial digital control systems (including dependences description) [11–14].

A network is constructed considering the causality and temporal relationship between the system elements. These elements are Process Nodes (PN), Condition Nodes (CN), Condition Edges (CO), Causality Edges (CE), Transfer Boxes (TB), and Transition Boxes (TT). More information is found in references [5, 8, 9, 11, 12, 15].

The physical system and control system main elements are the PN of the model. The discrete behavior of these elements is represented by CN [5]. TB and TT reflect the time and causality relationships between the variables [5].

Decision tables, each one associated with its respective TB/TT, are defined reflecting the possible states combination between the model variables [5].

The analysis consists in defining a top event of interest and finding out how the elements can possible combine their states, presented in the model [11].

DFM works with the concept of prime implicants [11, 13, 15, 16], which are the minimum combinations of variable states causing the top event of interest. The set of prime implicants can be used to represent the various states in which the system can be found [11].

Examples of DFM methodology and its details can be found in references [12–15]. There are applications on software failures on digital control systems, human errors, failures of control systems in nuclear power plants, and failures in spatial digital control systems. This work presents a simplified example [5, 9, 11] based on a current PWR pressurizer [5].

The proposed system has the same functionality implemented by a digital system, but with some simplifications and assumptions in the controlled plant. This system and its modeling are presented on references [5, 9, 11]. It contains heaters, sprays, a relief valves, and a safety valve. Failure modes considered for each component. **Figure 1** illustrates the proposed digital system. **Table 1** summarizes the system control logic, where P is the pressure, HT is the heaters, SP is the sprays, RV is the relief valve, and SV is the safety valve.

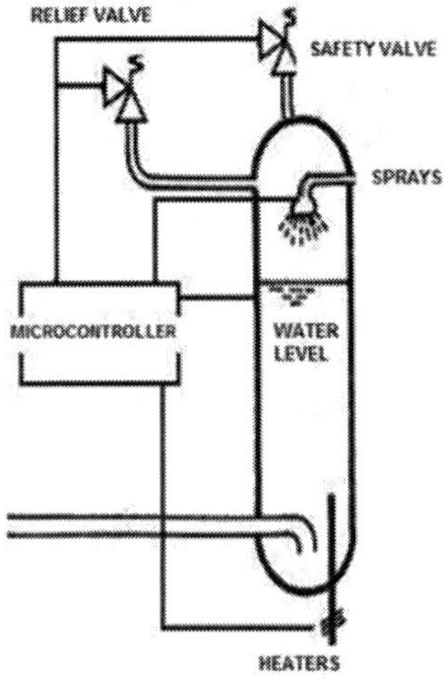

Figure 1. Proposed digital system.

P	HT	SP	RV	SV
Very low	On	Off	Closed	Closed
Low	On	Off	Closed	Closed
Lower	On	Off	Closed	Closed
Normal	Off	Off	Closed	Closed
Higher	Off	On	Closed	Closed
High	Off	On	Opened	Closed
Very high	Off	On	Opened	Opened

P: pressure; HT: heaters; SP: sprays; RV: relief valve; SV: safety valve.

Table 1. System control logic.

The system has four mechanisms of pressure control triggered by a microprocessor that runs a control logic through a software. These actuators, heating control, spraying control, and the two valve controls, are the key parameters of the control system, and therefore they will become PN in the DFM model as well as the pressure variable, which is the key parameter of the controlled process. These variable states are discretized as shown in **Table 2**, where SS is the sensor state; HTS is the heaters state; SPS is the sprays state; RVS is the relief valve state; and SVS is the safety valve state.

PN	State	CN	State
P	Very high (169–175 bar)	SS	Failed high
	High (166–169 bar)		Normal
	Higher (160–166 bar)		Failed low
	Normal (156–160 bar)	HTS	Failed on
	Lower (148–156 bar)		Normal
	Low (140–148 bar)		Failed off
	Very low (131–140 bar)	SPS	Failed on
RV	Opened		Normal
	Closed		Failed off
SV	Opened	RVS	Failed opened
	Closed		Normal
HT	On		Failed closed
	Off	SVS	Failed opened
SP	On		Normal
	Off		Failed closed

Table 2. Model process and conditions nodes.

SS	P	HT	RV
Normal	Very high	Off	Opened
	High	Off	Opened
	Higher	Off	Closed
	Normal	Off	Closed
	Lower	On	Closed
	Low	On	Closed
	Very low	On	Closed
Failed low	–	On	Closed
Failed high	–	Off	Opened

Table 3. Model TB 1.

http://dx.doi.org/10.5772/64649

The next step consists in interconnecting the model variables through transfer and transition boxes. Each of these elements has an associated decision table showing the causality relationship that exists between the variables.

The group of heaters and relief valve action logic is shown on the decision table linked to a TB (**Table 3**). The decision table related to a TT is shown in **Table 4**. This decision table shows the control mechanisms of the system [5].

P	HT	SP	RV	SV	P+
Very low	Off	Off	Closed	Closed	Very low
	Off	Off	Closed	Opened	Very low
Low	Off	On	Opened	Opened	Low
	On	Off	Closed	Closed	Lower
Normal	On	Off	Opened	Opened	Lower
	On	On	Closed	Closed	Lower
Very high	On	On	Closed	Opened	Lower
	On	On	Opened	Opened	Normal

Table 4. Model TT 1.

Var	State	Prob
SS	Failed high	0.033
	Failed low	
HTS	Failed on	0.018
	Failed off	
SPS	Failed on	0.046
	Failed off	
RVS	Failed opened	0.004
	Failed closed	
SVS	Failed opened	0.007
	Failed closed	
P	Very high	<10E-166
	High	<10E-96
	Higher	<10E-14
	Normal	9.0 10E-1
	Lower	9.2 10E-2
	Low	<10E-81
	Very low	<10E-295

Table 5. Model variable probabilities.

The DFM model provides a quantitative analysis of the results from the state probabilities of its variables. Using failure data from reference [17] and the probability distribution estimated for pressure, the probabilities were obtained and are shown in **Table 5**.

For control devices in continuous mode, 1 year of operation time in a nuclear power plant has been considered calculation. For control devices in demand mode, one demand operation has been considered. Generic failure modes for each device have been considered.

The pressure probabilities in each state were calculated from the probability density function in each interval.

Regarding the analysis, the top event "Pressure Very Low", representing one of the failures in the pressurizer control and later reactor trip is one of the top events of interest [5, 9, 11].

The toolset DYAMONDA® [15], from ASCA® Inc., was utilized.

The prime implicants or, in other words, the smallest number of combinations of variable states in the system that lead to the failure top event are searched. Setting the sentence "Pressure Very Low @ t = 0", where t = 0 is a notation indicating the end of the analysis time, the results are 32 prime implicants.

Assuming boundary conditions consisting of a proper work of the level sensor and heaters off and running, the result is the prime implicant shown in **Table 6** [5, 9, 11].

Prime Implicant Probability = 1.0609E-06
Pressure was Normal at time −1
Sensor State was Normal at time −1
Heaters State was Normal at time −1
Safety Valve State was Failed Opened at time −1
Relief Valve State was Failed Opened at time −1
Sprays State was Failed On at time −1
Sprays state was failed on at time −1

Table 6. Prime implicant for "pressure very low."

For this prime implicant, valve and, spray failures lead the pressure to "Very Low". Not even the fact that the level sensor is in "Normal," as are the group heaters, allows an increase of pressure to compensate the drop provided by the other mechanisms.

The replacement of analog loops by digital systems is gradual and, therefore, several digital systems still coexist with analog systems in various industrial plants. It is necessary that the results of failure analysis in digital systems can be incorporated into the existing probabilistic safety analysis reports related to analog loops. Only then it will be possible to perform uncertainty and importance analyses, for example, on these results, such as those carried out for other fault trees.

The results of the DFM meet this requirement. One can incorporate them by using a traditional tool in failure analysis, as the SAPHIRE code [18], for instance. This procedure is illustrated below.

The SAPHIRE code requires a text file to be imported in an extension. Ftl written in a specific format. Taking as an example, the results of the top event "Pressure Very Low", the. Ftl would be written as follows [9]:

pressure_very_low

= pressure_very_low or

pressure_very_low_subsystem_1

pressure_very_low_subsystem_2

pressure_very_low_pressurizer

etc

...

pressure_very_low _pressurizer or

prime_implicant_1

prime_implicant _1 and

pressure_normal_t-1

heaters_normal_t-1

sensor_normal_t-1

sprays_failed_on_t-1

reliefvalve_failed_opened_t-1

safetyvalve_failed_opened_t-1

where "pressure_very_low" is the top event, "pressure_very_low_subsystem1, 2, etc..." represent the trips of "Very_Low" pressure in the other analog systems, and "pressure_very_low_pressurizer" represents the trip of the digital pressurizer control.

More details regarding incorporation on PSA can be found on references [4, 8], where guidelines are made available.

DFM can be used to identify system software failures reflected in the model on the definition of some decision tables through its two modes (inductive and deductive), as shown in references [8, 19]. Once the deductive mode is utilized, one can utilize the inductive mode, step by step, to verify the correctness of the software logic.

DFM can also incorporate Human Reliability (HRA) on the system failure analysis, as shown in reference [20].

3. MARKOV/CCMT approach

Markov/CCMT [4, 21–23] is an approach that combines Markov stochastic processes with the CCMT to represent the dependencies between failure events that can originate from the dynamic interactions between the digital I&C system and the controlled process and also among the different components of the digital I&C system itself.

Markov processes can treat dependencies among events, like common-cause failures, shared-load components, and also repair.

CCMT [22–24] is a systematic procedure to describe the dynamics of both linear and nonlinear systems in discrete time and discretized system state space (like Markov processes do).

CCMT provides a very effective means to account for epistemic uncertainties, nonlinear aspects of the system dynamics, and stochastic fluctuations in dynamic system operation. CCMT produces a model that is compatible with the Markov process approach for representing failures [20, 22, 23].

The conventional Markov chain represents the stochastic evolution of a system through the transition probabilities among possible system states. Transitions between states can be represented graphically by directed links (edges) through Markov transition diagrams. Even if failure data are not available, a Markov/CCMT model can be used in both the inductive and deductive steps (that is, identification of accident sequences and safety system failure analysis, respectively) of a PSA. The results from the former can be used to obtain the relations between initiating and top events or operational state (cause-consequence relations) and the results from the latter to investigate the primary causes that lead to a specific top event or system state [4].

Importance analyses (frequency ordering of sequence events or components) can be carried out using standard PSA tools [4, 18]. If failure data are available, then the scenario frequency and top event probability can be quantified. The Markov/CCMT model can be integrated into standard PSAs using standard PSA tools [4, 8, 18, 24].

A full Markov/CCMT discretizes the whole system in states defined by the user and shows all the possible transitions between these states. The analysis is carried out by defining top events or initialing events of interest and system behavior observation. It may not be computational feasible to construct large models with Markov/CCMT (generally models with several thousands of system states) [4, 23, 24].

The steps in applying Markov/CCMT are (a) construct the Markov/CCMT model to represent the system of interest; (b) analyze the Markov/CCMT model; and (c) quantify the deductive and the inductive analytical results. These steps are described below [4].

The input to the Markov/CCMT model construction is the set of discretized system states. These states are identified from a Failure Mode and Effect Analysis (FMEA), as well as the system control logic. One must define mutually exclusive intervals (just like the process carried out in finite difference methods) for continuous process variables. These intervals are called cells. Then, throughout simulations (defining final and initial conditions as well as a time-step interval), the transition probabilities between cells are found. The state transition probabilities of the system must also be simulated and combined with the former continuous variables' transition probabilities. Although some of the steps in model construction have been mechanized, general purpose software for model construction is not yet available [4].

Reference [8] shows some limitations of the methodology. These limitations comprise computational difficulties arising from the volume of model states defined (model complexity) as well as time step and mission time definition on the analysis. Also, Markov/CCMT requires a substantially larger amount of technical knowledge compared to that needed for a traditional event tree/fault tree analysis [4]. The methodology produces a large amount of data; therefore, some postprocessing of the results is required. Here, it is presented a simplified example of application of the methodology to an adapted digital control system of the water level of a typical PWR steam generator [10].

In the adapted digital system, the water level is measured by two-level sensors and their average signal is fed to the controller, which compares it to the set point. The difference is fed to a PI "Proportional-Integral" control routine that generates a correction signal, which controls a motorized feedwater valve and the water that enters the steam generator. From this adaptation, a simulation of the system was built and the Markov/CCMT methodology was applied to the system.

Failure mode		**Effects**	**Failure rate (/h)**
MC1	Signal loss of one sensor	Computer operates solely with the signal of the remaining sensor.	λ_1^{MC} 16.4×10^{-7}
MC2	Signal loss of both sensors	Computer maintains the control valve completely open.	λ_2^{MC} 8.2×10^{-7}
MC3	Processing failure of the data received by the computer	Control is transferred to the Backup Computer.	λ_3^{MC} 1.2×10^{-6}
MC4	Failure to communicate with the valve	Signal fed to the valve is 0.0 V, keeping it completely closed.	λ_4^{MC} 1.8×10^{-6}

Table 7. FMEA of the main CPU.

The next step is to perform an FMEA of this system. In this case, only its main components were considered. Failures induced by external phenomena, such as fires and radiation were not considered. Also, component repair or replacement was not considered. These restraints are not taken into account in a complete PSA. The failure rates were taken from reference [25].

Two computers work together to ensure proper system operation. In case a failure occurs in the Main CPU, the Backup CPU assumes control of the system. Failure modes of the sensors as well as failure modes of the CPUs may be considered, since the consequences of these failures are the same [4]. **Table 7** presents the FMEA of the Main CPU and **Table 8** presents the FMEA for the Backup CPU.

It is now possible to build the Markovian transition diagrams for each of the system components, based on the Failure Modes and Effect Analyses. Since the two CPUs work together, their transition diagrams are also built together.

Failure mode		Effects	Failure rate (/h)
BC1	Signal loss of one sensor	The computer operates solely with the signal of the remaining sensor.	λ_1^{BC} 16.4 × 10^{-7}
BC2	Signal loss of both sensors	The computer maintains the control valve completely open.	λ_2^{BC} 8.2 × 10^{-7}
BC3	Processing failure of the data received by the computer	Automatic control of the process is lost and the valve is maintained closed.	λ_3^{BC} 1.2 × 10^{-6}
BC4	Failure to communicate with the valve	The signal fed to the valve is 0.0 V, keeping it completely closed.	λ_4^{BC} 1.8 × 10^{-6}

Table 8. FMEA of the backup CPU.

Other failure modes are possible for the CPUs but, in order to simplify the analysis, they were ignored. They must be considered in a full PSA.

Table 9 presents the Failure Mode and Effects Analysis of the Feedwater Valve. As was said with respect to the CPUs, other failure modes for the Feedwater Valve are possible but were ignored in order to simplify the analysis.

Failure mode		Effects	Failure rate (/h)
V1	The valve gets stuck completely closed.	The feedwater flowrate is 0, 0 and the water level decreases continuously.	λ_1^{VPC} 1.7 × 10^{-5}
V2	The valve gets stuck completely open.	The feedwater flowrate is max and the water level increases continuously.	λ_2^{VPC} 1.7 × 10^{-5}

Table 9. FMEA for the feedwater valve.

For example, the following assumptions were made for the states transitions of the CPUs: (1) the transfer of control between the two CPUs is made instantly once the Main CPU reaches state MC3; (2) the only other failure mode that is possible after the failure of one of the sensors is the failure of the other sensor; (3) the Backup CPU can only fail after it begins operating.

Figure 2 presents the Markov transition diagram for the Feedwater Valve, and **Figure 3** presents the Markov transition diagram for both the Main CPU and the Backup CPU.

http://dx.doi.org/10.5772/64649

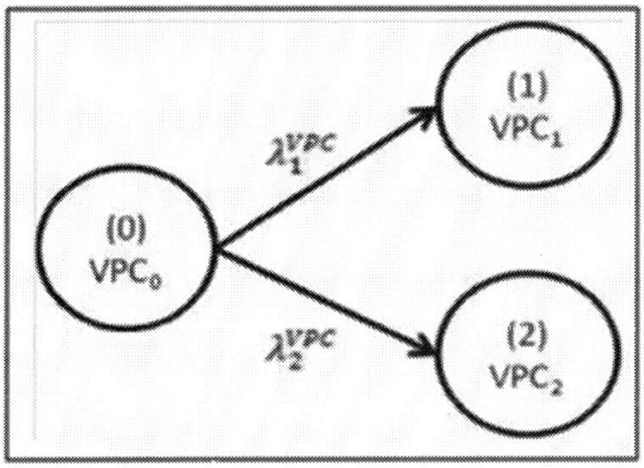

Figure 2. Markov transition diagram for the Feedwater Valve.

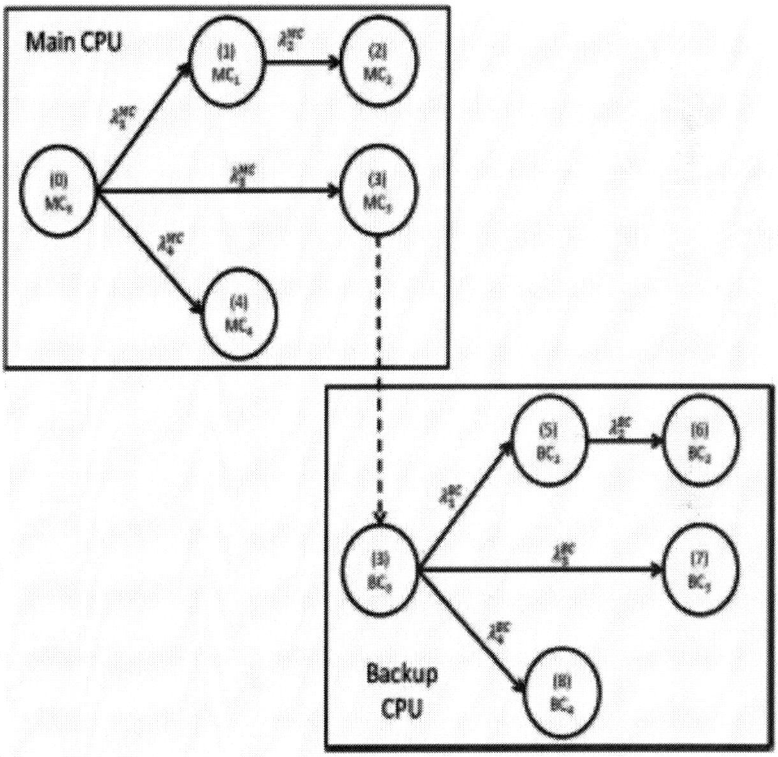

Figure 3. Markov transition diagram for the Main CPU and the Backup CPU.

From the transition diagrams, sets of differential equations are obtained. These sets of differential equations were solved using the finite difference method.

It is necessary to define a time step that must be the same for both transition diagrams. The time step must respect the following condition Eq. (1):

$$\Delta t \leq \frac{1}{\lambda} \tag{1}$$

Therefore, since the largest transition rate of the whole system is $\lambda_1^{VPC} + \lambda_2^{VPC} = 3,\ .4 \times 10^{-5}$ failures/h, the time step must respect

$$\Delta t \leq 29411.76 \text{ h} \tag{2}$$

Respecting this condition, the time step was chosen to be 10 h. It was chosen this value because it was long enough so that changes in the behavior of the system could be observed and small enough so that it could account for the changes in the operation scenario.

The next stage is applying CCMT to the system. Its first step is the Controlled Variables States Space (CVSS) partitioning, where the sole Controlled Variable for this example is the Steam Generator water level. **Table 10** shows the cells of the CVSS that were chosen for this study. These cells are subsequently divided into four subcells ($P = 4$).

$j = 1$	$x \leq 11.2$ m	Failed low
$j = 2$	11.2 m $< x \leq$ 11.7 m	Low
$j = 3$	11.7 m $< x \leq$ 12.2 m	Normal-low
$j = 4$	12.2 m $< x \leq$ 12.7 m	Normal-high
$j = 5$	12.7 cm $< x \leq$ 13.2 cm	High
$j = 6$	$x >$ 13.2 cm	Failed high

Table 10. Cells of the CVSS.

Once the subcells are defined, the probability $g(j|j', nc', nv', k)$ (i.e., the probability that the water level goes from cell Vj' to cello Vj given that it was at cell Vj', the CPUs were at state nc' and the valve was at state nv' at instant $t = k.\Delta t$) may be obtained. The simulation of the system is used for this purpose.

The simulation is adjusted so that the CPUs are at state nc', the valve at state nv', and the initial water level is at the midpoint of each of the subcells of Vj'. The number A of arrivals at cell Vj is observed and $g(j|j', nc', nv', k)$ is obtained through Eq. (3):

$$g(\mathrm{j}|\mathrm{j}',\mathrm{n}',k)=\frac{A}{P} \quad (3)$$

The probability of occurrence of Top Events and the reliability of the system are obtained from equations as follows:

The probability that the system is in cell Vj at $t = (k+1).\Delta t$, given that it was in cell Vj′ at time $t = k.\Delta t$ is [4]

$$q_{\mathrm{j}}(k+1\mid \mathrm{j}',k)=\sum_{n'=1}^{\mathrm{N}} g(j|\mathrm{j}',\mathrm{n}',k)\,h_{\mathrm{n}'}(k) \quad (4)$$

where $h_{n'}(k)$ is the probability that the component was at state n′ at $t = k$, obtained from the Markov model. Therefore,

$$p_{\mathrm{j}}(k+1)=\sum_{j'=1}^{\mathrm{J}} q(j,k+1|\mathrm{j}',k).p_{\mathrm{j}'}(k) \quad (5)$$

Since the cells cover the whole CVSS and are mutually exclusive and exhaustive, it is possible to state that

$$\sum_{j=1}^{\mathrm{J}} p_{\mathrm{j}}(k)=1 \quad (6)$$

Having defined the Top Events, i.e., the cells where the system is considered failed (Vi), it is possible to obtain the probability that the system is failed in an instant:

$$p_{\mathrm{ET}}(k)=\sum_{i=1}^{\mathrm{I}} p_{\mathrm{i}}(k) \quad (7)$$

Therefore, the reliability of the system can be obtained from

$$R(k)=1-\sum_{i=1}^{\mathrm{I}} p_{\mathrm{i}}(k)=1-p_{\mathrm{ET}}(k) \quad (8)$$

K	*t*	**P1(k)**	**P5(*k*)**	**PET(*k*)**
0	0	0.0	0.0	0
1	10	0.0	0.0	0
2	20	0.0	0.0	0
3	30	3.5E-08	1.78955E-08	5.3E-08
4	40	2.7E-06	1.1427E-07	2.8E-06

Table 11. Probability of occurrence of a top event.

Table 11 and **Figure 4** present the resulting Top Events occurrence probability, and **Table 12** and **Figure 5** present the resulting reliability of the system.

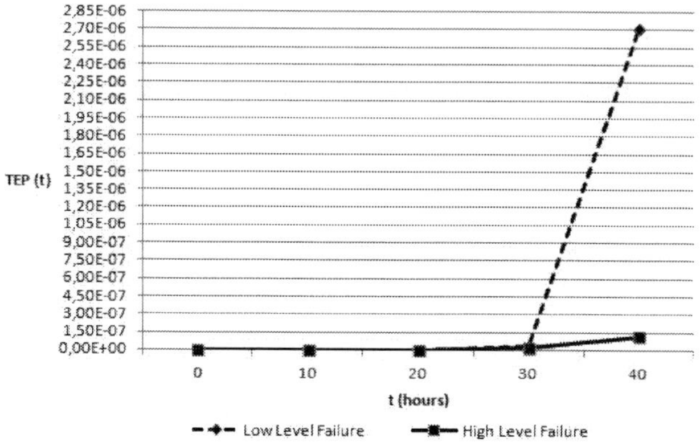

Figure 4. Probability of occurrence of a Top Event.

k	*t*	PET(*t*)	*R*(*t*)
0	0	0	1.00
1	10	0	1.00
2	20	0	1.00
3	30	5.3E-08	9.9999995E-01
4	40	2.8E-06	9.9999718E-01

Table 12. Reliability of the digital water level control system.

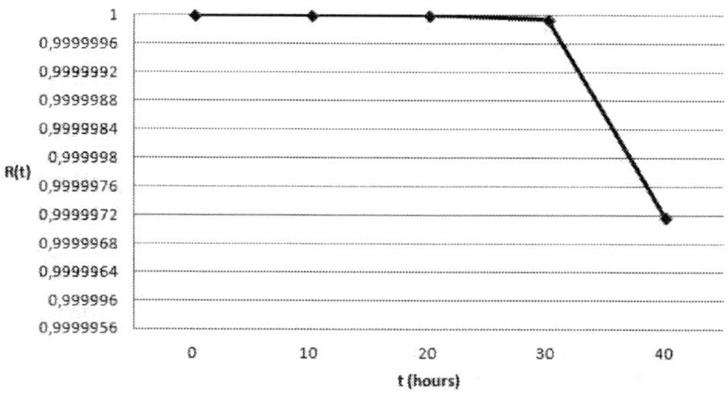

Figure 5. Reliability of the digital water level control system.

http://dx.doi.org/10.5772/64649

From the results it is possible to obtain information regarding the development of the reliability of the digital water level control system created for this study. Observing **Figure 4**, it is possible to verify that the failure with the largest probability of occurrence is low water level. In spite of the failure rates for both failure modes of the valve being the same, the failure modes of the CPUs increase the probability that the system fails low.

It is important to observe that the data in reference [25], used to obtain the failure rates of the system components, were published in 1988. Since its publication, I&C system components have been constantly improved, consequently increasing their reliability.

4. Conclusions

Appropriate methods for assessing safety and reliability are the key to establishing the acceptability of digital I&C systems in safety and control systems of nuclear power plants by the regulatory side.

Reliability models suitable for digital I&C systems are in development process or in validation process.

The traditional approach of using fault trees does not consider the dynamic interactions present in those systems; therefore, it is necessary to find a reliability methodology that takes into account these issues without violating the existing requirements concerning safety analysis.

This work discusses the application of DFM and MARKOV/CCMT to model the reliability of digital systems. As stated previously, these methodologies fulfilled the most the requirements concerning these type of systems.DFM is effective in modeling the interactions of the various components of a digital system (physical devices and software, the latter being implicit in the logic driving one or more decision tables). Through prime implicants, it allows the visualization of possible system states, failed, or not. Its deductive analysis allows an efficient study of failures tracing the causes of a given top event. Its inductive analysis can be used in the mitigation of failures found in deductive analyses and for the verification of system specifications. It can also be used for FMEA preparation, investigating the consequences of given initial conditions.

A limitation of the methodology is that the knowledge of the whole system both for modeling and for mitigations is necessary. But once built, the system can be analyzed for various failure modes and top events of interest.

As many digital systems still coexist with analog loops, it is important that the results reported by any methodology can be incorporated into existing PSAs. Only then, uncertainty and importance studies, for example, can be developed for digital systems such as those performed for other systems in failure analysis.

As the main element of a digital system is the software (and the fact that it does not have a defined reliability approach), it is quite convenient the existence of tools that enable the verification of faults and subsequent corrections in these elements.

In what concerns the Markov/CCMT approach, we intend to apply it to a PWR steam generator control system in order to assess its capabilities. The Markov/CCMT model can be used in both the inductive and deductive steps (that is, identification of accident sequences and safety system failure analysis, respectively) of a PSA to produce respectively the cause–consequence relations (event sequences and scenarios) between initiating events and top events, or operational states and the prime implicants leading to a specified top events or operational states. The ability of DFM to find the most probable causes for a specific Top Event can be used to determine the initial conditions for Markov/CCMT, which results in more detailed probabilistic data of the system's reliability behavior in relation to time. However, this methodology demands a higher computational effort than usual as the complexity (i.e., the number of components and failure states) of the system increases.

The models presented are relevant for Risk Informed decisions taken by the regulatory side where PSA models and results complement the primary deterministic requirements (regarding structures, systems, and components) to be met by the utility in the licensing process.

Author details

Jonathan M. O. Pinto[1*], Ian B. Gomes[2], Pedro L. C. Saldanha[1], Eustério B. Furieri[1] and Paulo F. F. e Melo[2]

*Address all correspondence to: jonathan.pinto.ufrj@gmail.com

1 National Commission of Nuclear Energy, Rio de Janeiro, RJ, Brazil

2 Graduate Program of Nuclear Engineering, COPPE, Federal University of Rio de Janeiro, Rio de Janeiro, RJ, Brazil

References

[1] IAEA. Modern Instrumentation and Control for Nuclear Power Plants: Guidebook. Vienna: International Atomic Energy Agency; 1999.

[2] Hashemian H. M. Nuclear Power Plant Instrumentation and Control. In: P. Tsvetkov, editor. Nuclear Power—Control, Reliability and Human Factors. Texas: Intechopen; 2011. DOI: 10.5772/18768.

[3] NRC. Digital Instrument and Controls. Washington, DC: Nuclear Regulatory Commission; 2011.

[4] Aldemir T., Stovsky M. P., Krischenbaum J., Mandelli D., Bucci P., Mangan L. A., Miller D. W., Sun X., Ekici E., Guarro S., Yau M., Johnson B., Elks C., Arndt S. A. S. Dynamic Reliability Modeling of Digital Instrumentation and Control Systems for Nuclear Reactor Probabilistic Risk Assessments, NUREG/CR-6942. Washington, DC: Nuclear Regulatory Commission; 2007.

[5] Pinto J. M. O., Frutuoso e Melo P. F., Saldanha P. L. C. A DFM/ATHEANA Human Failure Analysis of a Digital Control System for a Pressurizer. In: Proceedings of the European Safety and Reliability Conference, Taylor & Francis, Netherlands; 2013.

[6] Stamatelatos M. Probabilistic Risk Assessment Procedures Guide for NASA Managers and Practitioners. Washington, DC: NASA; 2002.

[7] Furieri E. B. Internal Guideline on Review and Assessment of Digital I&C System. Brazil: National Commission of Nuclear Energy, CNEN; 2016.

[8] Aldemir T., Miller D. W., Stovsky M. P., Kirschenbaum J., Bucci P., Fentman A. W., Mangan L. T. Current State of Reliability Modeling Methodologies for Digital Systems and Their Acceptance Criteria for Nuclear Power Plant Assessment, NUREG/CR-6901. Washington, DC: Nuclear Regulatory Commission; 2006.

[9] Pinto J. M. O., Frutuoso e Melo P. F., Saldanha P. L. C. A Dynamic Failures Evaluation of a Simplified Digital Control System for a Nuclear Power Plant Pressurizer. In: Proceedings of the European Safety and Reliability Conference, Taylor & Francis, Greece; 2010.

[10] Gomes I. G., Frutuoso e Melo P. F., Saldanha P. L. C. A Cell-to-Cell Markovian Model for the Reliability of a Digital Control System of a Steam Generators. In: International Nuclear Atlantic Conference, ABEN, Brazil; 2013.

[11] Pinto J. M. O., Frutuoso e Melo P. F., Saldanha P. L. C. A DFM/Fuzzy/ATHEANA Human Failure Analysis of a Digital Control System for a Pressurizer. Nuclear Technology. 2014;188:20–33. DOI: 10.13182/NT13-48.

[12] Aldemir T., Stovsky M. P., Krischenbaum J., Mandelli D., Bucci P., Mangan L. A., Miller D. W., Sun X., Guarro S., Yau M., Johnson B., Elks C., Arndt S. A., Dion J., Nguyen Q., Ekici, E. A Benchmark Implementation of Two Dynamic Methodologies for the Reliability Modeling of Digital Instrumentation and Control Systems, NUREG/CR-6985. Washington, DC: Nuclear Regulatory Commission; 2009.

[13] Yau M., Apostolakis G., Guarro S. The Use of Prime Implicants in Dependability Analysis of Software Controlled Systems. Reliability Engineering and System Safety. 1998;62:23–32.

[14] Guarro S., Yau M., Apostolakis G. Demonstration of the Dynamic Flowgraph Methodology using the Titan II Space Launch Vehicle Digital Flight Control Software. Reliability Engineering and System Safety. 1995;49:335–353.

[15] Guarro S., Yau M., Motamed M. Development of Tools for Safety Analysis of Control Software in Advanced Reactors. Washington, DC: Nuclear Regulatory Commission; 1996.

[16] Garret C. J., Apostolakis G. Automated Hazard Analysis of Digital Control Systems. Reliability Engineering and System Safety. 2002;77:1–17.

[17] IEEE. Equipment Reliability Data for Nuclear-Power Generating Stations. New York: IEEE and John Wiley & Sons; 1984.

[18] Smith C. L., Wood S. T., Galyean W. J., Schroeder J. A., Beck S. T., Sattison M. B. Systems analysis Programs for Hands-On 17 Integrated Reliability Evaluations (SAPHIRE) Summary Manual, NUREG/CR-6116. 18 Washington, DC: Nuclear Regulatory Commission; 2008.

[19] Guarro S., Yau M., Motamed M. Development of Tools for Safety Analysis of Control Software in Advanced Reactors, NUREG/CR-6465. Washington, DC: Nuclear Regulatory Commission; 1996.

[20] Aldemir T., Kirschenbaum J., Mandelli D., Bucci P., Mangan L. A., Miller D. W., Sun X., Guarro S., Yau M., Arndt S. A., Ekici, E. Probabilistic Risk Assessment Modeling of Digital Instrumentation and Control Systems Using Two Dynamic Methodologies. Reliability Engineering and System Safety. 2010;95:1011–1039.

[21] Aldemir T. Computer-Assisted Markov Failure Modeling of Process Control Systems. IEEE Transactions on Reliability. 1987;R-36:133–144.

[22] Hsu C. S. Cell-to-Cell Mapping: A Method of Global Analysis for Nonlinear Systems. New York: Springer-Verlag; 1987.

[23] Aldemir T. Utilization of the Cell-to-Cell Mapping Technique to Construct Markov Failure Models for Process Control Systems. In: Probabilistic Safety and Assessment and Management, PSAM-1, Elsevier, Greece; 1991.

[24] Aldemir T., Bucci P., Mangan L. A., Kirschenbaum J., Mandelli D., Arndt S. A. Incorporation of Markov Reliability Models for Digital Instrumentation and Control Systems into Existing PRAs. In: Proceedings of NPIC&HMIT 2006, American Nuclear Society, La Grange Park, IL; 2006.

[25] IAEA. Component Reliability Data for Use in Probabilistic Safety Assessment. Vienna: International Atomic Energy Agency; 1988.

Chapter 3

Force Estimation for Teleoperating Industrial Robots

Enrique del Sol Acero

Additional information is available at the end of the chapter

http://dx.doi.org/10.5772/63788

Abstract

As the energy on the particle accelerators or heavy ion accelerators such as CERN or GSI, fusion reactors such as JET or ITER, or other scientific experiments is increased, it is becoming increasingly necessary to use remote handling techniques in order to interact with the remote and radioactive environment.

Traditionally, the remote handling techniques employed for bilateral teleoperation in the nuclear industry have been based on mechanically linked manipulators, backdrivable slaves or robotic devices equipped with a force or torque sensor. In this chapter, a bilateral control system based on a sensorless force-position architecture is introduced. This method avoids the use of force/torque sensors, whose electronic content makes them very sensitive to radiation. Its main purpose is to teleoperate industrial robots, which due to their well-known reliability, easiness to be adapted to harsh environments, cost-effectiveness and high availability, are considered as an interesting alternative to expensive custom-made solutions for remote handling tasks.

The proposed control technique implements a Luenberger-sliding observer of the slave robot as a force estimator, in order to employ a bilateral control based on force-position. A set of experiments demonstrates the applicability of this approach for estimating external forces acting on a hydraulic manipulator. The implementation of these techniques is straightforward and the results obtained during the experiments achieve an estimation error lower than 10%. This research develops an alternative method for teleoperating industrial robots whose teleoperation in radioactive environments would have been impossible in a different way.

Keywords: force estimation, industrial, sensorless, non-backdrivable, teleoperation, robots, radiation

1. Introduction

Most of bilateral control architectures developed to employ industrial robots for remote handling operations make use of force/torque sensors. The main reason for this, is the need of implementing any type of force-position bilateral control when teleoperating non-backdrivable devices. The force sensors are typically placed on the robot's end-effector, which implies that only external forces on that end can be measured. These devices also require additional wiring in the robot and cannot withstand the dose rates of the high-energy scientific facilities due to the utilisation of electronics [1]. Moreover, force sensors can be expensive and can increase the production cost of the robot. Therefore, a different research line seeks to develop an approach where the benefits of a force-sensing equipment are obtained without the need of using such devices.

Conventional master-slave devices have exploited one of the main requirements for bilateral teleoperation which is the backdrivable design of the manipulators. This characteristic facilitated the use of the positional error between master and slave, to estimate the external forces acting on the slave side. Nevertheless, the conventional industrial robots are non-backdrivable due to their mechanical properties such as, high reduction gears, high friction or non-backdrivable gear design, i.e. worm gears. Specific solutions of rad-hard dexterous and backdrivable manipulators are costlier than standard industrial solutions. The approach presented in this research looks into the possibility of adapting conventional robots to be deployed in these facilities. It would be very useful to take advantage of the big stock of industrial manipulators on the market and, through basic modifications in order to ensure radiation resistance, achieve a sensorless remote handling solution at a competitive price. This research looks into force estimation methods which can be applied to these devices and it is mainly focused on disturbance observers.

The area of research involving disturbance observers provides a useful framework for the problem of estimating external forces acting on a manipulator. Disturbance observers have been widely proposed for motion control and collision control applications [2–4], for determining disturbance forces such as friction. Estimation techniques based on observers for robot motion control were carried out by Ohishi et al. [5–7] using a nominal model of the robot. In this work, a disturbance torque is calculated by subtracting the nominal torque to the motor torque provided by the actuators while performing position control. The value of the nominal torque is calculated with a nominal inertia for every link. This method seeks to decouple the joint control by treating the effect of coupled inertia, Coriolis torque, friction and external effects as a disturbance torque. This basically consists of a feed-forward torque control with the nominal values of inertia. No distinction between the effect of external forces and the coupled inertia, Coriolis and friction is done. The method was tested with a 3-DOF robot.

The first observers for robots which use the complete manipulator model were implemented by Nicosia and Tomei and a large amount of research has been derived from their findings. Their aim was to design observers to perform robotic control without using velocity measurements which tend to introduce a large amount of noise [8]. The dynamic model of a manipulator can be written in the following way:

$$u = H(q)\ddot{q} + C(q,\dot{q}) + \tau_g(q) + \tau_f(\dot{q}) \tag{1}$$

where

q: is the vector of joints' values.

u: denotes the vector of motor input torques exerted in each joint

H(q): is the symmetric positive definite robot inertia matrix which is bounded for any q.

$C(q,\ \dot{q})$: is the centrifugal and Coriolis forces matrix in the Christoffel form.

$\tau_g(q)$: is the gravity forces vector.

$\tau_f(\dot{q})$: is the friction torques vector, $\tau_f(\dot{q}) = F \cdot \dot{q}$

Assuming the joint displacements as the output variables of the robot system, the observer output would be the following:

$$y = q \tag{2}$$

And defining the observed state as $\hat{y}$ and the observation error as $\tilde{y} = y - \hat{y}$, the proposed observer is described by:

$$\begin{cases} \dot{\hat{x}}_1 = \hat{x}_2 + k_D \tilde{y} \\ \dot{\hat{x}}_2 = H^{-1}(y)\left[-C\left(y, \dot{\hat{x}}_1\right)\dot{\hat{x}}_1 + u + k_P \tilde{y} - \tau_g(q) - F\dot{\hat{x}}_1\right] \\ \hat{y} = \hat{x}_1 \end{cases} \tag{3}$$

where k_D is a positive scalar constant and k_P is a symmetric positive definite matrix. In [8] it is proved the convergence of this observer by finding an appropriate Lyapunov's function, if the joints' velocities are assumed to be bounded and the initial observation error belongs to a suitable region of attraction.

Afterwards, Hacksel and Salcudean [9] employed the mentioned observer to estimate external forces on robots by splitting the total force in two terms, the control force and the environmental force: $f = f_{con} + f_{env}$. On the robot state, the term f is applied, while in the observer, only the known control force f_{con} is taken into account. By calculating the observer's estimation error, they yield to:

$$H(q)\ddot{\tilde{x}}_1 + C(q,\dot{q})\dot{\tilde{x}}_1 + C\left(q,\dot{\hat{x}}_1\right)\dot{\tilde{x}}_1 = -K_p\tilde{x}_1 - K_v H(q)\dot{\tilde{x}}_1 + u_{env} \tag{4}$$

which has an equilibrium point that acts as a stretched spring:

$$\tilde{x}_1 = K_p^{-1} u_{env} \tag{5}$$

It was found that, in equilibrium, the external force can be assumed to be proportional to the observation error and established the conditions for that to happen. From [8], they obtained the condition of bounded joint velocities. Also, if $k_c > 0$ is such that $\| C(q, \dot{q}) \| \leq k_c \| \dot{q} \|$ and $k_v > \frac{k_c M}{\lambda_{min}(H)}$, then the equilibrium point, $[\tilde{x}_1, \dot{\tilde{x}}_1] = [0, 0]$, is asymptotically stable, and a region of attraction is given by (6).

$$S = \left\{ x \epsilon \mathbb{R}^{2N}: \|x\| < \sqrt{\sigma_{min}(H_d) / \sigma_{max}(Hd)} \left(\frac{\lambda_{min}(H) k_v}{k_c} - M \right) \right\} \tag{6}$$

where $H_d = diag[K_p, H(q)]$, and σ_{min} and $\sigma_{\max}$ denote the minimum and maximum singular value, respectively. A constant environmental force can shift the equilibrium from $[\tilde{x}_1, \dot{\tilde{x}}_1] = [0, 0]$ to $[\tilde{x}_1, \dot{\tilde{x}}_1] = [K_p^{-1} u_{env}, 0]$ and has a shifted region of attraction as in (6) [9].

The same approach is employed again in [10] in order to predict the external forces acting in an ABB IRB2000 robot at the Robotics Lab, in Lund. The ABB control hardware has been replaced by an external VME-based control computer. They established that external forces at robot end-effector can be estimated with the following expression:

$$\phi_2 \ddot{\tilde{x}}_1 + \phi_1 \dot{\tilde{x}}_1 + \phi_0 \tilde{x}_1 = J^T F \tag{7}$$

with J being the robot's jacobian, and the φ_i functions taking the following values: $\phi_2 = H(x_1)$

$\phi_1 = C(x_1, \dot{x}_1) + C(x_1, \dot{\hat{x}}_1) + \tau_f + H(x_1) K_1$

$\phi_0 = K_2$

The environmental force is then estimated by:

$$\hat{F} = J^{T\dagger}(x_1) \phi_0 \tilde{x}_1 \tag{8}$$

with † denoting the matrix pseudo-inverse.

This observer has the advantage of not assuming a measurement of the joint velocities. However, it has the following drawbacks [11]:

- It needs to compute the Coriolis matrix for different input values, and also the friction effects separately.
- It assumes a perfect model of the manipulator, because otherwise, the observation errors will be manifested has an external force offset.

- Means of calculating the observer gains K_i are not provided.
- A good value of the external force is only guaranteed at steady state, this is when $\dot{x}_1 \simeq 0$, and $\ddot{x}_1 \simeq 0$. The Coriolis term is very hard to compute or measure and the force estimation may have large error and slow response to external force steps.

Different approaches based on robust observers [11–15] were also focused on avoiding the smaller stability margins of the disturbance observers during motion control [16]. Particularly interesting is the work of Colome et al. in [11] during their experiments with a cable-driven robot called WAM. They use an observer based again in [8], where only the inertial term is calculated with an a-priori knowledge of the robot and the rest is learnt by methods such as locally weighted projection regression (LWPR) and local Gaussian process (LGP). These approaches allow to improve the model even when the system is in operation. The observer makes use of the position and velocity errors with the related differentiation errors due to the numerical differentiation. They also find high complexity driving the robot with low control gains due to the static friction and cogging effects which are impossible to learn by the algorithm.

The proposed observer in [11] it is based in [17], and it estimates the state and the disturbance at the same time. The robot state space is represented in (9) while the observer state space equations are in (10).

$$\dot{x} = Ax + B(x)d + \Gamma^*(u,x) \tag{9}$$

where d is the disturbance external torque with the sign changed, and $A = \begin{bmatrix} 0 & I \\ 0 & 0 \end{bmatrix}$, $B = \begin{bmatrix} 0 \\ H^{-1}(x_1) \end{bmatrix}$ and $\Gamma^*(u_c, x) = \begin{bmatrix} 0 \\ \Gamma(u,x) \end{bmatrix}$, where, $\Gamma(u_c, x) = M^{-1}(x_1)[u_c - C(x_1, x_2)x_2 - \tau_f - \tau_g]$. While the state observer is defined in the following way:

$$\dot{\hat{x}} = A\hat{x} + B\hat{d} + K(x - \hat{x}) + \Gamma^*(u,\hat{x}) \tag{10}$$

With this, the external force estimation is derived and it yields:

$$\hat{d} = M(\hat{x}_1)\left(\dot{\hat{x}}_2 + \Sigma(x_2 - \hat{x}_2)\right) + \hat{n}(\hat{x}_1, \hat{x}_2) - u_c \tag{11}$$

where $\hat{n}(\hat{x}_1, \hat{x}_2)$ is the learned function which comprises the Coriolis Effect, friction torque and gravity torque and Σ is a set of gains. With this approach, the measurement of the joint velocity is necessary, but at the same time, no requirements for the system to be in equilibrium are given. The approximate value of the learned function will appear as an error in the contact force estimation, although this may happen in most of the model-based observers.

Different techniques are based on Ohishi's previous work and have employed the adaptive disturbance observer scheme [18], testing the proposed method for a 2-DOF planar robot. This research presents a novel approach in which a simple disturbance observer is developed with the nominal model of a robot. This model matches with Ohishi's work in the sense that the nominal inertia of each axis is used as a constant inertia matrix with only diagonal terms. Additional torque due to the coupled inertia, Coriolis, friction, etc. is considered torque disturbance, together with the external torque. In absence of external forces, the disturbance observer is used to calibrate a complete model of the robot by adjusting it, using the gradient method. Once the model is calibrated, it is used to compute in real time the external force by subtracting the model output to the observer output. The main drawback of this algorithm is the need of using the velocity and acceleration values in real time, in order to estimate the external forces, and the errors in the dynamic model which will introduce noise in the force estimation. Nevertheless, this method involves an improvement with respect to Ohishi's previous work, solving the lack of estimation of some torque components, which is accomplished with the use of the model.

In [19], a H^{∞} robust force observer is designed with the objective of controlling a robot joint by joint and considering all the force effects, except the nominal inertia, as a disturbance. This research completes Ohishi's work in robot control with robust observers. As mentioned earlier, the external force is estimated inside the entire disturbance, its independent determination being impossible.

Kalman filter has also been used to estimate external disturbances. In [20], the adaptive Kalman filter (AKF) is employed to estimate the disturbances of a 2-DOF robot. The particular advantage of using this method is the continuous updating of the noise covariance during the disturbance estimation process. Unfortunately, this research does not detail the effect of considering a 6-DOF robot without having the complete model. The theoretical solution works well with 1-DOF and DC motor, since all the disturbance is due to external torque effects. However, when considering a 6-DOF robot, if the complete model is not used, it would be difficult to distinguish the external torque from the internal torques caused by un-modelled effects.

Additionally, in [20], an alternative approach based on disturbance observers is used where a PID-like observer gain is employed to guide the observer convergence. The drawbacks of this method are similar to AKF implementation due to the lack of complete model for a 6-DOF robot.

Canudas de Wit and Slotine introduced the concept of sliding observers for robot manipulators [21]. The sliding observers had been used before to control highly non-linear processes using a non-linear control action. This technique has been good for controlling certain systems where the control chattering is not important, as in motor control, but cannot be used when no chattering is allowed. In state observers it is clear that discontinuities in control action are not important since it is not a real system and the chattering problem is not crucial. They prove the exponential convergence of sliding state observers under some circumstances and show the results when applying a time-varying gain observer. This technique is excellent when the exact model of the system is not known since observation errors tend to zero asymptotically.

Sliding observers have also been used in teleoperation to estimate velocities and forces in the presence of delays as in [22], where the only use position measurements. However, these algorithms were only tested during simulation and no real tests are provided.

In [23], three non-conventional state observers are compared, these are: high-gain observers, sliding mode and non-linear extended state observers. The high-gain observer [24] of a plant described by (12) is indicated by (13).

$$\ddot{y} = f(y, \dot{y}, w) + k \cdot u \tag{12}$$

$$\begin{cases} \dot{\hat{x}}_1 = \hat{x}_2 + h_1(y - \hat{x}_1) \\ \dot{\hat{x}}_2 = f_0 + b_0 u + h_2(y - \hat{x}_1) \end{cases} \tag{13}$$

where f represents the dynamics of the plant and disturbance, w is the unknown input disturbance, u is the control action and y is the output that can be measured. f_0 is a nominal model of the function f. With this, the estimation error equations are described by (14).

$$\begin{cases} \dot{\tilde{x}}_1 = -h_1\tilde{x}_1 + \tilde{x}_2 \\ \dot{\tilde{x}}_2 = -h_2\tilde{x}_1 + \delta(x, \tilde{x})\tilde{x} = \begin{bmatrix} x_1 - \hat{x}_1 \\ x_2 - \hat{x}_2 \end{bmatrix} \end{cases} \tag{14}$$

where $\delta(\cdot) = f(\cdot) - f_0(\cdot)$. The convergence of the error is achieved in absence of disturbance if the observer gain matrix is designed such that the matrix A_0 is Hurwitz,that is, for every positive constants, h_1 and h_2. In the presence of δ, the observer gains are adjusted as (16).

$$A_0 = \begin{bmatrix} -h_1 & 1 \\ -h_2 & 0 \end{bmatrix} \tag{15}$$

$$h_1 = \frac{\gamma_1}{\varepsilon}, \quad h_2 = \frac{\gamma_2}{\varepsilon}, \tag{16}$$

where $0 < \varepsilon \ll 1$, and the gains γ_1 and γ_2 can be determined via pole placement.

The sliding observer is explained later and no more detail will be given here. Both high-gain observer and sliding require some knowledge of the plant dynamics. An alternative method termed non-linear extended state observer has been created by Han [25] as follows. The plant in (12) is firstly augmented as:

$$\begin{cases} \dot{x}_1 & = & x_2 \\ \dot{x}_2 & = & x_3 + b_0 u \\ \dot{x}_3 & = & f(y, \dot{y}, w) \\ y & = & x_1 \end{cases} \tag{17}$$

where f is an extended state, x_3. Here both f and its derivative are assumed unknown. By making f a state, it is now possible to estimate it using a state estimator. Han proposed a non-linear observer for (17) as follows:

$$\begin{cases} \dot{z}_1 = z_2 + \beta_1 g_1(e) \\ \dot{z}_2 = z_3 + \beta_2 g_2(e) + b_0 u \\ \dot{z}_3 = \beta_3 g_3(e) \end{cases} \tag{18}$$

where $e = y - z_1$ and z_1 is the estimation of the function f. Then, $g(\cdot)$ is defined as a modified exponential gain function:

$$g_i(e, \alpha_i, \delta) = \begin{cases} |e|^{\alpha_i} sign(e), & |e| > \delta \\ \dfrac{e}{\delta^{1-\alpha_i}}, & |e| \le \delta \end{cases} \quad \delta > 0, \tag{19}$$

As α_i is chosen between 0 and 1, g_i yields high gain when error is small. δ is a small number to limit the gain in the neighbourhood of the origin. Starting with linear gain $g_i(e, \alpha_i, \delta) = e$, the pole placement method can be used for the initial design of the observer, before the non-linearities are added to improve the performance.

The comparison of these three types of observers is accomplished in [23], proving best performance for the non-linear extended observer and followed closely by the sliding gain observer.

In parallel with the force estimation techniques, based on disturbance observers, another research approach that implements sensor fusion has been developed to reduce the noise levels of the force sensors used in teleoperation. In [26, 30], the information from a force sensor is fused with an accelerometer measurement in order to eliminate the effect of the tool inertia in the force sensor measurements. This sensor fusion is performed with the Kalman filter. In [27], data from force sensors and position encoders are fused. In [28, 29], data gathered by means of a force sensor are combined with visual information to estimate position measurements between a grasped object and other objects in the environment.

2. A new general approach for teleoperation

An overview of the framework where this research is set is detailed next. A general approach for bilateral control must consider situations when the external variables are either measured or estimated. **Figure 1** represents an approach of a bilateral teleoperation where only conventional positional and force feedback are considered. Also, no delay in transmission of the information is taken into account. The operator (human) exchanges forces and torques with the master device, in such a way that they both share their position, $x_h = x_m$, at all time. While the operator applies position commands and reaction forces, the haptic master conveys the external forces, measured or estimated from the environment, assistive and dragging forces, to the operator.

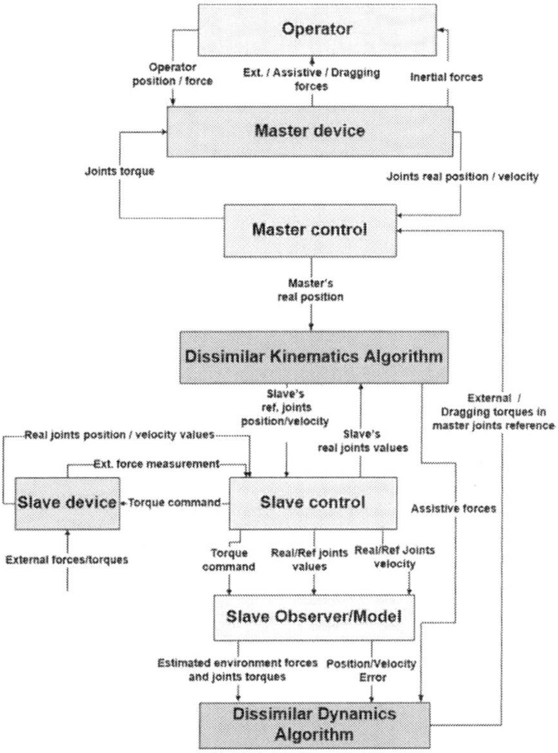

Figure 1. General control scheme for a bilateral system for dissimilar master-slave.

The measured or estimated forces, which are transmitted to the human, have been previously processed in the dissimilar dynamics block and sent back to the master controller as reference torques for the master joints. The assistive forces are those artificially created and conveyed to the operator in order to facilitate the teleoperation tasks. These can be vibratory, kinaesthetic or from different type and their objective is to guide the operator in his movement along the master's workspace. On the other hand, the dragging forces are unintentional forces created in some control architectures where the force feedback depends on the positional and velocity errors. This is due to the fact that, in some control schemes, such as position-position, a positional error is required in order to produce a torque that moves the slave manipulator towards the master's pose and vice versa. In these cases, the operator would feel a resistive force as if he was continuously pulling from the haptic device. Finally, the inertial forces arise by the fact that the master device is not ideal. This presents mass and inertia which will induce a reaction force to the movement.

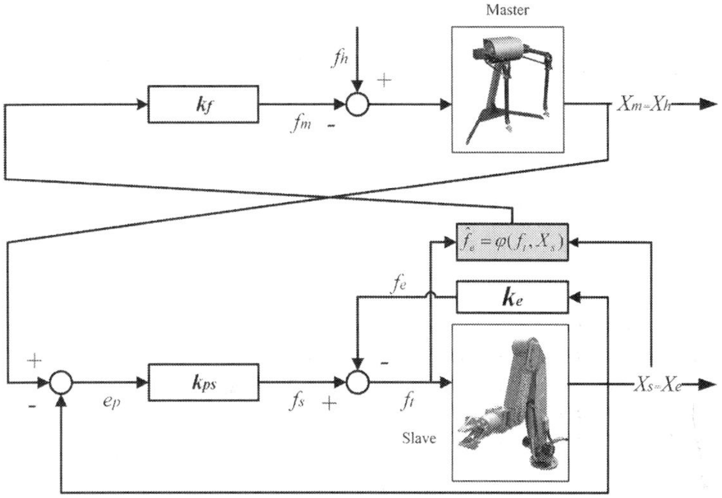

Figure 2. Proposed force-position bilateral control for teleoperating non-backdrivable slaves.

In the most common scenario, the master control system would receive the positional feedback from the master device and send the appropriate joint torque to it. The assistive forces are calculated in the dissimilar kinematics block in order to correct the trajectory of the human operator in a way that the movement is always performed inside the slave's workspace. Afterwards, these are processed in the dissimilar dynamics block to be transformed into the joint space. The remaining forces are calculated by the dissimilar dynamics block depending on the external forces or control scheme utilised. This block typically employs the master's Jacobian to transform the external forces and torques from Cartesian space to the master's joints space. The dissimilar kinematic block interfaces the master's control with the slave's control in a way that the master's end-effector pose and position are mimicked by the slave's end-effector as much as possible. The slave's control will close the loop with the slave device by controlling its position by means of torque commands applied on its actuators.

A state observer of the slave is introduced here as a general scenario for those control schemes where a force has to be estimated without using force sensors—the central topic of this chapter. In a common scenario, the observer would receive the torque command issued to the slave device, and all the available feedback from it, such as position, velocity or acceleration. With this information, it will estimate the value of the external forces and torques applied on the slave, if any. Afterwards, the dissimilar dynamic block transforms all the forces from the slave's reference to the master's reference.

The bilateral control presented here is displayed in **Figure 2**, where the force/torque sensor is substituted by a dynamic model of the robot or a force observer. The central idea is to convey to the operator the estimation of environmental forces as if they were measured by the sensor. Several approaches can be used to perform this estimation, but most of them make use of the knowledge of the slave's dynamic model, the commanded torque and the state space variables of the manipulator.

As described in Section 1, some approaches try to reduce the complexity of the model and implement a learning algorithm to avoid the analytic calculation [11], some others are based on Kalman [22–24, 30, 27] or Luenberger [9, 10], observers, but almost all of them need at least a basic model of the slave manipulator.

3. Estimation of external forces for robots

In this section, a review of the main methods for force estimation is carried out, starting from an off-line evaluation of the robotics dynamics equation. A set of experiments accomplished by means of a hydraulic manipulator is explained, highlighting the benefits and drawbacks of this approach. Afterwards, a Luenberger observer of the robot is designed and tested for estimating external forces and compared with the off-line approach. This observer is based on the one presented by Nicosia and Tomei in [8] which was adapted by Hacksel and Salcudean [9] for force estimation. This method is considered one of the main techniques for force estimation so far, and presents clear advantages over the evaluation of the robot dynamics equation. Following this, research is conducted towards the search of robust estimators with zero offset in absence of external forces, in a way that the human operator does not receive unnecessary stimuli that could lead to tiredness and lack of concentration. The main advance here comes with the adaptation of sliding observers for force estimation in teleoperation. Their use improves the results obtained with simpler Luenberger observers.

3.1. Evaluation of the forward dynamics equation

As the forces and torques applied on the master device are proportional to those applied to the slave in bilateral control using force channel, the estimation of the robot end-effector torques in a sensorless system is crucial. In this section, to obtain the force information from the disturbance signal, the external torques are estimated using the robot dynamic equation (20) modified to take into account the external effect.

$$\tau_m = H(q)\ddot{q} + C(q,\dot{q})\dot{q} + \tau_g(q) + \tau_f(\dot{q}) + \tau_{ext} \quad (20)$$

where τ_m is the vector of motor torques exerted in each joint, *H(q)* is the robot inertia matrix, which is a function of the joints' values, $C(q,\dot{q})$ is the Coriolis and centripetal forces vector, which also depends on the joints' values and velocities. τ_g is the gravity forces vector depending on the robot position. τ_f is the friction torques vector, which in general terms, is also dependent on the joints' velocities. Finally, τ_{ext} is the vector of external torques on each joint.

The external forces can be estimated by applying the kinematic information contained in the robot Jacobian and obtaining (21).

$$T_{ext} = J^{T^{\dagger}}(\tau_m - H(q)\ddot{q} + C(q,\dot{q})\dot{q} + \tau_g(q) + \tau_f(\dot{q})) \quad (21)$$

where T_{ext} is the vector of forces and torques ejected in the robot end-effector and expressed in the base coordinates system and *J* is the robot jacobian with † denoting the matrix inverse or pseudo-inverse when corresponds.

When a force estimation is needed in online mode, i.e. for teleoperation purposes, a real-time estimation of the speed and acceleration should be accomplished. When a tachometer is available on the robot, there is no need of differentiation of the position measurements; however, this is not the case of most of manipulators, and velocity and acceleration have to be obtained from position measurements. Also, generator-type tachometers and encoder-based velocity measurement electronics often provide unsatisfactory outputs at very slow velocities due to noise and low resolution [31] and they are not compatible with radioactive environments.

It has been proved in the literature [32] that a recommended sampling time of 1 kHz should be used for teleoperation when requiring force feedback. Therefore, any method implemented for obtaining the velocity data should not introduce a delay superior than 1 ms.

The simplest velocity estimation method is the Euler approximation that takes the difference of two sampling positions divided by the sampling period. Typically, the position measurements are taken with encoders or resolvers, which contain stochastic errors that result in enormous noise during the velocity estimation by the Euler approximation when the sampling period is small and the velocity low [31]. Different alternatives have been tried which utilise more backwards steps to reduce the noise but introducing a small delay. In [33], a first-order adaptive method is shown which is able to vary the backward steps depending on the speed. Also, in [34] it has been found that three steps are the best for a sampling rate of 2500 Hz in their experiments with an encoder of 655,360 pulses per revolution. They also implemented a Kalman observer and non-linear observers, obtaining the same results than an averaging of the Euler formula. In [35], a Kalman filter is tested assuming a normal distribution of the position error. In [31], a dynamic method which varies the samples used for averaging depending on the speed is developed with very good results.

Given a desired relative accuracy (r_j) of the velocity calculation, with encoder measurements by the formula (22) taken from [31], it is possible to derive the required amount of time for obtaining a velocity measurement. This is assuming that the velocity is not calculated with two consecutive samples, but with two samples separated by a certain number of backwards steps j in order to increase the velocity resolution. For an incremental encoder with resolution R, if the position $q(t)$ is sampled with a sampling period T, and for $k = 1, 2, \ldots$, the discrete sampled position at time kT is given by $\theta(k)$. The relative accuracy is given by (22).

$$r_j = \left|\frac{\hat{v}_j - v_j}{\hat{v}_j}\right| < \left|\frac{2R}{\theta(k) - \theta(k-j)}\right| = \left|\frac{1}{\theta(k) - \theta(k-j)}\right| 2R = 2 / s_j \tag{22}$$

where v_j is the real velocity and $\hat{v}_j$ is estimated with the measurements. For example, in order to obtain a relative accuracy of $r_j = 2\%$, $s_j = 100$, i.e. 100 past pulses have to be traced back on the velocity calculation. If this is to be achieved with an encoder of 10.000 lines/rev, the elapsed angular space for 100 pulses would result to be 3.6°. With a motor running at 1 rpm, the required amount of time for completing that angular slot is 10 ms. This amount of delay is detrimental for a good bilateral performance.

The scheme used in this section for obtaining the smoothed position, velocity and acceleration makes use of a Savitzky-Golay filter due to its good properties for smooth differentiation. A conventional low-pass filter can be utilised for smoothing the torque data since no differentiation is needed.

3.1.1. Force estimation results of a hydraulic manipulator by direct evaluation of the dynamics equation

To evaluate the previous method, an identification procedure based on damped least mean squares, with optimisation of the parameters, was implemented for the hydraulic manipulator from Kraft Telerobotics as shown in **Figure 3**. This allowed to obtain a complete model of the manipulator as described by equation (21).

The experimental setup was composed of the following elements:

- 1 x KRAFT GRIPS hydraulic telemanipulator.
- 1 x NI-PXIe-8108 Real Time controller.
- 1 x PC running Labview 2011, © National Instruments, interfacing with the PXI.
- 1 x Force/Torque sensor, ATI, Gamma SI-130-10.
- 1 x Resilient interface with an elastic constant of 5000 [N/m].

The manipulator was mounted with an elastic interface attached on the robot end-effector with an ATI force sensor between them, in order to verify the effectiveness of the proposed approach (see **Figure 4**). This allowed to evaluate the accuracy of the estimation during a wide dynamic range, and identify the occurrence of estimation offsets. Initially the robot was commanded to a pose with the end-effector approximately perpendicular to the horizontal plane. An up-down movement was accomplished, compressing the elastic interface by commanding joint 2, while the PID controllers of each joint maintained the positions of the other joints. This configuration was chosen with the objective of maintaining the spring as perpendicular to the plane as possible. The duration of the compression movement was approximately 4 s.

Figure 3. KRAFT GRIPS hydraulic telemanipulator.

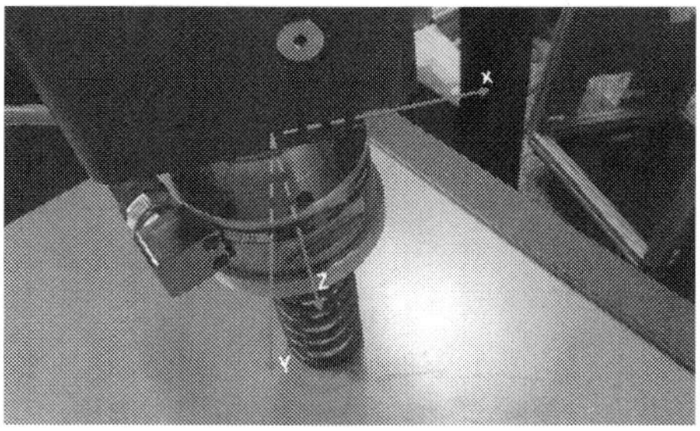

Figure 4. Robot's end-effector reference system equipped with the ATI force sensor and an elastic interface.

Figures 5–7 present the result of this experiment, comparing the estimated motor torque for the given dynamics with the real torque exerted by the actuators. The external torque has been calculated by subtracting the estimated torque from the measured one. During the compression effort, the model only estimates the dynamics given by the movement accomplished by the robot, that is, the inner torque, ignoring the existence of external elements. However, the measured torque takes into account the real effort exerted by the joints which considers the addition of external forces and torques plus the torques required for moving the robot. During this test, the main effort was accomplished by joints 2 and 3.

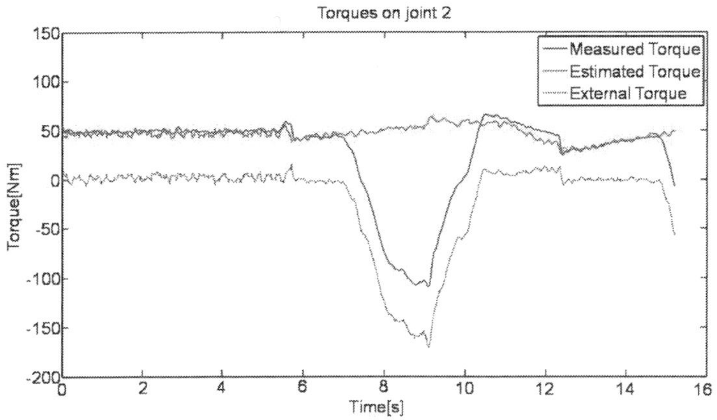

Figure 5. Measured and estimated motor torques for joint 2. The dashed line represents the external torque caused by the compression effort in joint 2.

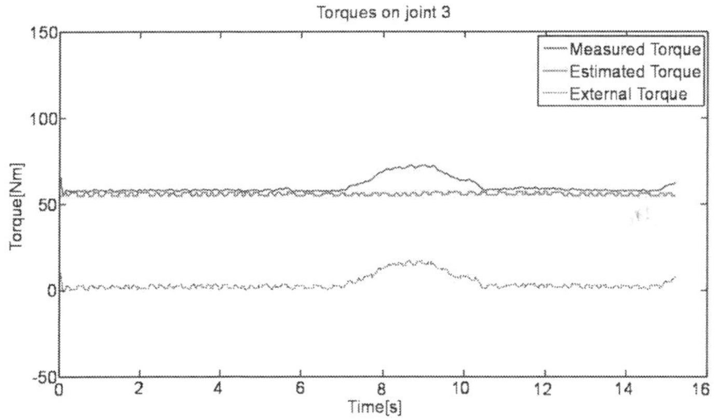

Figure 6. Measured and estimated motor torques for joint 3. The dashed line represents the external torque caused by the compression effort in joint 3.

The major issue to overcome when applying this method is the differentiation of position and velocity to obtain the joints' velocity and acceleration respectively. In this experiment, the sampling rate has been 1 kHz and an offline Savitzky-Golay filtering has been applied to smooth the position and differentiate it. Performing this operation in real time, with conventional low pass filters, would lead to either unaffordable delays or prohibitive estimation errors. The former would cause an unstable teleoperation. However, it would be required due to the noisy positional feedback and the noise amplification effect of the differentiation process.

Therefore, an increased sampling frequency up to a minimum of 4 kHz would help to reduce the delay caused by filtering, allowing the bilateral system to have any delay lower than 1 ms. Also, the application of more advanced smoothing techniques would be desirable. This issue motivated the development of force estimation techniques based on state observers. A state observer was found to be useful in order to avoid position differentiation and the undesirable effects produced by it.

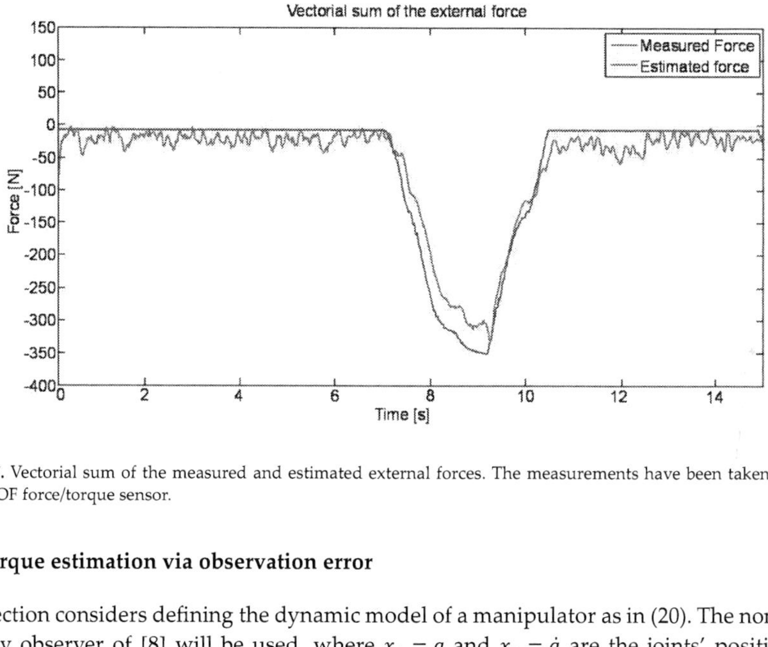

Figure 7. Vectorial sum of the measured and estimated external forces. The measurements have been taken with the ATI 6-DOF force/torque sensor.

3.2. Torque estimation via observation error

This section considers defining the dynamic model of a manipulator as in (20). The non-linear velocity observer of [8] will be used, where $x_1 = q$ and $x_2 = \dot{q}$ are the joints' position and velocity respectively. The state space representation of the robot dynamics is then the following:

$$\begin{cases} \dot{x}_1 = x_2 \\ \dot{x}_2 = H^{-1}(x_1)[-C(x_1,\dot{x}_1)\dot{x}_1 - \tau_g(x_1) - \tau_f(\dot{x}_1) + \tau_m - \tau_{ext}] \end{cases} \tag{23}$$

Assuming that only joint's positions are measured and without accounting explicitly for the external forces, it is possible to construct a non-linear observer by copying the manipulator dynamics. The output variable will then be x_1.

$$\begin{cases} \dot{\hat{x}}_1 = \hat{x}_2 + k_1\tilde{x}_1 \\ \dot{\hat{x}}_2 = H^{-1}(x_1)[-C(x_1,\dot{\hat{x}}_1)\dot{\hat{x}}_1 - \tau_g(x_1) - \tau_f(\dot{\hat{x}}_1) + \tau_m + k_2\tilde{x}_1] \\ \tilde{x}_1 = x_1 - \hat{x}_1 \end{cases} \tag{24}$$

where k_1 and k_2 are the Luenberger (observer) gains and they will be symmetric and definite positive gains, properly selected to place the poles of the linearised system into the desired positions. Using the results given in [8–10], one can demonstrate that the dynamics of the observation error can be expressed as in (25).

$$\varnothing_2\ddot{\tilde{x}}_1 + \varnothing_1\dot{\tilde{x}}_1 + \varnothing_0\tilde{x}_1 = \tau_{ext} \tag{25}$$

where $\varnothing_2 = H(x_1)$, $\varnothing_1 = C(x_1, \dot{x}_1) - \pi(x_1, \dot{\hat{x}}_1) + \tau_f(\dot{\tilde{x}}_1) + H(x_1)k_1$ and $\varnothing_0 = k_2$. And thus, in the equilibrium, the expression in (25) could be simplified to (26), which provides an expression to estimate the external torques when the velocity and acceleration are small.

$$\tau_{ext} = k_2\tilde{x}_1 \tag{26}$$

Let us now apply the same reasoning as in [10] with an extended Luenberger-sliding observer to see how the forces and torques can be estimated when in steady state. By including the sliding gains, one can yield to the Luenberger-sliding observer for robots represented in Eq. (27), where k_1 and k_2 are the Luenberger gains,which will be symmetric and definite positive gains, properly selected to place the poles of the linearised system into the desired positions. k_3 and k_4 are the sliding gains. K_3 can be seen as a boundary of the steady state error and k_4 is chosen to be higher than the modelling error.

$$\begin{cases} \dot{\hat{x}}_1 = \hat{x}_2 + k_3 sgn(\tilde{x}_1) + k_1\tilde{x}_1 \\ \dot{\hat{x}}_2 = H^{-1}(x_1)\left[-C(x_1,\dot{\hat{x}}_1)\dot{\hat{x}}_1 - \tau_g(x_1) - \tau_f(\dot{x}_1) + \tau_m + k_4 sgn(\tilde{x}_1) + k_2\tilde{x}_1\right] \end{cases} \tag{27}$$

with $\tilde{x}_1 = x_1 - \hat{x}_1$.

After operating with the Coriolis torques and friction torques, it is possible to get the expression for the observer error:

$$\begin{cases} \dot{\tilde{x}}_1 = \tilde{x}_2 - k_1\tilde{x}_1 - k_3 sgn(\tilde{x}_1) \\ \dot{\tilde{x}}_2 = H^{-1}(x_1)\left[-C(x_1,\dot{x}_1)\dot{x}_1 + C(x_1,\dot{\hat{x}}_1)\dot{\hat{x}}_1 - \tau_f(\dot{\tilde{x}}_1) - \tau_{ext} - k_2\tilde{x}_1 - k_4 sgn(\tilde{x}_1)\right] \end{cases} \tag{28}$$

By differentiating and combining the two terms, the expression for the dynamics of the position error is obtained.

$$\begin{aligned}\ddot{\tilde{x}}_1 &= \dot{\tilde{x}}_2 - k_1\dot{\tilde{x}}_1 - k_3\mathrm{sgn}(\dot{\tilde{x}}_1)\\ &= H^{-1}(x_1)[-C(x_1,\dot{x}_1)\dot{x}_1 + \pi(x_1,\dot{\hat{x}}_1)\dot{\hat{x}}_1 - \tau_f(\dot{\hat{x}}_1) - \tau_{ext} - k_2\tilde{x}_1 - k_4\mathrm{sgn}(\tilde{x}_1)] - k_1\dot{\tilde{x}}_1 - k_3\mathrm{sgn}(\dot{\tilde{x}}_1)\end{aligned} \tag{29}$$

Collecting the terms of (29), it yields:

$$\o_4\ddot{\tilde{x}}_1 + \o_3\dot{\tilde{x}}_1 + \o_2 sgn(\dot{\tilde{x}}_1) + \o_1\tilde{x}_1 + \o_0 sgn(\tilde{x}_1) = \tau_{ext} \tag{30}$$

where

$$\o_4 = H(x_1) \tag{31}$$

$$\o_3 = C(x_1,\dot{x}_1) - \pi(x_1,\dot{\hat{x}}_1) + \dot{\hat{x}}_1(\dot{\hat{x}}_1) + H(x_1)k_1 \tag{32}$$

$$\o_2 = H(x_1)k_3 \tag{33}$$

$$\o_1 = k_2 \tag{34}$$

$$\o_0 = k_4 \tag{35}$$

And thus, on equilibrium, the external torques can be estimated using (31).

$$\tau_{ext} = k_2\tilde{x}_1 + k_4 sgn(\tilde{x}_1) \tag{36}$$

Although this theoretical result seems feasible during steady state force estimation, it is not adequate for practical implementation due to the likely strong chattering of the sliding action. In order to avoid this effect of the sliding control, several methods have been developed in the literature. These are summarised in [36] and are divided into two main types: gain modification algorithms and structural methods. In this research, a gain modification algorithm based on boundary layer solution is employed. This has been done by varying the value of the k_4 gain depending on the torque predicted via Luenberger observer only; in this way (31) is converted to (32).

$$\tau_{ext} = k_2\tilde{x}_1 + \xi k_4 sgn(\tilde{x}_1) \tag{37}$$

http://dx.doi.org/10.5772/63788

$$\begin{cases} \xi = 0 & if \left|k_2 \tilde{x}_1\right| < \tau_{threshold} \\ \xi = \dfrac{\left|k_2 \tilde{x}_1 - \tau_{threshold}\right|}{\tau_{threshold}} & if \left|k_2 \tilde{x}_1\right| \geq \tau_{threshold} \end{cases} \tag{38}$$

In addition to this transformation, ξ is saturated to a maximum value which is 1. This allows a progressive increase of the effect of the non-linear observer action in a way that the chattering is avoided.

3.2.1. Experimental results on force estimation implementing Luenberger and Luenberger-sliding observers

The same experimental setup as in Section 3.1.1 has been employed here. During a similar scenario, the KRAFT manipulator was commanded to different poses, carrying an elastic interface and the ATI force/torque sensor between the interface and the last link. The objective of this test was to validate the estimators presented earlier and to compare the performance between the two observers. During this test, the robot was teleoperated in free space by a human operator during approximately 25 s and then placed in the parking position before disconnection. At intermediate positions during its trajectory, the robot was forced to compress the spring against a horizontal surface.

Luenberger observer gains	
K_1	50
K_2	$100 \cdot$diag([1.5, 7, 2.3029, 0.345, 0.2918, 0.0651]) (*)

Table 1. Luenberger observer gains used during the experiment. (*) The function diag() indicates a diagonal matrix composed by the elements between brackets.

A Luenberger observer was tuned with the gains shown in **Table 1**. The motor torques during this operation are represented in **Figure 8**, and the external torques predicted with this observer are shown in **Figure 9**. The observer behaves as expected, and after a period of convergence of approximately 8 s, it reaches the steady state and performs a stable force estimation. It is clear that this algorithm decouples the external torque from the efforts due to different actions other than the external. Although the estimation is still not perfect, the method explained here exhibits good performance and clearly improves the results of the method based on evaluating the robot's dynamics equation since it can be implemented during real time for teleoperation purposes. Increasing the gains not only improves the average of the estimated torques, but it also increases the noise of the estimation. A compromise must be reached when tuning the observer gains.

The inaccuracies found when implementing this algorithm, especially in the form of estimation offsets in absence of external forces, led this research towards the search of a more robust estimator which was not affected in such a way by the modelling errors. The sliding observers were found to be an extremely effective solution with easiness of implementation.

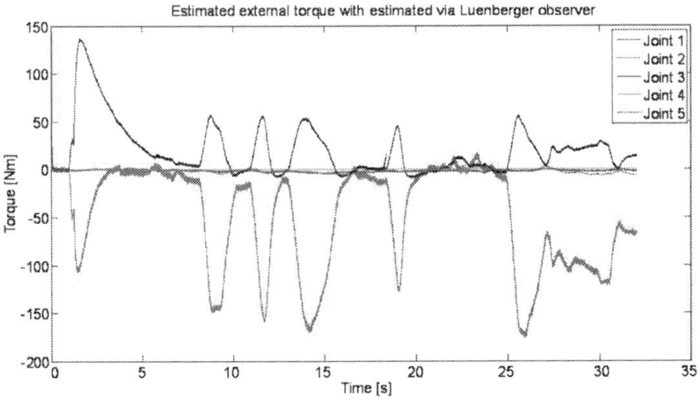

Figure 8. Motor torques during the spring compression test. The values represented here include the gravity, inertial and Coriolis torque and also the action of external torques and forces.

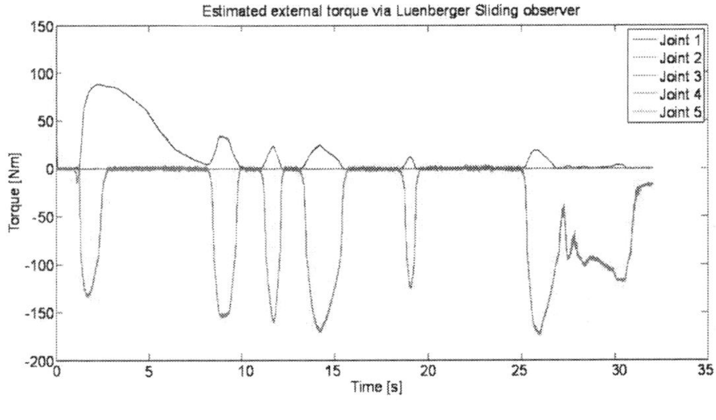

Figure 9. External torques predicted using the Luenberger observer during the spring compression test. Three different parts can be distinguished here, e.g. the pre-convergence stage, where estimation of external torques appears even in the absence of external forces. This only occurs during the first seconds of estimation until the observer converges to zero error. Afterwards, four impacts are performed on a plane surface where the spring is compressed; these conform to the second stage. Finally, after 25 s, a period of instability is shown when the robot was placed on hold position and disconnected to finalise the experiment.

These estimators were previously used when controlling highly non-linear processes and when only a rough model of the system was known. A Luenberger-sliding observer was thus designed and tuned with the gains from **Table 2**. Predicted external torques are shown in **Figure 10**. One can appreciate great differences with respect to the simpler version of the observer illustrated in **Figure 9**. Offsets and unmodelled torques have almost disappeared, resulting in a much clearer estimation.

http://dx.doi.org/10.5772/63788

Luenberger-sliding observer gains	
K_1	$50\cdot\text{diag}([1,1,1,1,1,1])$
K_2	$60\cdot\text{diag}([1.5;8;1;0.345;0.2918;\ 0.0651\ ])$ (*)
K_3	0.01
K_4	$25\cdot\text{diag}([1,2,0.9,1,1,1])$

Table 2. Gains used on the Luenberger-Sliding observer during the spring compression test. (*) The function diag() indicates a diagonal marix composed by the elements between brackets.

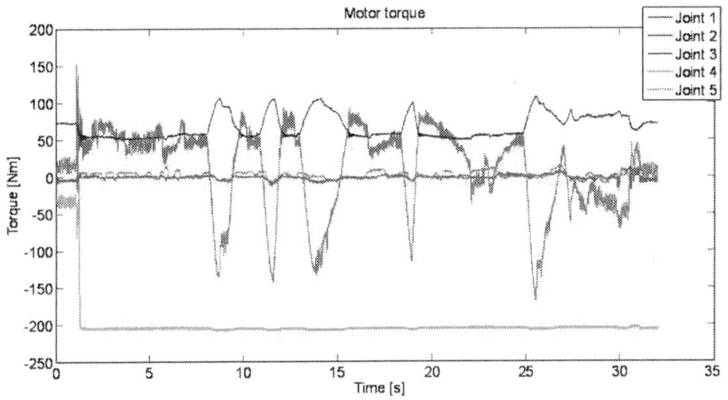

Figure 10. External torques predicted using Luenberger-sliding observer.

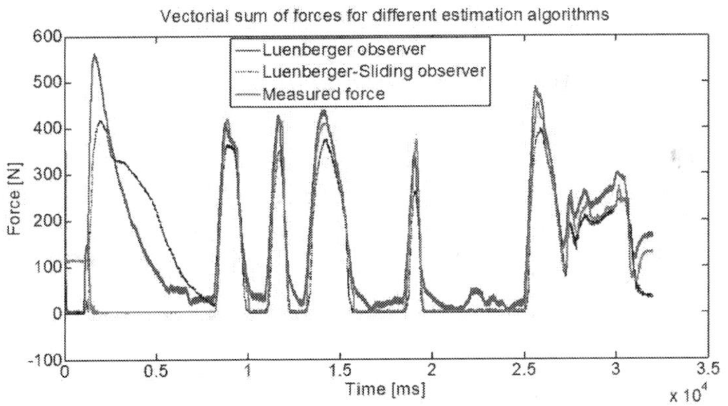

Figure 11. Comparison of force magnitude for estimations based on Luenberger observer and Luenberger-sliding observers. Validation against measurement performed with a 5-DOFATI force/torque sensor.

In **Figure 11**, comparative results for the force estimation between Luenberger and Luenberger-sliding observers are shown. One can check that estimations carried out without the sliding action present offset errors due to modelling inaccuracies. These offsets disappear when implementing the sliding-observer as a result of a more robust action, and a clearer force estimation is achieved after the convergence period. An average error of 10% has been achieved during dynamic impact when using the sliding action. In the absence of external forces, the estimation error is negligible.

4. Conclusions

During the development of this chapter, the theoretical basis for the external force estimation for teleoperation has been established. The main algorithms have been introduced during the review of the state of the art, and three methods have been developed further.

It was proved that the evaluation of the robotics dynamics equation was not feasible for real-time force estimation due to the noise caused by the differentiation, unless the position was sampled at a much higher frequency than the one used for the bilateral loop. This approach should only be used when estimating forces during an off-line process, e.g. during the determination of the dynamics of a new end-effector placed on the robot.

This chapter introduced the use of Luenberger observers for estimating the internal state of a robot manipulator, a common mathematical tool. However, this observer has been proved to be also useful for force estimation by demonstrating that the observation error is proportional to the external force.

These observers were used to estimate external forces by means of the observation error. One of the contributions of this method is that the position differentiation and filtering is not needed anymore. This avoids having either a noisy velocity and acceleration or a detrimental delay if filtering techniques are used. The former would lead to noisier and less accurate force estimation which would deteriorate the transparency and performance of the teleoperation. Presence of a delay greater than 1 ms is considered in the literature [32] as a source of instabilities during the bilateral control, and then, it cannot be tolerated.

It has been shown that the only use of a Luenberger observer does not provide accurate results when the robot model is not perfectly known, which is the most common scenario. Experimental tests were performed with a Kraft manipulator, showing that although a decoupling of the external force was possible, incorrect torque offsets were introduced when the model was not perfect. This conducted the research towards the search of a more robust observer, more reluctant to model inaccuracies. A simple but powerful non-linear mathematical tool, called sliding observer, was identified. This type of estimator was previously used to control highly non-linear processes and it was typically implemented when the model of the system was not totally known. The main disadvantage of this observer is the chattering effect provoked by the switching behaviour around the zero torque. This effect creates a high content of noise on the estimation. However, the strong switching action was smoothed by varying the sliding gains, depending on the value of the external torques which are previously obtained by the simpler Luenberger observer.

The proposed solution provides successful results, allowing the sliding action to reduce the offset error almost totally, with minimum chattering. The results were shown by estimating external forces on a manipulator and validating them against the measurements taken by a 6-DOF force/torque sensor. During the tests performed thorough spring compression, the average error on force estimation during the impact was 7% for the Luenberger estimator and 10% for the Luenberger-sliding. Direct comparison of the accuracy value is not fair since the offset errors on the Luenberger observer tend to decrease the amplitude error observed during the impact, i.e. the estimation is moved upwards.

To summarise, a new method for estimating the external forces based on Luenberger-sliding observers has been presented here, proving its application for bilateral teleoperation. This method is able to perform accurate estimations with zero offset and delay, which makes it adequate for bilateral teleoperation, especially for non-backdrivable manipulators without force sensing equipment.

Author details

Enrique del Sol Acero

Address all correspondence to: e.delsol.acero@gmail.com

Technical University of Madrid, Madrid, Spain

References

[1] E. Del Sol, R. Scott, and R. King. "A sensorless virtual slave control scheme for Kinematically dissimilar master-slave teleoperation". In Proceedings of HOTLAB. 2012, Marcoule, France.

[2] M.T. White, M. Tomizuka, and C. Smith. "Improved track following in magnetic disk drives using a disturbance observer". In IEEE/ASME Transactions on Mechatronics. 2000, vol. 5, pp. 3–11.

[3] A. Sabanovic and I. Khalil. Sensorless torque/force control. In Advances in Motor Torque Control, Dr. Mukhtar Ahmad, editors. 2011, InTech, Croatia, DOI: 10.5772/20741. Available: http://www.intechopen.com/books/advances-in-motor-torque-control/sensorless-torque-control

[4] K. Fujiyama, R. Katayama, T. Hamaguchi, and K. Kawakami. "Digital controller design for recordable optical disk player using disturbance observer". In IEEE Proceedings of

6th International Workshop on Advanced Motion Control. 2000, Nagoya, Japan, pp. 141–146.

[5] M. Nakao, K. Ohnishi, and K. Miyach. "A robust decentralized joint control based on interference estimation". In Proceedings on IEEE International Conference on Robotics and Automation, Raleigh, NC, March 1987, vol. 4, pp. 326–331.

[6] Murakami T et al. "Torque sensorless control in multidegree of freedom manipulator". In IEEE Transactions on Industrial Electronics. 1993, vol. 40, no 2, pp. 259–265.

[7] K. Ohnishi, S. Masaaki and M. Toshiyuki. "Motion Control for advanced mechatronics". In IEEE/ASME Transactions on Mechatronics. 1996, vol. 1, no 1, pp. 56–67.

[8] S. Nicosia and P. Tomei. "Robot Control by using only joint position measurements". In IEEE Transactions on Automatic Control. 1990, vol. 35, no. 9, pp.1058–1061.

[9] P. J. Hacksel and S. E. Salcudean "Estimation of environmental forces and rigid body velocities using observers." In IEEE International Conference on Robotics and Automation, 1994, pp. 931–936, San Diego, CA, USA.

[10] A. Alcocer, A. Robertsson, A. Valera, and R. Johansson. "Force Estimation and control in robot manipulators". In Proceedings of the 7th Symposium on Robot Control (SYROCO 2003). 2003 Sept. 1–3, Wroclaw, Poland. pp. 31–36.

[11] A. Colome, D. Pardo, G. Alenya, and C. Torras. "External force estimation during compliant robot manipulation". In IEEE International Conference on Robotics and Automation (ICRA). 2013, May 6–10; Karlsruhe, Germany, pp. 3535, 3540.

[12] C.J. Kempf and S. Kobayashi. "Disturbance observer and feedforward design for high-speed direct-drive position table". In IEEE Transactions on Control System Technology. 1999, vol. 7, pp. 513–526.

[13] K.S. Eom, I.H. Suh, and K.C. Wan. "Disturbance observer based path tracking of robot manipulator considering torque saturation". In Mechatronics. 2000, vol. 11, pp. 325–343.

[14] X. Chen, F. Toshio and K.D. Young. "A new nonlinear robust disturbance observer". In Systems & Control Letters. 2000, vol. 41, no. 3,pp. 189–199.

[15] J.R. Ryoo, D. Tae-Yong, and J.C. Myung. "Robust disturbance observer for the track-following control system of an optical disk drive". In Control Engineering Practice. 2004, vol. 12, pp. 577–585.

[16] S. Komada, N. Machii, T. Hori. "Control of redundant manipulators considering order of disturbance observer". In IEEE Transactions on Industrial Electronics. 2000, vol. 47, pp. 413–420.

[17] Liu, Chia-Shang and Huei Peng. "Inverse dynamics based state and disturbance observers for linear time-invariant systems". In Journal of Dynamics systems Measurement and Control. 2002, vol. 124, pp. 375–381.

[18] K.S. Eom, I.H. Suh, W.K. Chung, and S.R. Oh. "Disturbance observer based force control of robot manipulator without force sensor". In Proceedings of IEEE International Conference on Robotics and Automation. New York: IEEE Press. 1998, pp. 3012–3017.

[19] K. Ohishi, M. Miyazaki, M. Fujita and Y. Ogino. "Hinf observer based force control without force sensor". In Proceedings of Industrial Electronics, Control and Instrumentation. 1991. IECON'91, 1991 International Conference on Industrial Electronics, Control and Instrumentation, Kobe, Japan, pp. 1049–1054.

[20] L. Sang-Chul and A. Hyo-Sung. "Sensorless torque estimation using adaptive Kalman filter and disturbance estimator". In IEEE/ASME International Conference on Mechatronics and Embedded Systems and Applications (MESA). 2010, Qingdao, China, pp. 87–92.

[21] C. Canudas de Wit and J.J.E. Slotine."Sliding observers for robot manipulators". In Automatica. 1991, vol. 27, no. 5, pp. 859–864 .

[22] J.M. Daly and D.W. Wang. "Bilateral teleoperation using unknown input observers for force estimation". In IEEE American Control Conference, ACC'09. 2009, pp. 89–95.

[23] W. Wang and Z. Gao. "A comparison study of advanced state observer design techniques". In Proceedings of the 2003 American Control Conference. IEEE, 2003, vol. 6, pp. 4754–4759.

[24] H.K. Khalil. "High-gain observers in nonlinear feedback control. New directions in nonlinear observer design". In Lecture Notes in Control and Information Sciences. 1999, vol. 24, no. 4, pp. 249–268.

[25] J. Han. "A class of extended state observers for uncertain systems". In Automatica. 1998, vol. 34, no. 6, pp. 757–764.

[26] J.G. García, A. Robertsson, J.G. Ortega, and R. Johansson. "Estimacion de la fuerza de contacto para el control de robots manipuladores con movimientos restringidos" ("Contact force estimation for the control of robot manipulators with constrained movement"). RIAII, 2007, vol. 4. no. 1, pp. 70–82.

[27] J.G. Garcia, A. Robertsson, A. Valera, and R. Johansson. "Sensor fusion for compliant robot motion control". In IEEE Transactions on Robotics. 2008, vol. 24, no. 2, pp. 430–441.

[28] T. Ishikawa, S. Sakane, T. Sato, and H. Tsukune."Estimation of contact position between a grasped object and the environment based on sensor fusion of vision and force". In IEEE/SICE/RSJ International Conference on Multisensor Fusion and Integration for Intelligent Systems. 1996, pp. 116–123. IEEE, 1996. doi: 10.1109/MFI.1996.572167

[29] Y. Zhou, B.J. Nelson, and B. Vikramaditya. "Fusing force and vision feedback for micromanipulation". In Proceedings of the IEEE International Conference on Robotics and Automation. 1998, vol. 2, pp. 1220, 1225, 16–20 May 1998. doi: 10.1109/ROBOT.1998.677265

[30] T. Kröger, D. Kubus, and F.M. Wahl. "Force and acceleration sensor fusion for compliant manipulation control in 6 degrees of freedom". In Advanced Robotics. 2007, vol. 21, no. 14, pp. 1603–1616.

[31] G. Liu. "On velocity estimation using position measurements". In Proceedings of the American Control Conference, Anchorage, AK May 8–10. 2002, vol. 2, pp. 1115–1120.

[32] M.M. Dalvand, and S. Nahavandi. "Improvements in teleoperation of industrial robots without low-level access". In 2014 IEEE International Conference on Systems, Man and Cybernetics (SMC). 2014, San Diego, CA, USA, pp. 2170–2175.

[33] F. Janabi-Sharifi, V. Hayward, and C-S.J. Chen. "Discrete-time adaptive windowing for velocity estimation". In IEEE Transactions on Control Systems Technology. 2000, vol. 8, no. 6, pp. 1003–1009. doi: 10.1109/87.880606

[34] A. Jaritz, and M.W. Spong. "An experimental comparison of robust control algorithms on a direct drive manipulator". In IEEE Transactions on Control Systems Technology. 1996, vol. 4, no. 6, pp. 627–640. doi: 10.1109/87.541692

[35] P.R. Belanger, P. Dobrovolny, A. Helmy, and X. Zhang. "Estimation of angular velocity and acceleration from shaft-encoder measurements". In The International Journal of Robotics Research. 1998, vol. 17, no. 11, pp. 1225–1233.

[36] H. Brandtstädter, Sliding Mode Control of Electromechanical Systems, PhD dissertation for Technische Universität München, 2008.

Chapter 4

Human Movement Control

David Balderas and Mario Rojas

Additional information is available at the end of the chapter

http://dx.doi.org/10.5772/63720

Abstract

Control theory is used to design automatic systems, which are able to maintain a desired behaviour despite of the disturbances. It is present in different machines we use every day; in fact, technical systems in our homes and all the industries are hard to imagine today without these concepts. Moreover, the same theories can be used for modelling life processes as a collection of inputs, outputs, plants and control loops. Feedback is one of the main concepts behind control; in particular, several examples of physiological control mechanisms for regulating life aspects can be found in the human anatomy, for example, blood pressure, cholesterol levels, body movements, the equilibrium, etc. Those processes can be damaged by the aging effects, diseases, accidents or when the mechanism has been broken and cannot be recovered naturally; consequently, it will be required external assistance. A relative new field in control theory is related with developing technology for helping with physiological and medicals problems. However, in comparison with machines, those physiological processes are highly nonlinear, with delays and slow responses. Another problem is when human becomes the operators using their capacities of decision making to close the control loop, as they are prone to errors and mistakes. For those reasons, the biomedical system needs to be carefully designed and several aspects have to be considered. This chapter gives a small review of some internal and external control processes within the human body and discusses how to interact with them for designing biomedical devices. Under this design scheme, a practical application of a smart electric wheelchair for assisting persons with strong disabilities is presented. These assistive robotic systems are in close contact with the user, and thus, it is determinant to have a user-friendly relation between the human and the interface. Therefore, intuitive interfaces were included in the design and an intelligent navigation assistant to guarantee a collision-free path.

Keywords: human–machine interaction, control, feedback, biomedical control, sensors, rehabilitation, homeostasis, human anatomy

1. Introduction

Nowadays, it is difficult to imagine a lot of systems working without control, as its application simplifies everyday tasks. It helps to make processes [16] more efficient and faster than those made by hand. Examples are found in different areas: automotive, home appliances, industrial production, financial transactions and medical processes.

Even though control theory was initially developed for physical systems by mathematicians, physicists and engineers, it can be applied to model and explain physiological systems. This does not imply that all the control theories fit exactly into biologic systems, since most of them contain essential nonlinearities. However, an approximate solution can be found for particular cases by looking similarities between linear and nonlinear characteristics [1–4]. It is worth mentioning that from the engineering control perspective, it is searched an optimal result and the system is normally well defined; on the contrary, in physiological control systems, it is searched for an approximate value between boundaries and the system is unknown or hard to define. That is a consequence of the physiological differences between individuals.

Control processes are present in biological systems with their own inputs and outputs. In particular, the human body and the environment are sensed by natural transducers, which provide neural impulses to special areas of the cerebral cortex. After being interpreted by the brain, orders are sent to the muscles to contract and glands to secrete, with the aim to maintain homeostasis. This automatic process controls different mechanisms in the human body, and they will be described in Sections 2.1 and 3.

Human control includes systems with feedback (exteroceptive or proprioceptive), and two categories are considered: indirect or direct. Indirect or automatic means that the individual has no control over a regulatory internal process or the received technology (e.g. implants). On the other hand, direct human interaction with machines, tools, instruments or interfaces requires a series of actions to control the system. These actions start with an initial stimulus to the muscles, joints or tendons; thus, the sensors provide information about the movement that has to be done in order to alter or maintain the stimulus for the next step. In this way, movements follow a sequence that terminates when the task has been accomplished.

It is important to distinguish that in conventional control machines; negative feedback is explicitly subtracted from the reference point. On the other hand, in physiological control systems, negative feedback is embedded in the plant [5] and it is hard to know the set point.

Furthermore, the applied methods in today's systems have evolved from sequential logic to artificial intelligence. In addition, the role of human operators has evolved too, from manually adjusting the system to control supervision. The feedback information, usually displayed in a computer or in an industrial panel, can be interpreted by a human operator or by specialized software to drive the actuators that regulate the process.

In order to motivate the design of new technologies for healthcare, this chapter presents an overview of concepts related with biomedical control. First, it is presented an overview of the nervous systems and some biological processes to understand what happens internally with

http://dx.doi.org/10.5772/63720

the body control. Those processes are interpreted as inputs, outputs, blocks, feedback loops, and transfer functions. Then, it is explained how humans act as operators and their limitations; and therefore, what considerations should be done to interact with devices. Finally, with all these in mind, a case study of assistive technology is presented.

2. Nervous system

The human body is a complex machine that poses many sub-systems interacting each other and a main control to make efficient this interaction: the nervous system. For an effective control, the nervous system takes inputs from all the sensors in the body. The sensors send information by nerve impulses that travel to the brain through the spinal cord. Then, according to the nature of the stimulus, there is a reaction sent to the effectors: contractions in the muscles and secretions in glands. Examples of the interaction between the nervous and other systems can be seen in **Table 1**.

System	Muscular action	System reaction
Skeletal system	Receptors send sensory input from bones and joints to brain	Protect sense organs. Store Ca^2 for muscle function
Respiratory system	Regulate breathing rate	Provide Oxygen. Gets rid of CO_2 produce by neurons
Muscular system	Controls muscle contractions. Receive information of muscles	Move eyes. Permit speech. Creates facial expressions
Cardiovascular system	Controls nerves that regulate the heart. Controls dilatation of blood vessels. m	Blood vessels deliver nutrients and oxygen. Remove waste
Digestive system	Control contractions for digestive track movements	Provide nutrients for grow, maintenance and repair
Urinary system	Control muscle contraction that permits urination	Eliminates creatinine. Kidneys maintain levels of Na^+, K^+ and Ca^{2+} needed for nerve conduction
Endocrine system	Innervates certain glands secretion. The hypothalamus is part of these systems	Hormones are involved in the development of the brain
Integumentary system	Nerves regulate size of cutaneous blood vessels. Activate sweat glands and pili muscles	Skin protects the nerves. Helps regulating the temperature. Send information from skin receptors
Reproductive system	Starts puberty. Control erections. Control contraction of the uterus and ducts carrying gametes	Sexual hormones masculinize or feminize the brain. Influence sexual behaviour

Table 1. Nervous system and its interaction with another systems.

The nervous system is described by two main components: the central nervous system (CNS) integrated by the brain and the spinal cord, and the peripheral nervous system (PNS) that includes sensory neurons, ganglia and the nerves connected to the CNS. Both systems work together to capture information from the current state of the body and from the environment. The brain is the main control centre and interprets all the collected information. The communication between the body and the brain is made through the PNS. The PNS is divided into the somatic and the autonomic nervous system. The somatic or voluntary nervous system consists of nerves that connect the spinal cord with muscle effectors and sensory receptors. The autonomic nervous system regulates involuntary processes like the breathing rate or the blood pressure. This classification makes possible to distinguish the characteristics of human control.

2.1. Autonomic physiological control

Before describing these systems, it is necessary to state some of the differences between conventional and physiological control. First, in conventional control, it is intended to design for accomplishing a specific task and fine tune of the parameters is needed for optimal results. In comparison, physiological control is versatile and accomplishes many tasks at the same time. Second, conventional systems are well defined and their state variables may be independent. In contrast, physiological systems are usually unknown and difficult to analyse, as these systems are highly dependent between each other. Furthermore, in conventional control, it is normal that the feedback is directly subtracted from the input, and under this scheme, it is clear the use of the feedback. However, in physiological systems, the feedback is embedded within the plant and it is not clearly observed. Lastly, it is intended that the engineering systems do not change over time; meanwhile, physiological systems are adaptive to the changing environment. A summary of these differences can be seen in **Table 2**.

Conventional control	Physiological control
Designed to accomplish a specific task	Built in versatility
Fine tune for optimal results	Capable of doing several jobs
System is generally known	Unknown and difficult to analyse
Independent	Cross-coupling among different systems
Direct feedback	Adaptive to plant change
Preferred linearity	Highly nonlinear
Explicitly feedback	Feedback embedded in the plant

Table 2. Difference between conventional and physiological.

To develop every day activities, humans need to control the intake and outtake of energy within the system. The body converts the consumed food and the breathed air into the required energy. For this conversion to work, it is necessary a system to takes the food, another one to transform it, another to distribute it and one more to controls all of them. In fact, this conversion is done by the digestive, cardiovascular and respiratory systems; and they are controlled by the nervous system. Although there are many other systems for controlling the processes within the human body (e.g. reproductive, lymphatic, endocrine systems, etc.), they will not be discussed in this chapter due to their specificity.

2.2. Homeostasis

Homeostasis is the maintaining of stable, internal conditions of the human body within specific limits [7–9, 27]. To maintain these conditions, it is required negative and positive feedback. Negative feedback works by detecting changes using sensing mechanism or receptors, and thus, a control centre evaluates the changes and activates mechanisms to correct it. Once the condition has returned to normal, the corrective action is stopped (**Figure 1**).

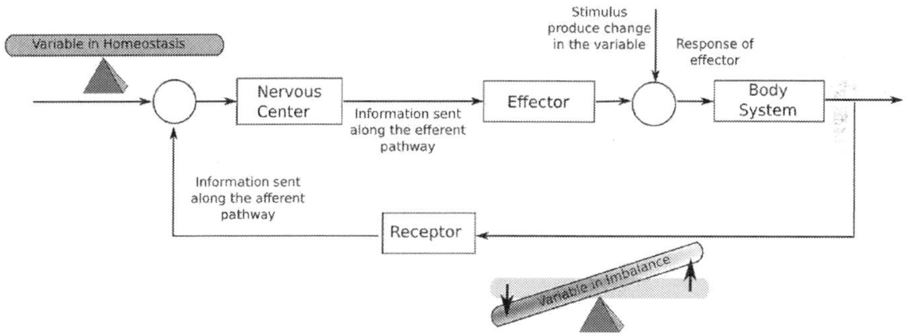

Figure 1. Conceptual scheme of the control of homeostasis system. It is intended to achieve a balance. When this balance is broken, the nervous system activates one of its effectors to correct the situation.

An example of how the human body maintains homeostasis using negative feedback is the glucose concentration on the blood. After a meal, the body increases the glucose by the absorption from the digestive track. To compensate this glucose intake, the alpha cells in the pancreas secrete insulin, a substance which stimulates the liver and muscle cells in order to absorb the excess. Moreover, after certain activity the glucose may drop, in this case the beta cells in the pancreas secrete glucagon, which stimulates the liver to release the stored glucose. Once the levels have returned to normal, the secretion of glucagon stops.

Positive feedback intensifies a condition beyond normal limits: in childbirth, a hormone (oxytocin) is released to intensify and speed up every contraction. The increase in contractions releases more of the hormones, intensifying and speeding up even more. The cycle stops once the child has born and the positive feedback stops. Another examples of positive feedback are lactation and blood clotting where extra production is needed.

2.3. Digestive system control

The digestive system controls the food breakdown into small molecules, which can be absorbed by the body. This is done during several processes: the ingestion of the food is followed by the propulsion, which is performed by moving the food along the digestive track by contracting and relaxing the smooth muscles. Within the body, the food is separated into smaller molecules by mechanic movements and chemical decomposition. As a result, the nutrients can be absorbed by diffusion or active transportation into the blood stream. The unabsorbed material is disposed through the anus. The digestive system is composed of mouth, pharynx, oesophagus, stomach, small intestine and large intestine. It may also use accessory organs such as teeth and tongue, salivary glands, liver, gallbladder and pancreas. Regulation of the digesting system is controlled by neural reflexes and hormones (gastrin, secretin, cholecystokinin and glucose insulinotropic peptide), see **Figure 2**.

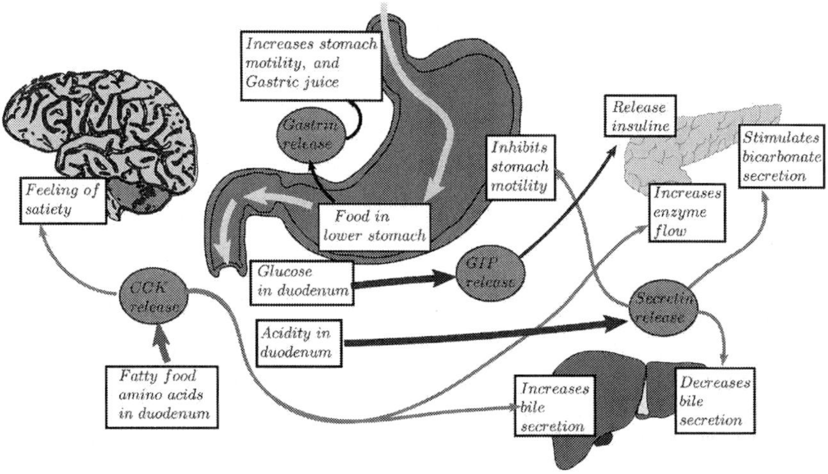

Figure 2. Conceptual scheme of the digestive system with all the different hormones and what they control.

Some of the functions of these hormones are regulate the appetite if the stomach is full (CCK), regulate the insulin released into the body by detecting the sugar levels in the duodenum (Glucose insulinotropic peptide), change the mobility of the stomach if food is detected in the lower stomach (Gastrin), adapt the bile as a consequence of the acidity in the duodenum (Secretin) and many others. It is worth mentioning that those are not the unique tasks and that these hormones adapt and compensate each other to work better.

2.4. Cardiovascular control

The cardiovascular system is composed of blood, blood vessels and the heart. It is in charge of distributing nutrients, hormones and oxygen through the body, as well as removing metabolic

http://dx.doi.org/10.5772/63720

waste. It also regulates the temperature, helps to protect the body and regulates the pH. In normal situations, the heart beats without nervous control; but, when there is a change due to exercise or trauma, it is altered by the cardiovascular centre located inside the medulla. A reflex response occurs when there is a change in the blood pressure or the chemistry within the body. This makes the cardiovascular centre to stimulate or inhibit the cardioacceleratory centre, the cardioinhibitory centre and the vasomotor centre until equilibrium or homeostasis is reached [10] (**Figure 3**).

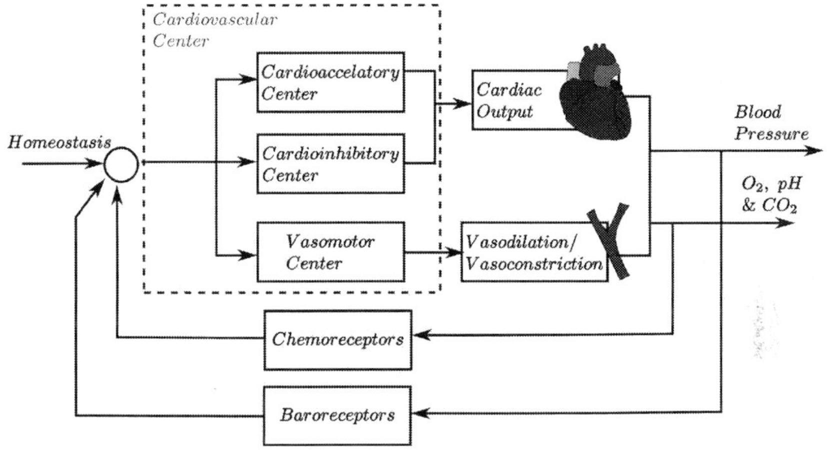

Figure 3. Conceptual scheme of the cardiovascular control with its sensors, what they control and what they alter.

2.5. Respiration control

Respiration is the intake of the air, in order to absorb the oxygen necessary for metabolic processes in the body. Respiration is done by the contraction of the intercostal muscles and the diaphragm. The areas in the brain in charge of stimulating the contraction are called respiratory centres. These centres are the medullary inspiratory centre, the pheumotaxic and the apneustic areas. The medullary inspiratory centre, located in the medulla oblongata, controls the contraction by stimulating rhythmically the nerves of the external intercostal muscles and the diaphragm. The expiration occurs when the muscles relax, except if the breathing is happening fast; in these cases, the expiration is done by stimulating the expiratory muscles: the internal intercostal muscles and the abdominal muscles. The pheumotaxic and the apneustic areas are in charge of inhibiting or stimulating the inspiratory centre, first to avoid the lungs for over inflating and second to prolong the contraction of the inspiratory muscles.

There are three sensors that have influence over the stimulus generated by the respiratory centres: the stretch receptors, the central and the peripheral chemoreceptors. The stretch receptors, located in the walls of the bronchi and bronchioles, inform when the lungs are expanded to their physical limit, stop stimulation to the inspiration muscles and start expiration. The central chemoreceptors send a signal to increase the air intake when they detect changes in the cerebrospinal fluid acidity, caused by the entrance of CO_2 from the plasma. Finally, the peripheral chemoreceptors monitor the acidity in the blood caused by an increase of pH or pCO_2, or a decrease in pO_2.

3. Neuromusculoskeletal system

The human skeletal and muscular systems create the forces to perform several tasks. Generally speaking, this system is the one that allow us to interact with the directly. In order to activate the muscles, it is required an electrical current that comes from the nervous system, which can be seen as a control apparatus that poses a linkage system (body segments), actuators (muscles), sensors (proprioceptive and tactile sensors, visual and vestibular system) and the controller (CNS), see **Figure 4**.

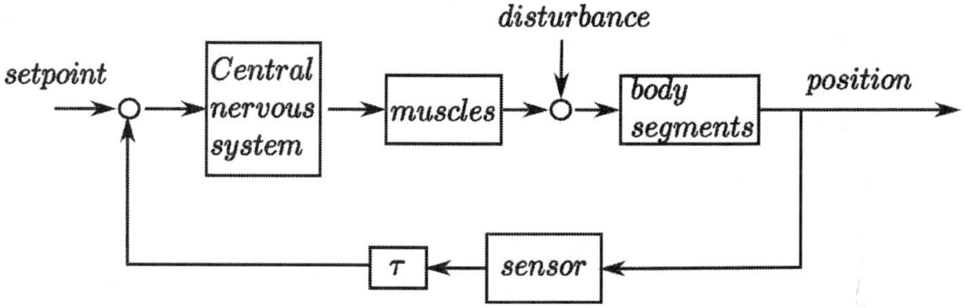

Figure 4. Conceptual scheme of the neuromusculoskeletal system where the nervous system controls the muscles that would move the bones and that would send information about its state back to the brain.

The CNS controls the system through "wires" conducting electrical currents called Nerves. To generate this loop, a desired position (set point) is created somewhere in the brain. This position is compared with the actual position of the limb and the CNS sends a neural signal to the correct muscles. The muscles, by means of contractions and relaxations, pull or release forces to the bone; thus, together start moving if there are no restrictions by the environment. An extra input in the system is the external forces or disturbances that act on the body, deviating it from the desired set point. The movements and positions are detected by the sensors located in muscles, joints, skin, etc. besides the visual and vestibular systems analysis.

To study this control system, it is required to analyse the biomechanical behaviour of the body. One of the biggest problems is that, without invasive techniques, it is hard to measure the necessary variables in living subjects. The problem complicates the analysis of the body mechanisms, since only external and a few internal signals can be measured.

http://dx.doi.org/10.5772/63720

The variables that are used in the description of any movement can be grouped as: kinematics, kinetics, anthropometry, muscle mechanics, electromyographic and the human senses [11].

Kinematics: The Kinematic variables only deal with movements, and they do not take into consideration the forces that cause that movement. These variables include linear and angular displacements, besides velocities and accelerations. They can be referred to another segment, anatomical land marks or a global coordinate system (normally outside the body). The skeletal system consists of joints, bones and ligaments; and it defines the degrees-of-freedom (DOF) of motion. In general, one bone referred to another has three rotations and three translations. These motions are limited by either another bone or by passive structures, such articular surfaces and ligaments. If one of the motions is limited or it is constrained to a small movement, the number of DOF is diminished by one. Once the reference is understood, the movements can be recorded and analysed. The movements are recorded using either a camera, markers, accelerometers, electromagnetic devices or a combination of them all.

Kinetics: Contrary to Kinematics, kinetics study the force that causes the movement. These forces can be either internal or external. Internal forces include muscle activity, the ligaments or friction from muscles and joints. Moreover, external forces come from the ground or from external loads. Kinetics includes the moments produced by forces, the mechanical power, and the energy changes in the human body.

Anthropometry: Anthropometry is used since the metrics of the body are necessary to create a good model. This model requires the mass of limb segments, the use of mass centres, centres of rotation, moments of inertia, angles of pull of muscles, muscle cross-sectional area and more.

Muscle Mechanics: Muscles are the ones that generate the internal forces to control the system. Their actuation is highly nonlinear, with varying possible forces according with its length and contraction velocity. Muscles also possess underlying properties as mass, viscosity and elasticity. These properties, either active or passive, need to be considered to construct a better model. Two basic muscle models are generally used: the Hill-type and the Huxley-type. The first one considers more the dynamical properties, while the second one goes one step beyond considering muscle contraction on micro-level.

Electromyographic: The brain [6] controls the activation of the muscles through an electrical signal, known as electromyography (EMG) which describes the precise contraction of each muscle. Besides, EMG signals give information about the joint activity of different types of muscle fibres and the fatigue state of the muscle.

Human sensors: Humans are filled with sensors for the correct control of the body (feedback). These sensors go from tactile, pressure and stretch, length and velocity in the muscle fibres, force sensors in the muscle tendons with even more global the use of the visual and vestibular system (see Section 3). Although there are many more sensors, they are not particular essentials for any motor control scheme.

The relationship between all this pathways and groups can be observed in **Figure 5**. Where the pathways interconnect to create a connection with excitations and inhibitions capable of generating movement. Some of these sensors can be seen in the Section 3.1. Have to be noted that although is in general command of the movement, there are still some reactions that are control peripherally. This is done as a reaction to harmful situations and prevents the body from damaging.

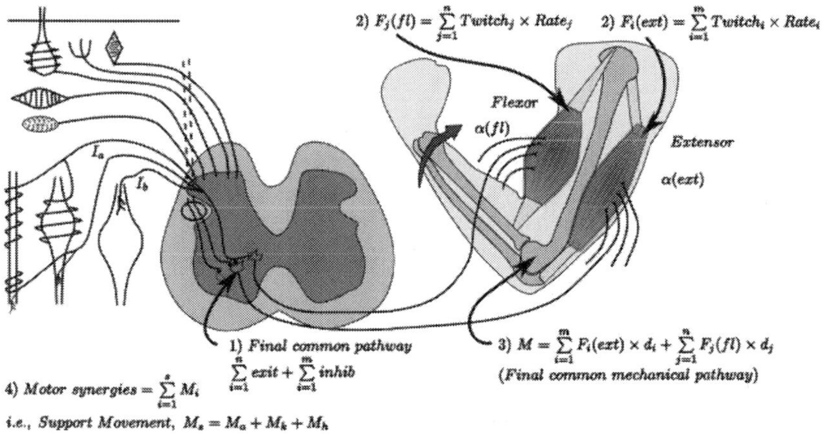

Figure 5. Neuromusculoskeletal integration. Four levels of integration in the neuromusculoskeletal system, which provides control of movement. (1) Summation of all neural excitatory/inhibitory inputs to the α motoneuron. (2) The tendon force resulting from the summation of all motor twitches from the recruitment of all active motor units. (3) The resulting movement of the agonist and antagonist muscle movements. (4) Combination of movements acting synergistically towards a movement.

3.1. Human perception

Human perception is related to our natural sensory system. In general, a sensor is a device that receives and responds to stimuli. The sensors are a fundamental part in control systems, as they provide information to the operator for compensation of variables against disturbances. The human body has several sensors for detection of sound waves, light rays, flavours, odours or physical contact. Those environmental signals are transduced by the sensory system into neural impulses for the brain.

In other words, the perception is the feedback for controlling external systems, since information from different variables in the environment is sensed at the same time. As an example, consider the activity of driving: the human operator senses the world by the vision (combining external aspects from the road and the car′s gauges), the somatosensory (both in the arms and legs), the equilibrium (mainly rotational movements) and the hearing (surrounding alerting sounds). The collected information is transduced into neural impulses that travel to the brain for interpretation and processing. Finally, decisions are made and orders are sent to the corresponding actuators. Particularly, adjustments in the steering and braking are achieved by moving our limbs.

The natural transducers in the human body are epithelial cell or neurons, classified by the type of stimulus they sense. Five main categories are distinguished: mechanoreceptors for detecting vibrations, tapping and pressure in the skin; photoreceptors located in the eye to detect light stimuli; chemoreceptors, which are present in smell and taste senses, and are stimulated by chemical reactions; Thermoreceptors to detect temperature changes in the skin; and pain receptors, located in the skin for detecting tissue damage.

Moreover, the human sensations are classified as the somatesthetic senses and the special senses. The former senses are located over wide areas of the body, and they communicate to the spinal cord first and then possibly with the brain. These sensations are known as cutaneous. The second category includes those senses to detect changes by specialized organs in the head, and they conduct information directly to the brain (the taste, the smell, the hearing, the equilibrium and the vision). A specialized area of the brain receives information from each sense, and thus the collected information from all the senses is interpreted together to perceive the environment.

3.2. The somatosensory system

Sensory receptors in skin, muscles, joints, tendons and some internal organs are connected with the dorsal column system by nerve fibres. Thus, the nerve impulses from those sensors are received by the somatosensory areas of the cerebral cortex. There are three types in this system:

Proprioceptors: These mechanoreceptors are specialized cells wrapped by nerve endings, which generate nerve impulses with the muscles stretching information. This information is used to maintain the muscle tone for the equilibrium and posture, despite of external forces acting over our body.

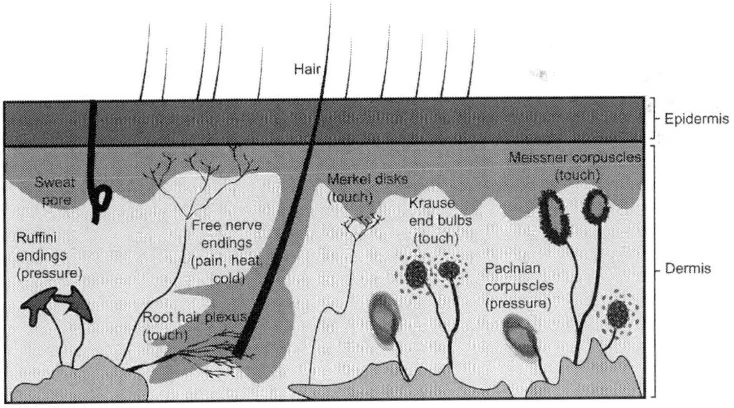

Figure 6. The sensory receptors contained in the skin layers. These receptors are connected with the dorsal column by nerve fibres.

Cutaneous receptors: The dermis is a skin layer which contains tiny receptors for the sensations of fine-touch, pressure, vibrations and temperature, as shown in **Figure 6**. The Meissner corpuscles, located in the most sensitive parts of the body, and the nerves around hair follicles are related with fine touch sensations. Moreover, the receptors to detect cutaneous pressure changes are formed by connective tissue and nerve fibres; there are three different types: Pacinian corpuscles, Ruffini endings and Krause end bulbs. Finally, warmth and cold temperatures are detected by free nerve endings in the epidermis. It is worth to mention that there are specialized receptors for cold and others for warmth.

Pain receptors: Nociceptors detect chemical substances, which are released when the tissue is damaged because of inflammation. Pain receptors are free nerve endings located within the skin and internal organs. These fibres enter the spinal cord and terminate in the dorsal horn.

3.3. The smell and the taste

The smell and the taste senses are very similar as both of them use chemoreceptors, which are the special cells that generate nerve impulses when they react with molecules present in food or air. The olfactory and taste anatomies, besides the chemoreceptors for those senses, are illustrated in **Figure 7**. Conceptual scheme of the digestive system.

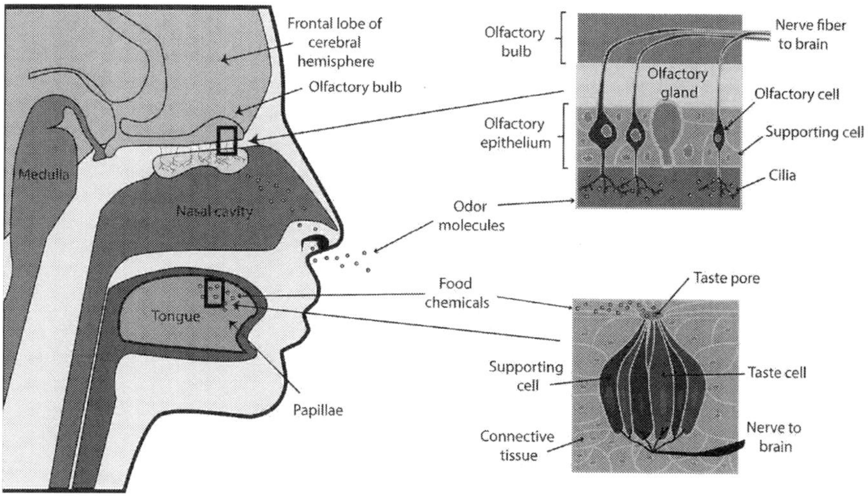

Figure 7. Conceptual scheme of the digestive system.

The olfactory cells are located in the olfactory epithelium, a special epithelial tissue in the superior nasal cavity. These cells end in thick protuberances, called cilia, which bear proteins for odour molecules. The cilia are sensitive only to one type of odour molecules; consequently, the activated neurons in the olfactory bulb area of the brain correspond to that class exclusively.

http://dx.doi.org/10.5772/63720

An odour contains different molecules, which stimulate a combination of different neurons. So on, those neurons are communicated by the olfactory tract with the olfactory areas of the brain to interpret odours.

For the case of the taste sense, the chemoreceptors are located on taste buds distributed on specialized papillae at the tongue. These cells end in protrusions, called microvilli, which bear receptor proteins for special molecules. According to the tongue area, the taste buds are more sensitive to particular tastes, and the brain is able to distinguish sour, salty, bitter and sweet tastes. The taste cells emit nerve impulses for the brain, who is able to integrate the incoming information from other taste buds to interpret the taste.

3.4. The vision

The eye is the organ responsible of vision for perceiving the world. The eyeball has three layers: the sclera, the choroid and the retina. There are two types of photoreceptors located in the retina: the rod cells and the cone cells. The rods are sensitive to low-intensity light; as a consequence, they are responsible for night vision. On the other hand, the cones are sensitive to high-intensity light and different wavelengths; thus, they are responsible for day vision. When acute vision is required, the light is focused in a special region of the retina called the fovea centralis, where a high density of cones is allocated.

The photoreceptors have membranous disks with special visual pigments. As the molecules in the membranes are stimulated by light, sequences of reactions provoke nerve impulses. The sensory fibres, going from the retina to the optic nerve, carry those impulses to the brain for interpreting the image. The parts described are shown in **Figure 8**.

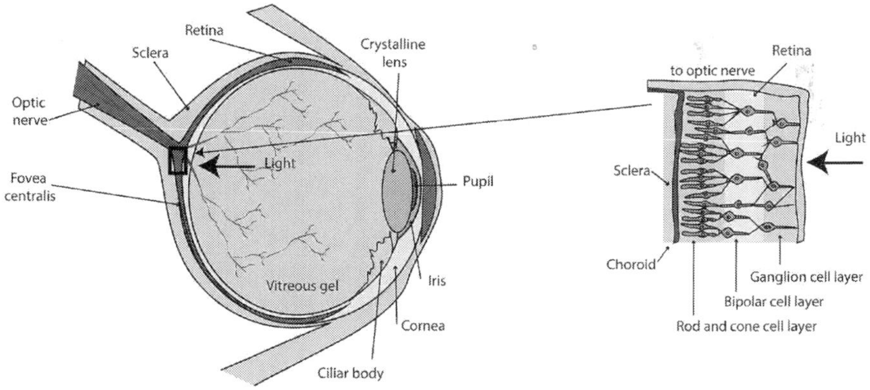

Figure 8. The eye anatomy. The enlargement of the area marked with a rectangle shows the retina layers, besides the rods, the cones and other supporting cells.

3.5. The hearing

The ear is the organ for hearing. The ear contains two sensory systems based in mechanoreceptors: the hearing and the equilibrium. The structure of the ear is divided in three parts: the outer ear, the middle ear and the inner ear, as shown in **Figure 9**. In the outer ear, sound waves are collected into the auditory canal. In the middle ear, those waves make vibrate the tympanic membrane and the auditory ossicles (malleus, incus and stapes). The ossicles amplify the sound and concentrate the sound waves from the tympanic membrane onto the oval window. The stapes strikes the membrane of the oval windows to pass the sound to the fluid contained in the inner ear.

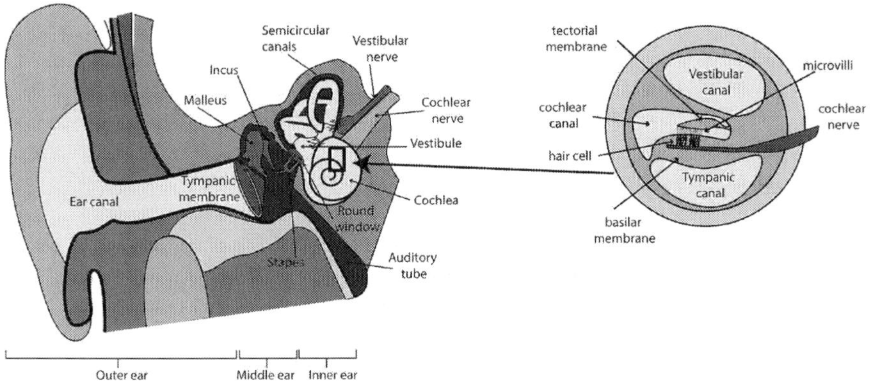

Figure 9. The ear anatomy and its parts. The enlargement of the area marked with a rectangle shows the cochlea cross section.

In the inner ear, there is a bony labyrinth, formed by semicircular canals, the vestibule and the cochlea. A spiral organ, called the organ of Corti, is located within the cochlea, and it contains hair cells, which are the receptor cells for auditory. When sound waves provoke vibration in the organ of Corti, the elasticity of the basilar membrane causes the hair cells to bend. The bending of the stereocilia causes an oscillating potential of the hair cells, firing intermittently the cochlear nerve. These impulses reach the auditory cortex of the brain to be interpreted as sounds.

3.6. The equilibrium

The semi-circular canals and the vestibule are the parts of the ear used to detect angular and linear acceleration of the head (shown in **Figure 10**). The brain interprets this information for maintaining rotational and gravitational equilibrium of the body.

Rotational equilibrium: There are three perpendicular semi-circular canals for sensing each dimension of the space. At the end of each canal, there are hair cells as the receptors, whose cilia is contained in a gelatinous part called cupula. When the head rotates, the cupula is

http://dx.doi.org/10.5772/63720

dragged with the movement and bends the cilia. As a consequence, impulses travel to the brain into the vestibular nerves.

Gravitational equilibrium: The utricle and saccule, located in the vestibule, are responsible for sensing the vertical or horizontal movement of the head. Those membranous contain hair cells, whose cilia is contained in a gelatinous material called otolithic membrane. The utricle is sensitive to horizontal (back–forth) movements, and the saccule is sensitive to vertical (up–down) movements. When the head or the body moves in those planes, the otholits in the utricle and saccule are dragged with the movement, bending the cilia and changing the nerve impulses.

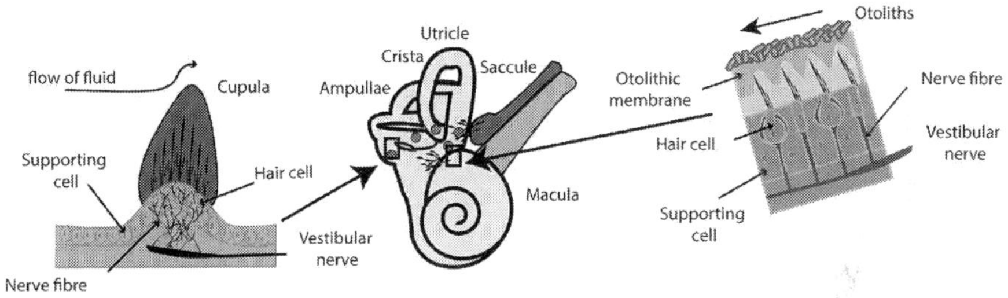

Figure 10. Receptors for equilibrium sense. The enlargement of the areas marked with a rectangle shows the rotation receptors in semicircular canal and the gravitational equilibrium receptors in the vestibule. Neuromusculoskeletal system.

3.7. Senses involved in a natural control mechanism: human gait

As an example of the motion control that humans can achieve is the walking mechanism. This mechanism is one of the most important control systems, allowing people to move within their environment. Walking has proven to be complex, hard to achieve and hard to replicate. Robot prototypes trying to mimic this behaviour had proved that this is not a trivial task because it has a high degree of complexity, it is unstable in many situations and it is easily disturbed. The control system for walking has many variables to analyse: where the joints are located, where the joints are located within each other, what force can they achieve, and what are the disturbances to compensate against them. To start the walking analysis, it is necessary to observe the cycle time, the step length, the walking velocity and the reference system. If that was not enough for completely understand walking, it is necessary to understand all the components that feedback the system: the pressure points, the muscle current situation as well as the incredible mechanism that allows us to control stability (vestibular system).

The vestibular system explained early is the one in charge of the sense of balance. This balance has the purpose of coordinating the movement. This means that, according to the sensation, it will correct and adjust every step during the walking. It also corrects when the position of a vehicle changes the orientation with respect to the gravity field by tilting the body based on this reference.

It is possible to observe the human movement control as a system that possesses several internal and external interaction. It uses inputs, muscular adjustments and disturbances, to initiate or deviate the movement. Humans try to compensate the disturbances by observing their muscles, their bones and the equilibrium currents states with the sensors, and the set point using the CNS.

4. Human as the operator

The feedback information, usually displayed in a computer or in an industrial panel, can be perceived and interpreted by a human operator, or by an automatic intelligent system to drive the actuators that regulate the process. In the block diagram shown in **Figure 11**, there are presented the two control options: manual and automatic/semi-automatic [12]. In the former case, the human operator acts as the controller, characterized by $g_c(t)$, and determines the control outputs u(t) for regulating the plant g(t). The process output y(t) has to follow the reference r(t) despite of the disturbances d(t) against the process. On the other hand, in the automatic/semiautomatic case, there is cooperation between the man and the machine to ensure the control goals. The artificial operator $g_{iac}(t)$ makes the control decisions, which are supported by the human with the information provided by the system, or the human operates the system with machine supervision programmed to minimize errors.

Figure 11. The block diagram of a control system.

Good examples of the cooperative control applications are found in complex multivariable systems. For instance, the action of flying an aircraft involves the control altitude, weighting, lifts, headings, drag, engine power, and many other variables [17]. Engineers know how to construct airplanes and engines; however, it is the nature of planes to be unstable, even the modern high-performance airplanes, but they rely on automatic control systems to maintain stability during the flight. Besides, modern airplanes involve the use of a lot of sensors to measure internal and external conditions, and several processes are controlled by on-board computers. It is impossible to imagine a commercial flight controller only by human operators.

http://dx.doi.org/10.5772/63720

Complexity in today's systems demands not only the control engineering, but other theories must be involved: human factors, human–machine interaction and cooperative control [13]. A brief description of these areas is presented next.

4.1. Human factors

Even if the cooperative scheme is manual or automatic, the human operators have the same role in control systems: to ensure the control goals efficiently and safely. As an element in the control loop, the operator response is attached to his experience, training or knowledge. Thus, the performance of the complete control system depends of the computing. Human factors are related with the understanding of the decision-making behaviour in humans. A description of their performance will help to design better interfaces and secure interaction in the control to minimize errors. This process was modelled by [14] at three different levels: the Skill-, Rule- and Knowledge-based levels.

Skill-based behaviour (SBB): Describes a performance which takes place without conscious control or attention, like a reflex. The operator's response is automatic because he is really familiarized with the situation, and it is executed with speed and accuracy. In this model, he is barely able to describe how to do the performance and what information is necessary.

Rule-based behaviour (RBB): The operator follows a sequence of subroutines previously used and documented. Also, other persons are able to communicate the process or follow it, as the process is well known or a list of instructions is available. Accuracy and speed are good, but not as in the SBB.

Knowledge-based behaviour (KBB): The operator is not familiarized with the situation and needs to establish a strategy to solve the problem. The operator has to consider different plans, based in his knowledge, and proceeds the execution with trial and error process. For those reasons, the KBB performance tends to be risky and slow.

It is desired that the operators' skills evolve from the KBB to the RBB, and then to the SBB which presents the lowest error rate. However, there are two fundamental aspects to be considered in the migration process: time and training level. As indicated in [32], to understand and take advantage of the human–machine interaction, it is important to understand the cognitive processes of humans.

4.2. Human–machine interaction

As an element in the system presented in **Figure 11**, the human–machine interface (HMI) closes the loop in the control process. The HMI provides visualization for the operator in order to monitor and control the variables. However, recent developments in technology have increased the complexity in control systems, including multiple inputs and processes running at the same time.

It was a common practice that machines were designed according technical requirements, without considering the needs and characteristics of the operator; however, that paradigm has changed into the user-centred design or adapting tools to the capabilities, limitations and needs of the human beings. Nowadays, ergonomics is a determinant factor in order to minimize human errors and to improve the operator's health and safety.

Ergonomics is concerned with the concept of "usability" or user-friendly in technical systems, machines and tools [29]. In order to be intuitive and easy to use, the HMI needs to embed the operator in the control feedback by visual, somatosensory, propioceptive or a combination of those interfaces. This multi-modality involves human senses stimulated directly by visual, auditory or haptic (kinestesic, tactile, temperature) interaction to confront the challenge of the human operator working closely in complex machines [30].

4.3. Cooperative control

Finally, the cooperative control systems incorporate decision support capabilities implemented with artificial intelligence techniques. The main idea using the information acquired by the sensors to feed computer algorithms and then execute the most suitable actions for the current conditions. These intelligent control techniques are applied to different engineering areas such as robotics, aeronautics, financial and household appliances.

Fuzzy Logic, Artificial Neural Networks, Neuro-Fuzzy Systems, Genetics Algorithms, among other techniques are known as Artificial Intelligence computational methods [15]. Those techniques are based on characteristics observed in biological systems; moreover, a system with artificial intelligence may have the abilities of learning from experience, adapting to environment conditions, recognizing patterns, using knowledge and other tasks of intelligent beings. Artificial control [5] techniques can improve the control performance and the system autonomy.

Fuzzy Logic (FL): This technique uses vague data to make decisions, in a similar ways humans do. It uses linguistic descriptions for the variables and IF–THEN rules connected with logic operators.

Artificial Neural Networks (ANN): The ANNs are mathematical models which emulate the learning process in biological neurons. They are able to be trained in order to learn and acquire knowledge. Their application is pattern recognition, values prediction, data validation and classification.

Neuro-Fuzzy Control: This technique combines the characteristics of Fuzzy Logic Systems and Artificial Neural Networks, and thus, these systems are able to make decisions with vague information and are able to learn and adapt to the problem conditions.

Genetic Algorithms (GA): This is an optimization method based on biologic evolution principles. GAs are used to numerically evaluate functions and to obtain minimum and maximum values. Genetic programming techniques are used to find approximate solutions in different applications like economics, materials, computer-aided design, among others.

http://dx.doi.org/10.5772/63720

5. Biomedical control applications

A specific field in control engineering is related with biological and medical systems, explored in recent years to develop technology to impact on human life. Biomedical control is relatively new, but there are solid applications that demonstrate the usability of control theory for solving medical problems.

Physiological control mechanism maintains homeostasis in the human body; however, they could be compromised by a disease or an accident, as well as by the effects of aging. When the physiology control mechanism has been broken and cannot be recovered naturally, it is required external assistance to help in the restoration. This can be either achieved by drug dosing, therapies or medical devices for assistance.

There are mainly three areas to cover when talking to biomedical control:

- Drug delivery
- Medical instrumentation
- Rehabilitation engineering

While the drug delivery tries to recover homeostasis by creating biological reaction by means of chemical or biological changes, medical instrumentation and rehabilitation engineering try to recover it by means of physical reconstruction, mechanical assistance, external stimulation or changes over the environment.

5.1. Drug delivery

Drugs can be used to control how internal systems work (e.g. glucose, blood pressure, heart rate, etc.). Although drugs are intended to correct an abnormal behaviour, they can still create negative effects within the body (causing toxicity or side effects), so it is important that they are administrated in the correct dosage. Drugs are also required to be delivered when they are required and not just in any random moment, so they have a mayor impact and not just some reduced effect. One final case of drug delivery is the use of Anaesthesia that is of high importance during surgery or pain control. The fact that drugs have to fulfil different activities and have to be regulated translates into an adaptation of the drug dosage depending on their concentration and effects. The basic understanding over drug release mechanisms includes dissolution, diffusion, osmosis and ion exchange-based mechanisms.

Drug time delivery has change over the past decades, changing from a simple intake of pills in certain periods of time (e.g. twice-a-day), to using smart polymers that are environmentally sensitive, to currently using drugs that are sensitive to changes in concentrations of the body (like glucose or pH) and only release when needed.

Like previously said, it is important part of drug delivery is to the area that they are attacking. One important aspect is, for example, what system they are regulating and what side effects they can create. For example, when trying to reduce the blood pressure, an infusion of sodium nitroprusside is injected that rapidly will reduce the heart pressure, the problem is that its effects fade quickly and they can only be applied in certain time to avoid cyanide poisoning. It has been proposed to insertion control the release of that drug to counteract this effect and have extended periods of time with lower blood pressure.

Another example of drug delivery is trying to help the immune system. The immune system is in charge of protecting the body against diseases. These systems must detect pathogens and viruses, and distinguish them from other organisms that are not infectious. But there are cases that these systems are not capable of working against the intruders of the body, like in the case of HIV. A way to counteract the damage by this virus is by a therapy known as antiretroviral. The intention of this is to reduce the viral replication limiting the transmission of the HIV virus, as well as limit the possibility of acquisition [18]. The main problem of this therapy is the high amount of drugs introduced into the body at the same time, which limits the adherence of the therapy. To improve the benefits of this treatment, it has been proposed that the drug delivery is adjusted by using viral plasma levels.

A final example on how drug delivery control is of importance is the use of anaesthesia. Anaesthesia in general tries to control hypnosis, analgesia and relaxation of the body. These variables have to be adapted using EEG, heart rate, CO_2 and blood pressure as feedback signals, to adjust the anaesthetics, muscle relaxants, ventilation parameters, Nacl and others. The adjustment is normally done by an anaesthesiologist that acts like a feedback controller [19]. This could be change to an automatic control, which would in return improve parts of the complex decision process, providing the drug delivery and avoiding overusing. Resulting in a less drug consumption and shortening the time spent recovering from the anaesthesia.

5.2. Medical instrumentation

There exist several external variables, like temperature and humidity that affect the state of the body (e.g. temperature, heart rate, breath and humidity of the skin). They are normally regulated using heaters and humidifiers which act over the environment. The problem is that these variables change slowly, which can be overshoot, and in the case of humidity, it cannot be easily measured to correctly adapt it. The control of these variables has to constantly observe the inner state as well as the outer parameters to adjust and avoid overshooting.

One of the most important parts during a surgery is the feedback the surgeon can get through his eyes, hands and specially instruments. This feedback has to be sufficient to avoid unnecessary grasping or cutting and good enough that do not reduce performance [20]. This effect has become even more pronounce with current technology, like as robotics and minimal invasive surgery, where the surgeon cannot directly feel the object he/she is grasping. In these cases, a different type of feedback has to be provided to the surgeon that replace the one that was lost or enhance the one that remains. A normal approach is to try to transmit directly the touch of the tools to the handle using haptic (or tactile feedback) to the surgeon. Another type of feedback can be using visual or audial stimulation using video recordings of the surgery. These technologies can be added into a more robust system, which makes possible to have minimal invasive surgery and the specially to incorporate robotics into the surgery.

http://dx.doi.org/10.5772/63720

5.3. Rehabilitation engineering

The aims of the rehabilitation engineering are to develop devices and methods for helping individuals with disabilities in their everyday tasks, and helping to recover lost functions because of diseases. For instance, rehabilitation engineers build assistive devices like wheelchairs, scooters and prostheses for helping in everyday tasks. Moreover, control theory, signal acquisition and signal processing are combined to solve the problem of controlling powered prostheses, which can replace deficient or amputated extremities [21]. Efficient and intuitive interfaces are needed for controlling artificial limbs with body signals. High accuracy and quick response in these assistive devices will improve the quality of living for persons with disabilities.

Another application of rehabilitation engineering is the functional electrical stimulation (FES), in order to control or recover body functions by electric signals. Voltage pulses are applied to the muscles searching for correction of clinic dysfunctions. Besides, neuromuscular stimulation is used to electrically activate nerve cells. The FES has been successfully used in stroke rehabilitation, spinal cord injuries, head injuries, limb motor dysfunctions and neurological disorders.

Finally, biofeedback is used to consciously control body functions that are normally regulated automatically, like blood pressure, heart rate and temperature. By monitoring its heart rate, electroencephalographic or muscle activity, a trained patient is able to regulate certain anomalies, like migraines, attention deficit, hyperactivity disorder, epilepsy, diabetes, high blood pressure and incontinence. However, the feedback performance depends of the accuracy in the variable measurements and data presentation.

Research in rehabilitation engineering involves the development of new devices and techniques, like robotics for aiding in therapies, intelligent assistive devices for rehabilitation and mobility, virtual reality simulations for physical and cognitive rehabilitation, sophisticated interfaces for enabling severely disabled patients to interact with everyday devices, among others.

6. Case study: the smart wheelchair

This section presents the implementation of an assistive device considering the human operator aspects presented above. As an element in the control system, the operator takes part in the control loop to share navigation tasks with an artificial intelligence. Through his human senses, the operator is able to plan and correct a route to reach a desired place. At the same time, a running algorithm uses distance sensors to avoid collisions with objects. The whole system takes advantage of both, the human and the artificial intelligence, to minimize errors in the navigation process.

A smart wheelchair is a rehabilitation engineering application developed to assist persons with strong disabilities. The smart wheelchairs incorporate sensors, specialized software and mobile robot techniques to solve some mobility problems. Many prototypes have been implemented in different institutions around the world [22, 31]. These assistive robotic systems are in close contact with the user, as both of them share the same space; consequently, it is determinant to have a user-friendly relation between the human and the machine, and intuitive interfaces for users without knowledge of technical aspects [23, 28].

According to Ref. [24], it is recommended a collaborative or semi-autonomous control for driving the smart wheelchair. Under that scheme and despite of his disabilities, the user is still able to command the system by himself and plan routes to destinations meanwhile an intelligent assistant guarantees a collisions-free trajectory. As a result, the semi-autonomous control complements the user's skills without replacing him completely.

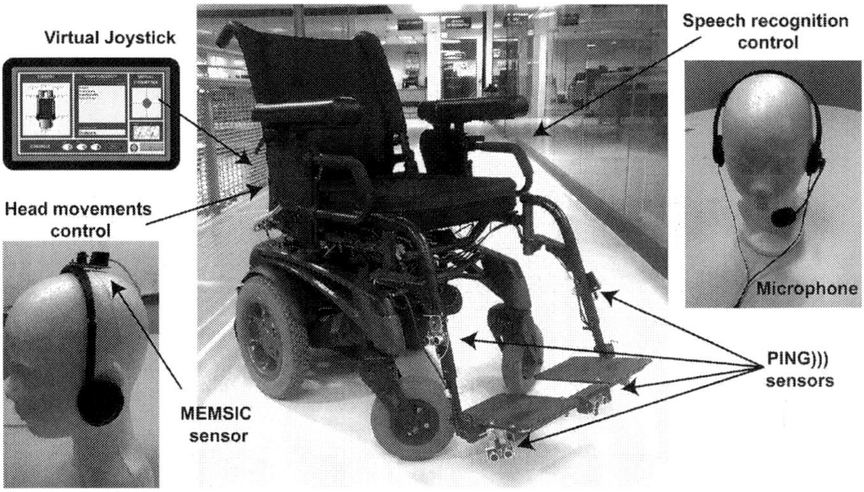

Figure 12. Semi-autonomous wheelchair.

The semi-autonomous smart wheelchair presented in **Figure 12** uses speech recognition and head movements detection as alternative interfaces to steer and manoeuvre. An obstacles avoidance controller is included, based on fuzzy logic control and range sensors as those implemented successfully in Ref. [25, 26]. In the prototype, developed at Tecnologico de Monterrey Campus Ciudad de Mexico, eight ultrasonic sensors were distributed around the wheelchair for a complete coverage and the distance measurements are the inputs for the controller. The fuzzy logic algorithm makes the navigation decisions similarly to a human operator; thus, when an object is detected near to the wheelchair, the control reduces the wheelchair speed and modifies the orientation carefully. The controller and the data acquisition routines were implemented in a Field Programmable Gate Array (FPGA), included in a Compact-RIO 9103, for high-speed processing. This device shares the data with the HMI running in a laptop with a touch screen to interact easily. The HMI shows the sensors indicators, virtual buttons to select among the interfaces and text indicators with instructions for the user.

As indicated, the user is able to operate the smart wheelchair in normal or assisted navigation; and by any of the available interfaces: virtual joystick, head movements or speech commands. The virtual joystick is similar to a real joystick, but it can be personalized according to the user requirements. With this interface, the user moves the cursor from its home position in the vertical or horizontal directions of the workspace. Moreover, the head movements control is used to command the wheelchair by head movements, as illustrated by **Figure 13**. This interface uses a tilt sensor, mounted in the headset presented in **Figure 12**, which detects movements in the 'x' and 'y' axes. This interface uses a function for mapping the sensor data into useful voltages for softly moving the wheelchair. Finally, the speech recognition interface uses nine voice commands to operate the wheelchair: 'action', 'move', 'run', 'stop', 'forward', 'backward', 'left', 'right and 'down'. They are classified as attention and orientation instructions. With the attention instructions, the user selects discrete or continuous movements; and after that, an orientation instruction starts the movement. As an example, the wheelchair displaces during 2 s by commanding 'Move' and then 'Forward'. In the case of 'run', the wheelchair moves continuously and accumulates orientation instructions to change the speed and orientation. The voice commands are obtained by the headset microphone shown in **Figure 13**.

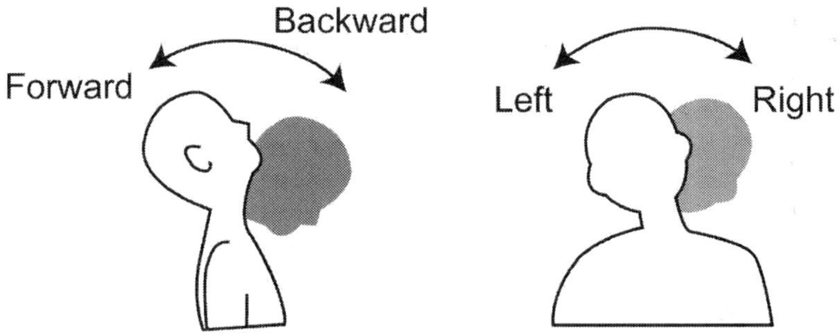

Figure 13. Head movements for commanding the wheelchair.

7. Discussion

Control engineering has been widely applied for creating technology, not only to make life more comfortable, but to improve life quality and life expectancy. Research has been done to develop applications in order to achieve those objectives. Even though these theories can be used to study and describe physiological systems, several considerations need to be done as there are important differences between these and conventional engineering.

Furthermore, it is imperative to study the cases where humans need to interact for closing the control loop. However, humans are prone to errors and their cognitive processes are limited by factors such as training, knowledge, speed reaction, and experience. For those cases, external assistance is recommended to complete safely the control goals.

The smart wheelchair presented is a clear example of a complete control system, which involves human factors, human–machine interaction and artificial intelligence. The user-centred design was applied for the interfaces to be comfortable and useful, besides the use of the HMI is very intuitive. The artificial intelligent algorithm helps the user to be involved in the system control, to monitor the environment variables and to complete the navigation.

Undoubtedly, biomedical control applications have proven to be very useful; however, that is not the only science field to create biomedical devices. Thus, the research continues in developing new technology applied to improve monitoring, therapies and helping patients. Hence, it is needed research on the developments of new sensory systems, drug delivery, robotics, assistive devices and new materials. Obviously, the technology needs to work under unfavourable conditions and being compatible with the human anatomy. Finally, the research must be oriented by other important factors, like the balance between cost and robustness in order to have affordable products.

Author details

David Balderas[*] and Mario Rojas

*Address all correspondence to: dc.balderassilva@itesm.mx

Monterrey Institute of Technology and Higher Education, Mexico City, Mexico

References

[1] Rosen, R. Control theory and biological systems. The Bulletin of Mathematical Biophysics. 1964;26(4):389–390. doi:10.1007/BF02484237

[2] Doyle III, Francis J. and Bequette, B. Wayne and Middleton, Rick and Ogunnaike, Babatunde and Paden, Brad and Parker, Robert S. and Vidyasagar, Mathukumalli{/Authors PT}. {PT ArticleTitle}Control in biological systems{/ArticleTitle PT}. {PT JournalTitle}The Impact of Control Technology{/JournalTitle PT} Vol. 1, pp- 57-68, IEEE Control Systems Society, {PT Year}2011{/Year PT}.

[3] Ingalls, BP, Iglesias, PA. Control Theory and Systems Biology. The MIT Press, Cambridge Massachusetts, 2010. doi:9780262013345

[4] Awrejcewicz, J. Biological and mechanical systems in modern control theory. Communications in Nonlinear Science and Numerical Simulation. 2011;16(5):2203–2204. doi: 10.1016/j.cnsns.2010.06.005

[5] Huang, C-N, Chung, H-Y. Applications of Control Theory in Biomedical Engineering. National Central University, Chungli Taiwan.

[6] Longenbaker, S. Mader's Understanding Human Anatomy & Physiology. McGraw-Hill Higher Education; Columbus OH, 2013.

[7] Bernard, C. De la Physiologie Generale. Hachette, Paris 1872.

[8] Cannon, WB. The Wisdom of the body. WW Norton & Co; USA, 1932.

[9] Novosel'tsev, VN. Homeostasis and health: analysis from a standpoint of the control theory. Automation and Remote Control. 2012;73(5):841–851.

[10] Lewis, MJ, Short, AL, Lewis, KE. Autonomic nervous system control of the cardiovascular and respiratory systems in asthma. Respiratory Medicine. 2006;100(10):1688–1705. doi:10.1016/j.rmed.2006.01.019

[11] Winter, DA. Biomechanics and Motor Control of Human Movement. John Wiley & Sons; New Jersey, 2009.

[12] Hacisalihzade, SS. Biomedical Applications of Control Engineering. Springer, Berlin Heidelberg 2013.

[13] Pere Ponsa, Ramon Vilanova, Marta Díaz and Anton Gomà (2008). A Human Factors Approach to Supervisory Control Interface Improvement, Robotics Automation and Control, Pavla Pecherkova, Miroslav Flidr and Jindrich Dunik (Ed.), InTech, DOI: 10.5772/5840. Available from: http://www.intechopen.com/books/robotics_automation_and_control/a_human_factors_approach_to_supervisory_control_interface_improvement Rasmussen, Jens. Skills, rules, and knowledge; signals, signs, and symbols, and other distinctions in human performance models. Systems, Man and Cybernetics, IEEE Transactions on. 1983;1(3):257-266.

[14] Rasmussen, J. Skills, rules, and knowledge; signals, signs, and symbols, and other distinctions in human performance models. IEEE Transactions on Systems, Man and Cybernetics. 1983;1(3):257–266.

[15] Ponce-Cruz, P, Ramirez-Figueroa, FD. Intelligent Control Systems with LabVIEW. Springer Science & Business Media; 2009.

[16] Frank, PM. Advances in Control: Highlights of ECC. Springer Science & Business Media; London, 2012.

[17] Fiset, J-Y. Human–Machine Interface Design for Process Control Applications. ISA; USA, 2009

[18] Cohen, MS, Chen, YQ, McCauley, M, Gamble, T, Hosseinipour, MC, Kumarasamy, N, Hakim, JG, Kumwenda, J, Grinsztejn, B, Pilotto, JHS, et al. Prevention of HIV-1 infection

with early antiretroviral therapy. New England Journal of medicine. USA, 2011;365(6): 493-505.

[19] Park, K. Controlled drug delivery systems: past forward and future back. Journal of Controlled Release. 2014;190:3–8. doi:10.1016/j.jconrel.2014.03.054

[20] Cosentino, C, Bates, D. Feedback Control in Systems Biology. CRC Press; 2011.

[21] Wellstead, P, Sreenath, S, Cho, K-H. Systems and Control Theory for Medical Systems Biology. IGI Global. PA USA, 2009;

[22] Simpson, RC. Smart wheelchairs: a literature review. Journal of Rehabilitation Research and Development.Washington DC, 2005;42(4):423.

[23] Bourhis, G, Agostini, Y. Man–machine cooperation for the control of an intelligent powered wheelchair. Journal of Intelligent and Robotic Systems. 1998;22(3–4):269–287.

[24] Nisbet, PD. Who's intelligent? Wheelchair, driver or both? Proceedings of the 2002 International Conference on Control Applications. 2002;2:760–765.

[25] Simpson, RC, Levine, SP. Voice control of a powered wheelchair. IEEE Transactions on Neural Systems and Rehabilitation Engineering. 2002;10(2):122–125.

[26] Pires, G, Nunes, U. A wheelchair steered through voice commands and assisted by a reactive fuzzy-logic controller. Journal of Intelligent and Robotic Systems. 2002;34(3): 301–314.

[27] Khoo, M. Physiological Control Systems: Analysis, Simulation, and Estimation. Press Series in Biomedical ed. doi: ISBN 0-7803-3408

[28] Yoshiyuki Noda, Akira Kawaguchi and Kazuhiko Terashima (2010). A Mechatronics Vision for Smart Wheelchairs, Mobile Robots Navigation, Alejandra Barrera (Ed.), InTech, DOI: 10.5772/8996. Available from: http://www.intechopen.com/books/mobile-robots-navigation/a-mechatronics-vision-for-smart-wheelchairs

[29] Baklouti, M, AbouSaleh, J, Monacelli, E, Couvet, S. Human Machine Interface in Assistive Robotics: Application to a Force Controlled Upper Limb Powered Exoskeleton. 2010.

[30] Imtiaz Ali Khan (2012). Ergonomic Design of Human-CNC Machine Interface, Human Machine Interaction - Getting Closer, Mr Inaki Maurtua (Ed.), InTech, DOI: 10.5772/26411. Available from: http://www.intechopen.com/books/human-machine-interaction-getting-closer/ergonomic-design-of-human-cnc-machine-interface {/DOI PT}

[31] Pedro Ponce, Arturo Molina and Rafael Mendoza (2012). Wheelchair and Virtual Environment Trainer by Intelligent Control, Fuzzy Controllers- Recent Advances in Theory and Applications, Dr. Sohail Iqbal (Ed.), InTech, DOI: 10.5772/48410. Available from: http://www.intechopen.com/books/fuzzy-controllers-recent-advances-in-

theory-and-applications/wheelchair-and-virtual-environment-trainer-by-intelligent-control

[32] Benigni Gladys and Gervasi Osvaldo (2012). Human-Machine Interaction and Agility in the Process of Developing Usable Software: A Client-User Oriented Synergy, Human Machine Interaction - Getting Closer, Mr Inaki Maurtua (Ed.), InTech, DOI: 10.5772/26025. Available from: http://www.intechopen.com/books/human-machine-interaction-getting-closer/human-machine-interaction-and-agility-in-the-process-of-developing-usable-software-a-client-user-ori{/DOI PT}

Chapter 5

Aircraft Landing Control Using the H-inf Control and the Dynamic Inversion Technique

Romulus Lungu and Mihai Lungu

Additional information is available at the end of the chapter

http://dx.doi.org/10.5772/62666

Abstract

The chapter presents the automatic control of aircraft during landing, taking into account the sensor errors and the wind shears. Both planes—longitudinal and lateral-directional—are treated; the new obtained automatic landing system (ALS) will consists of two subsystems—the first one controls aircraft motion in longitudinal plane, while the second one is for the control of aircraft motion in lateral-directional plane. These two systems can be treated separately, but in the same time, these can be put together to control all the parameters which interfere in the dynamics of aircraft landing. The two new ALSs are designed by using the H-inf control, the dynamic inversion, optimal observers, and reference models. To validate the new obtained ALS, one uses the dynamics associated to the landing of a Boeing 747, software implements the theoretical results and analyzes the accuracy of the results and the precision standards' achievement with respect to the requirements of the Federal Aviation Administration (FAA).

Keywords: Landing, H-inf control, Dynamic inversion, Observer, Reference model

1. Introduction

Landing is one of the most critical stages of flight; the aircraft has to perform a precise maneuver in the proximity of the ground to land safely at a suitable touch point with acceptable sink rate, speed, and attitude. During aircraft landing, the presence of different unknown or partially known disturbances in aircraft dynamics leads to the necessity of using modern automatic control systems. Sometimes, the conventional controllers are difficult to use due to the drastically changing of the atmospheric conditions and the dynamics of aircraft [1, 2]. In order to control aircraft landing, the feedback linearization has been used in [3], but the drawback of this method is that all the parametric plant uncertainties must appear in the same equation of the state-space representation. Other automatic landing systems (ALSs) use feed-forward neural networks based on the back propagation learning algorithms [4]; the main disadvantage is that the neural networks require a priori training on normal and faulty operating data. From the optimal synthesis' point of view, a mixed technique for the H_2/H_∞ control of landing has been introduced by Shue and Agarwal [5], while Ochi and Kanai [6] have used the H-inf technique for the same purpose; the negative point of these papers is the robustness of the controllers since the sensor errors and other external disturbances are not considered. The fuzzy logic has been also used to imitate the pilot's experience in compromising between trajectory tracking and touchdown safety [7]. In other studies [8], it has been proved that an intelligent on-line-learning controller is helpful in assisting different baseline controllers in tolerating a stuck control surface in the presence of strong wind.

The main drawback of all the papers dealing with aircraft landing is that the designed ALSs are designed either for the longitudinal plane or for the lateral-directional plane. Our work focuses on aircraft automatic control in the two planes, during landing, by using the linearized dynamics of aircraft, the H-inf control, and the dynamic inversion concept, taking into consideration the wind shears, the crosswind, and the errors of the sensors. Our aim is to design a new landing control system (both planes) which cancels the negative effect of wind shears, the crosswind, and the errors of the sensors. According to this work's authors, little progress has been reported for the landing flight control systems (using the H-inf control and the dynamic inversion) handling all the above presented problems.

The three phases of a typical landing procedure are: the initial approach, the glide slope, and the flare [1, 9]. The initial approach involves a descend of the aircraft from the cruise altitude to approximately 420 m (heavy aircraft). Aircraft pitch, attitude, and speed must be controlled during the glide slope path; its speed should be constant during this stage of landing. For a Boeing 747, the pitch should be between −5 and 5 degrees, while the sink rate should be 3 m/s. For the same type of aircraft, when the altitude is 20–30 m above the ground, a flare maneuver should be accomplished and, therefore, the slope angle control system is disengaged; during the flare, aircraft pitch angle is adjusted (between 0 and 5 degrees) for a soft touchdown of the runway. These issues will be achieved by the first system presented in this chapter—the one for the control of aircraft trajectory in the longitudinal plane. The motion of aircraft in lateral plane should be done without errors, this meaning the cancel of aircraft deviation with respect to the runway direction; for this purpose, flight direction automatic control systems are necessary; this issue will be achieved by the second system presented in this chapter—the one for the control of aircraft trajectory in the lateral-directional plane.

2. Design the first subsystem of the ALS (longitudinal plane)

2.1. Aircraft dynamics in longitudinal plane

The linearized dynamics of aircraft in longitudinal plane is described by the state equation [10]: $\dot{\boldsymbol{x}}_{long} = A_{long}\boldsymbol{x}_{long} + B_{long}\boldsymbol{u}_{long} + G_{long}\tilde{\boldsymbol{u}}_{long}$, with $\boldsymbol{x}_{long} = [\,u \quad w \quad q \quad \theta \quad H\,]^T$– the state vector, $\boldsymbol{u}_{long} = [\,\delta_e \quad \delta_T\,]^T$ – the command vector, while $\tilde{\boldsymbol{u}}_{long} = [\,V_{vx} \quad V_{vz}\,]^T$ is the vector of disturbances – V_{vx} and V_{vz} (the components of the wind velocity along the longitudinal and vertical axes of the aircraft [11]); in the above equations, u is the longitudinal velocity of aircraft, w – the vertical velocity, q – the pitch angular rate, θ – the pitch angle, H – aircraft altitude, while δ_e and δ_T are the elevator deflection and the engine command, respectively. Because the vertical velocity w is much smaller than u, one can consider the velocity in longitudinal plane to be $V=\sqrt{u^2+w^2}\cong u$ [10]; thus, the nominal value of V is considered to be $V_0 \cong u(0) = u_0$. The equations of the actuators are $\dot{\delta}_e=-\frac{1}{T_e}\delta_e+\frac{1}{T_e}\delta_{ec}$, $\dot{\delta}_T=-\frac{1}{T_T}\delta_T+\frac{1}{T_t}\delta_{Tc}$; δ_{ec} and δ_{Tc} are the commands applied to elevator engine, respectively. Considering δ_e and δ_T as new states, $\boldsymbol{x}_{long}$ and $\boldsymbol{u}_{long}$ become $\boldsymbol{x}_{long}=[u \quad w \quad q \quad \theta \quad H \quad \delta_e \quad \delta_T]^T$, $\boldsymbol{u}_{long}=[\delta_{ec} \quad \delta_{Tc}]^T$, while the new matrices $A_{long} \in R^{7\times 7}$, $B_{long} \in R^{7\times 2}$, and $G_{long} \in R^{7\times 2}$ are [10]:

$$A_{long}=\begin{bmatrix} a_{11} & a_{12} & 0 & a_{14} & 0 & b_{11} & b_{12} \\ a_{21} & a_{22} & a_{23} & 0 & 0 & b_{21} & b_{22} \\ a_{31} & a_{32} & a_{33} & 0 & 0 & b_{31} & b_{32} \\ 0 & 0 & 1 & 0 & 0 & 0 & 0 \\ 0 & a_{52} & 0 & a_{54} & 0 & 0 & 0 \\ 0 & 0 & 0 & 0 & 0 & -1/T_e & 0 \\ 0 & 0 & 0 & 0 & 0 & 0 & -1/T_T \end{bmatrix},\ B_{long}=\begin{bmatrix} 0 & 0 \\ 0 & 0 \\ 0 & 0 \\ 0 & 0 \\ 0 & 0 \\ 1/T_e & 0 \\ 0 & 1/T_T \end{bmatrix},\ G_{long}=\begin{bmatrix} g_{11} & g_{12} \\ g_{21} & g_{22} \\ g_{31} & g_{32} \\ 0 & 0 \\ 0 & 0 \\ 0 & 0 \\ 0 & 0 \end{bmatrix}. \qquad (1)$$

2.2. Wind shears' model

By using the velocities' spectrum and generator filters having as inputs white noises, one can define the vector $\tilde{\boldsymbol{u}}_{long}$ which corresponds to a stochastic process. In this work, the disturbances are considered to be the wind shears, the equations associated to them being [10, 11]: $V_{vx}=-V_{vx_0}\sin(\omega_0 t)$, $V_{vz}=-V_{vz_0}[1-\cos(\omega_0 t)]$, $\omega_0=2\pi/T_0$, where T_0 is the flight time period inside the wind shear, while V_{vx_0} and V_{vz_0} are the maximum absolute values of the wind velocities with respect to aircraft longitudinal and vertical axes, respectively.

In order to calculate the matrix G_{long}, one replaces $\tilde{\boldsymbol{u}}_{long} = 0$ in the aircraft dynamics and, after that, one replaces u with $(u - V_{vx})$ and w with $(w - V_{vz})$; the coefficients of the velocities V_{vx}, V_{vz} and, thus, the elements of the matrix G_{long} are obtained as follows: $g_{11}=-a_{11}$, $g_{12}=-a_{12}$, $g_{21}=-a_{21}$, $g_{22}=-a_{22}$, $g_{31}=-a_{31}$, $g_{32}=-a_{32}$.

2.3. The general form of the control law (longitudinal plane)

One considers the vector $\boldsymbol{z}_{long}=[H \quad u]^T=C'_{long}\boldsymbol{x}_{long}$ that contains the system-controllable output variables, while the vector $\bar{\boldsymbol{z}}_{long}=[\bar{H} \quad \bar{u}]^T$ contains the reference variables (the imposed values of the flight altitude and velocity). The system output vector is $\boldsymbol{y}_{long}$, chosen of the following form: $\boldsymbol{y}_{long}=[H \quad \dot{H} \quad u \quad \dot{u} \quad \theta \quad q]^T=C_{long}\boldsymbol{x}_{long}$. Taking into account the differential equations of the states H and u, obtained from aircraft dynamics, by using $\boldsymbol{x}_{long}$ and $\boldsymbol{u}_{long}$ the matrices $A_{long}, B_{long}, G_{long}$, one yields:

$$C'_{long} = \begin{bmatrix} 0 & 1 \\ 0 & 0 \\ 0 & 0 \\ 0 & 0 \\ 1 & 0 \\ 0 & 0 \\ 0 & 0 \end{bmatrix}^T, \quad C_{long} = \begin{bmatrix} 0 & 0 & 0 & 0 & 1 & 0 & 0 \\ 0 & a_{52} & 0 & a_{54} & 0 & 0 & 0 \\ 1 & 0 & 0 & 0 & 0 & 0 & 0 \\ a_{11} & a_{12} & 0 & a_{14} & 0 & b_{11} & b_{12} \\ 0 & 0 & 0 & 1 & 0 & 0 & 0 \\ 0 & 0 & 1 & 0 & 0 & 0 & 0 \end{bmatrix}. \tag{2}$$

Now, by using $\bar{z}_{long}$ and the dynamic inversion principle, $\bar{x}_{long}$ and $\bar{u}_{long}$ are calculated with respect to $\bar{z}_{long}$ and, after that, the vector $\bar{y}_{long}$ is obtained by means of the equations [11]: $\dot{\bar{x}}_{long} = A_{long}\bar{x}_{long} + B_{long}\bar{u}_{long}$, $\bar{z}_{long} = C'_{long}\bar{x}_{long}$, $\bar{y}_{long} = C_{long}\bar{x}_{long}$. The command law is calculated with the formula [10]:

$$u_{long} = \bar{u}_{long} + u_{\infty long}, \tag{3}$$

where $u_{\infty long}$ is the optimal command that is calculated by means of the H-inf method [12, 13], while the component $\bar{u}_{long}$ is calculated by using the dynamic inversion.

2.4. Design of the control law's first component (longitudinal plane)

A coordinates' change is achieved by means of the transformation matrix $T \in R^{7 \times 7}$ [11]:

$$\begin{bmatrix} \xi \\ \eta \end{bmatrix} = T x_{long}, \quad x_{long} = T^{-1}\begin{bmatrix} \xi \\ \eta \end{bmatrix}, \tag{4}$$

where ξ is a state vector consisting of the controlled variables and their derivatives, i.e. [11]: $\xi = \begin{bmatrix} z_1 & \dot{z}_1 & \cdots & z_1^{(r_1-1)} & z_2 & \dot{z}_2 & \cdots & z_2^{(r_2-1)} & \cdots & z_p & \dot{z}_p & \cdots & z_p^{(r_p-1)} \end{bmatrix}^T$, with $z_i^{(r_i-1)}$– the $(r_i - 1)$ order derivatives of z_i; for the aircraft dynamics in longitudinal plane, $z_1 = H$, $z_2 = z_p = u$. The state vector η consists of all the state variables not included in the vector ξ; considering n to be the dimension of the square matrix T, one can easily deduce the dimension of the vector η as $n{-}r = n{-}\sum_{i=1}^{p} r_i$, where the values of the relative degrees r_i, $i = \overline{1,\ 2}$, are to be deduced later.

For the obtaining of the relative degrees r_1 and r_2, the equations of $\dot{u}$ and $\dot{w}$ are differentiated until terms containing the two components of the control law $(\delta_{ec}, \delta_{Tc})$ appears in the expressions of the variables $\ddot{u}$ and $\ddot{w}$; by time derivation of the variables $\ddot{u}$ and $\ddot{w}$ (expressed by using aircraft dynamics), it results some terms containing the variables $.\delta_{ec}$ and $.\delta_{Tc}$; these can be expressed by means of equations $\dot{\delta}_e = -\frac{1}{T_e}\delta_e + \frac{1}{T_e}\delta_{ec}$, $\dot{\delta}_T = -\frac{1}{T_T}\delta_T + \frac{1}{T_T}\delta_{Tc}$; one obtains $\ddot{u}$ and $\ddot{w}$ as functions of δ_{ec}, δ_{Tc}, and other states. Thus, the relative degree of the state u is $r_2 = 2$. In order to obtain the relative degree of the altitude (H), one derivates the differential equation associated to H, i.e. $\dot{H} = a_{52}w + a_{54}\theta$, and obtains $\ddot{H} = a_{52}\dot{w} + a_{54}\dot{\theta}$. is obtained. Therefore, the relative degree of the altitude is $r_1 = 3$. The following equations result:

http://dx.doi.org/10.5772/62666

$$\begin{aligned}\ddot{u} &= a'_{11}u + a'_{12}w + a'_{13}q + a'_{14}\theta + a'_{16}\delta_e + a'_{17}\delta_T + \frac{b_{11}}{T_e}\delta_{ec} + \frac{b_{12}}{T_T}\delta_{Tc} + g'_{11}V_{vx} + g'_{12}V_{vz}\\ &\quad + g_{11}\dot{V}_{vx} + g_{12}\dot{V}_{vz},\\ \dddot{H} &= a'_{51}u + a'_{52}w + a'_{53}q + a'_{54}\theta + a'_{56}\delta_e + a'_{57}\delta_T + \frac{a_{52}b_{21}}{T_e}\delta_{ec} + \frac{a_{52}b_{22}}{T_T}\delta_{Tc} + g'_{51}V_{vx} + g'_{52}V_{vz}\\ &\quad + g''_{51}\dot{V}_{vx} + g''_{52}\dot{V}_{vz},\end{aligned} \tag{5}$$

with $a'_{11} = a_{11}^2 + a_{12}a_{21}$, $a'_{12} = a_{11}a_{12} + a_{12}a_{22}$, $a'_{13} = a_{12}a_{23} + a_{14}$, $a'_{14} = a_{11}a_{14}$, $a'_{16} = a_{11}b_{11} + a_{12}b_{21} - \frac{b_{11}}{T_e}$, $a'_{17} = a_{11}b_{12} + a_{12}b_{21} - \frac{b_{12}}{T_T}$, $g'_{11} = a_{11}g_{11} + a_{12}g_{21}$, $g'_{12} = a_{11}g_{12} + a_{12}g_{22}$, $a'_{51} = a_{54}a_{31} + a_{52}(a_{21}a_{11} + a_{21}a_{12} + a_{23}a_{31})$, $a'_{52} = a_{54}a_{32} + a_{52}(a_{21}a_{12} + a_{22}^2 + a_{23}a_{32})$, $a'_{53} = a_{54}a_{33}$, $a'_{54} = a_{52}(a_{22}a_{23} + a_{22}a_{33} + a_{21}a_{14})$, $a'_{56} = a_{54}b_{31} + a_{52}\left(a_{21}b_{11} + a_{22}b_{21} + a_{23}b_{31} - \frac{1}{T_e}b_{21}\right)$, $a'_{57} = a_{54}b_{32} + a_{52}\left(a_{21}b_{12} + a_{22}b_{22} + a_{23}b_{32} - \frac{1}{T_T}b_{22}\right)$, $g'_{51} = a_{54}g_{31} + a_{52}(a_{21}g_{11} + a_{22}g_{21} + a_{23}g_{31})$, $g'_{52} = a_{54}g_{32} + a_{52}(a_{21}g_{12} + a_{22}g_{22} + a_{23}g_{33})$, $g''_{51} = a_{52}g_{21}$, $g''_{52} = a_{52}g_{22}$.

Thus, the state vectors ξ and η are $\xi = [H \quad \dot{H} \quad \ddot{H} \quad u \quad \dot{u}]^T$, $\eta = [\theta \quad q]^T$. By means of the coordinates' change (4), considering $\tilde{\boldsymbol{u}}_{long} = 0$ and $\boldsymbol{u}_{long} = \bar{\boldsymbol{u}}_{long}$, aircraft dynamics gets the form [11]: $\begin{bmatrix}\dot{\xi}\\ \dot{\eta}\end{bmatrix} = \hat{A}_{long}\begin{bmatrix}\xi\\ \eta\end{bmatrix} + \hat{B}_{long}\bar{\boldsymbol{u}}_{long}$; $\hat{A}_{long} = TA_{long}T^{-1}$, $\hat{B}_{long} = TB_{long}$. If the matrices $\hat{A}_{long}$ and $\hat{B}_{long}$ are partitioned with respect to the dimensions of the vectors ξ and η, it results [4]: $\begin{bmatrix}\dot{\xi}\\ \dot{\eta}\end{bmatrix} = \begin{bmatrix}\hat{A}_{long\,11} & \hat{A}_{long\,12}\\ \hat{A}_{long\,21} & \hat{A}_{long\,22}\end{bmatrix}\begin{bmatrix}\xi\\ \eta\end{bmatrix} + \begin{bmatrix}\hat{B}_{long\,1}\\ \hat{B}_{long\,2}\end{bmatrix}\bar{u}_{long}$. Imposing $\xi = \bar{\xi}$, $\dot{\xi} = \dot{\bar{\xi}}$, with $\bar{\xi} = [\bar{H} \quad \bar{\dot{H}} \quad \bar{\ddot{H}} \quad \bar{u} \quad \bar{\dot{u}}]^T$, $\dot{\bar{\xi}} = [\bar{\dot{H}} \quad \bar{\ddot{H}} \quad \bar{\dddot{H}} \quad \bar{\dot{u}} \quad \bar{\ddot{u}}]^T$, the vector $\bar{\boldsymbol{u}}_{long}$ is obtained as: $\bar{\boldsymbol{u}}_{long} = \widehat{B}^{+}_{long_1}\left(\dot{\bar{\xi}} - \widehat{A}_{long_{11}}\bar{\xi} - \widehat{A}_{long_{12}}\eta\right)$, with $\widehat{B}^{+}_{long_1}$ – pseudo-inverse of the matrix $\widehat{B}_{long_1}$.

For the obtaining of the matrix T, the vectors ξ and are replaced in (4) and the following differential equations result: $\dot{H} = a_{52}u + a_{54}\theta$, $\ddot{H} = a_{52}\dot{w} + a_{54}\dot{\theta}$, $\dot{\theta} = q$, $\dot{u} = a_{11}u + a_{12}w + a_{14}\theta + b_{11}\delta_e + b_{12}\delta_T$, $\dot{w} = a_{21}u + a_{22}w + a_{23}q + b_{21}\delta_e + b_{22}\delta_T$; one yields:

$$\begin{bmatrix}H\\ \dot{H}\\ \ddot{H}\\ u\\ \dot{u}\\ \theta\\ q\end{bmatrix} = \underbrace{\begin{bmatrix}0 & 0 & 0 & 0 & 1 & 0 & 0\\ 0 & a_{52} & 0 & a_{54} & 0 & 0 & 0\\ a_{52}a_{21} & a_{52}a_{22} & (a_{54} + a_{52}a_{23}) & 0 & 0 & a_{52}b_{21} & a_{52}b_{22}\\ 1 & 0 & 0 & 0 & 0 & 0 & 0\\ a_{11} & a_{12} & 0 & a_{14} & 0 & b_{11} & b_{12}\\ 0 & 0 & 0 & 1 & 0 & 0 & 0\\ 0 & 0 & 1 & 0 & 0 & 0 & 0\end{bmatrix}}_{T}\begin{bmatrix}u\\ w\\ q\\ \theta\\ H\\ \delta_e\\ \delta_T\end{bmatrix}. \tag{6}$$

Replacing the vectors $\bar{\xi} = [\bar{H} \quad \bar{\dot{H}} \quad \bar{\ddot{H}} \quad \bar{u} \quad \bar{\dot{u}}]^T$ and $\dot{\bar{\xi}} = [\bar{\dot{H}} \quad \bar{\ddot{H}} \quad \bar{\dddot{H}} \quad \bar{\dot{u}} \quad \bar{\ddot{u}}]^T$ into equation $\bar{\boldsymbol{u}}_{long} = \widehat{B}^{+}_{long_1}\left(\dot{\bar{\xi}} - \widehat{A}_{long_{11}}\bar{\xi} - \widehat{A}_{long_{12}}\eta\right)$, one obtains

$$\bar{u}_{long} = \widehat{B}^{+}_{long_1}\left\{\begin{bmatrix}0 & 0 & \overline{\dddot{H}} & 0 & \overline{\ddot{u}}\end{bmatrix}^T - \widehat{A}'_{long_{11}}\bar{\xi} - \widehat{A}_{long_{12}}\eta\right\}, \tag{7}$$

where $\widehat{A}'_{long_{11}}$ is calculated from $\widehat{A}_{long_{11}}$ making the substitutions: $\widehat{a}'_{12} = \widehat{a}_{12} - 1$, $\widehat{a}'_{23} = \widehat{a}_{23} - 1$, $\widehat{a}'_{45} = \widehat{a}_{45} - 1$, the other elements of the matrices $\widehat{A}_{long_{11}}$ and $\widehat{A}'_{long_{11}}$ being the same; $\widehat{a}_{ij}$, $i, j = \overline{1, 5}$ are the elements of the matrix $\widehat{A}_{long_{11}}$.

Replacing (7) in $\dot{\eta} = \widehat{A}_{long_{21}}\xi + \widehat{A}_{long_{22}}\eta + \widehat{B}_{long_2}\bar{u}_{long}$, with $\xi = \bar{\xi}$, one obtains:

$$\dot{\eta} = \widehat{A}_{\eta}\eta + \widehat{B}_y\overline{\mathbf{Z}}, \tag{8}$$

where $\widehat{A}_{\eta} = \widehat{A}_{long_{22}} - \widehat{B}_{long_2}\widehat{B}^{+}_{long_1}\widehat{A}_{long_{12}}$, $\widehat{A}_{\xi} = \widehat{A}_{long_{21}} - \widehat{B}_{long_2}\widehat{B}^{+}_{long_1}\widehat{A}'_{long_{11}}$, $\widehat{B}_z\bar{\mathbf{z}}^{(r)}_{long} = \widehat{B}_{long_2}\widehat{B}^{+}_{long_1}\begin{bmatrix}0 & 0 & \overline{\dddot{H}} & 0 & \overline{\ddot{u}}\end{bmatrix}^T$, $\bar{\mathbf{z}}^{(r)}_{long} = [\bar{z}_1^{(r_1)} \ \ \bar{z}_2^{(r_2)}]^T = [\overline{\dddot{H}} \ \ \overline{\ddot{u}}]^T$, $\hat{B}_y = [\hat{B}_z \ \ \hat{A}_{\xi}]$, $\overline{\mathbf{Z}} = [\bar{\mathbf{z}}^{(r)}_{long} \bar{\xi}]^T = [\overline{\dddot{H}} \ \overline{\ddot{u}} \ \overline{H} \ \overline{\dot{H}} \ \overline{\ddot{H}} \ \bar{u} \ \overline{\dot{u}}]^T$. If one considers $\hat{B}_{long_2}\hat{B}^{+}_{long_1} = \begin{bmatrix}\hat{b}_{11} & \hat{b}_{12} & \hat{b}_{13} & \hat{b}_{14} & \hat{b}_{15} \\ \hat{b}_{21} & \hat{b}_{22} & \hat{b}_{23} & \hat{b}_{24} & \hat{b}_{25}\end{bmatrix}$ then $\widehat{B}_z = \begin{bmatrix}\hat{b}_{13} & \hat{b}_{15} \\ \hat{b}_{22} & \hat{b}_{25}\end{bmatrix}$ Thus, for the calculation of the command vector $\bar{u}_{long}$, one solves equation (8) and obtains the vector η and then uses the equation (7). From the expression of $\widehat{B}_z\bar{\mathbf{z}}^{(r)}_{long}$, it results: $\hat{B}^{+}_{long_1}[0 \ 0 \ \overline{\dddot{H}} \ 0 \ \overline{\ddot{u}}]^T = \hat{B}^{+}_{long_2}\hat{B}_z\bar{z}^{(r)}_{long}$, which, replaced in (7), leads to

$$\bar{u}_{long} = \widehat{B}_u^{-1}\left(\bar{\mathbf{z}}^{(r)}_{long} - \widehat{B}_{\xi}\bar{\xi} - \widehat{B}_{\eta}\eta\right), \tag{9}$$

with $\widehat{B}_u^{-1} = \widehat{B}^{+}_{long_2}\widehat{B}_z$, $\widehat{B}_{\xi} = \widehat{B}_u\widehat{B}^{+}_{long_1}\widehat{A}'_{long_{11}}$, $\widehat{B}_{\eta} = \widehat{B}_u\widehat{B}^{+}_{long_1}\widehat{A}_{long_{12}}$. Therefore, $\bar{u}_{long}$ can be obtained by means of equation (7) or by using equation (9).

2.5. Design of the control law's second component (longitudinal plane)

To calculate the second component of the control law u_{long}, one combines the aircraft dynamics, the equations associated to $z_1 = H$ and $z_2 = u$, as well as the equation of the output vector y_{long}:

$$\begin{bmatrix}\dot{x}_{long} \\ z_1 \\ z_2 \\ y_{long}\end{bmatrix} = \begin{bmatrix}A_{long} & B_{long} & G_{long} & 0_{(7\times6)} \\ C_{0long} & D_{01long} & 0_{(1\times2)} & 0_{(1\times6)} \\ C_{1long} & D_{11long} & 0_{(1\times2)} & 0_{(1\times6)} \\ C_{long} & 0_{(6\times2)} & 0_{(6\times2)} & D_{22long}\end{bmatrix}\begin{bmatrix}x_{long} \\ u_{long} \\ \tilde{u}_{long} \\ e_{long}\end{bmatrix}, \tag{10}$$

with $C_{0long} = [0 \ 0 \ 0 \ 0 \ 1 \ 0 \ 0]$, $C_{1long} = [1 \ 0 \ 0 \ 0 \ 0 \ 0 \ 0]$, $D_{01long} = [c_1 \ \ 0]$, $D_{11long} = [c_2 \ \ 0]$, the matrix C_{long} has the form (2), while $D_{22long} = I_6$ for the vector containing the sensor errors: $e_{long} = [e_H \quad e_{\dot{H}} \quad e_u \quad e_{\dot{u}} \quad e_\theta \quad e_q]^T$. The optimal control law has the form [10, 14]: $u_{\infty long} = -K_{\infty long}(\hat{x}_{long} - \bar{x}_{long})$, $K_{\infty long} = R_1^{-1} B_{long}{}^T P_\infty$, $R_1 = D_{11long}^T D_{11long}$; $u_{\infty long}$ minimizes the cost functional: $J_{long} = \frac{1}{2}\int_0^\infty z_2^T z_2 dt = \frac{1}{2}\int_0^\infty [x_{long}^T \underbrace{(C_{1\,long}^T C_{1\,long})}_{Q_1} x_{long} + u_{\infty\,long}^T \underbrace{(D_{11\,long}^T D_{11\,long})}_{R_1} u_{\infty\,long}]\, dt$.

The symmetric and positive defined matrix P_∞ is the stabilizing solution of the Riccati equation [15]:

$$A_{long}^T P_\infty + P_\infty A_{long} - P_\infty \left(B_{long} R_1^{-1} B_{long}^T - \mu_1^{-2} G_{long} G_{long}^T\right) P_\infty + Q_1 = 0. \tag{11}$$

Q_1 and R_1 are positive defined matrices, while μ_1 is a small enough positive scalar such that the Riccati equation (11) has a stabilizing solution [10]. To solve the H-inf control problem means to calculate the controller gain matrix ($K_{\infty\ long}$); the system has control inputs as well as disturbances; the control input (u_{long}) is the controller's output, this becoming the actuators' input. The disturbances of the system ($\tilde{u}_{long}$ and e_{long}) are the exogenous inputs [10, 12, 13]. The H-inf control problem means to find a controller for the generalized plant such that the infinity norm of the transfer function relating exogenous inputs to performance outputs is minimum. The controller gain matrix ($K_{\infty\ long}$) has the general form $K_{\infty long} = R_1^{-1} B_{long}^T P_\infty$ [10, 12, 13], the optimal control law $u_{\infty\,long}$ depending on $\Delta\hat{x}_{long} = \hat{x}_{long} - \bar{x}_{long}$; to estimate this signal and the state $\hat{x}_{long}$, one borrowed the observer presented in [14], i.e.: $\Delta\dot{\hat{x}}_{long} = A_{long}\Delta\hat{x}_{long} + B_{long}u_{long} + G_{long}\tilde{u}_{long} + L_{\infty long}\left(\Delta y_{long} - C_{long}\Delta\hat{x}_{long}\right)$. The observer gain matrix $L_{\infty long}$ is calculated with the formula: $L_{\infty long} = P_\infty^* C_{long}^T \left(D_{22long}^T D_{22long}\right)^{-1}$, with P_∞^* – the stabilizing solution of the Riccati equation [15]:

$$A_{long} P_\infty^* + P_\infty^* A_{long}^T - P_\infty^* \left(C_{long}^T C_{long} - \mu_2^{-2} Q_1\right) P_\infty^* + G_{long} G_{long}^T = 0; \tag{12}$$

μ_2 is a small positive scalar for which the Riccati equation (12) has a stabilizing solution.

3. Design the second subsystem of the ALS (lateral-directional plane)

3.1. Aircraft dynamics in lateral-directional plane

Before the start of the landing, two main stages in longitudinal plane (glide slope and flare), the pilot must cancel the aircraft lateral deviation with respect to the runway. This can be achieved by means of the second subsystem of the ALS designed in this chapter or by using other control systems for the flight direction control with radio navigation subsystem and equipment for the measurement of the distance between the aircraft and the radio markers. The linear model of the aircraft motion, in lateral-directional plane, can be described again by the state equation: $\dot{x}_{lat} = A_{lat}x_{lat} + B_{lat}u_{lat} + G_{lat}\tilde{u}_{lat}$, where $x_{lat} = [\beta \ p \ r \ \varphi \ \psi \ Y \ \delta_a \ \delta_r]^T$, $u_{lat} = [\delta_{a_c} \quad \delta_{r_c}]^T$, $\tilde{u}_{lat} = V_{vy}$, with β – aircraft sideslip angle, φ and ψ are the roll angle and the yaw angle, respectively, p – aircraft roll angular rate, r – the aircraft yaw angular rate, Y – aircraft lateral error, δ_a and δ_r – the ailerons and rudder's deflection angles, δ_{a_c} and δ_{r_c} – the roll and yaw commands (commands applied to the actuators), V_{vy} – the wind component having as direction—the aircraft the lateral axis, T_a and T_r – the effectors' time delay constants of the ailerons and rudder, respectively. The matrices A_{lat}, B_{lat}, and G_{lat} are [1]:

$$A_{lat} = \begin{bmatrix} a_{11} & a_{12} & a_{13} & a_{14} & 0 & 0 & b_{11} & b_{12} \\ a_{21} & a_{22} & a_{23} & 0 & 0 & 0 & b_{21} & b_{22} \\ a_{31} & a_{32} & a_{33} & 0 & 0 & 0 & b_{31} & b_{32} \\ 0 & 1 & 0 & 0 & 0 & 0 & 0 & 0 \\ 0 & 0 & 1 & 0 & 0 & 0 & 0 & 0 \\ -V_0 & 0 & 0 & 0 & V_0 & 0 & 0 & 0 \\ 0 & 0 & 0 & 0 & 0 & 0 & -\dfrac{1}{T_a} & 0 \\ 0 & 0 & 0 & 0 & 0 & 0 & 0 & -\dfrac{1}{T_r} \end{bmatrix}, \quad B_{lat} = \begin{bmatrix} 0 & 0 \\ 0 & 0 \\ 0 & 0 \\ 0 & 0 \\ 0 & 0 \\ 0 & 0 \\ \dfrac{1}{T_a} & 0 \\ 0 & \dfrac{1}{T_r} \end{bmatrix}, \quad G_{lat} = \begin{bmatrix} \dfrac{a_{11}}{V_0} \\ \dfrac{a_{21}}{V_0} \\ \dfrac{a_{31}}{V_0} \\ 0 \\ 0 \\ 1 \\ 0 \\ 0 \end{bmatrix}; \qquad (13)$$

For the design of the second optimal subsystem of the ALS, let us consider the vector $z_{lat} = [Y \ \ \beta]^T = C'_{lat} x_{lat}$—the vector of the system's controllable output variables and the vector $\bar{z}_{lat} = [\bar{Y} \ \ \bar{\beta}]^T$—the reference variables' vector, i.e. the desired values for the lateral deviation and the sideslip angle of the aircraft. The system's output vector is $y_{lat} = [Y \ \ \dot{Y} \ \ \beta \ \ \varphi \ \ p \ \ \psi \ \ r]^T = C_{lat} x_{lat}$; sensors' errors have been not taken into account here; knowing the forms of z_{lat} and y_{lat}, the matrices C_{lat} and C'_{lat} can be easily deduced.

3.2. The general form of the control law (lateral-directional plane)

The command law is similar to the one for longitudinal plane; it is calculated with the formula:

$$u_{lat} = \bar{u}_{lat} + u_{\infty lat}, \qquad (14)$$

where $u_{\infty lat}$ is the optimal command calculated by means of the H-inf method, while the component $\bar{u}_{lat}$ is calculated by using the dynamic inversion [3, 12, 13]. For the design of the signal $\bar{u}_{lat}$ there are used the dynamic inversion principle and the vectors $\bar{z}_{lat} = C'_{lat}\bar{x}_{lat}$, $\bar{y}_{lat} = C_{lat}\bar{x}_{lat}$, where $\bar{x}_{lat}$ is determined from the equation $\dot{\bar{x}}_{lat} = A\bar{x}_{lat} + B_{lat}\bar{u}_{lat}$.

3.3. Design of the control law's first component (lateral-directional plane)

First, one obtains the relative degrees of the variables $z_1 = Y$ and $z_2 = \beta$; these relative degrees are denoted here with r_1 and r_2, respectively. One derivates with respect to time the equations associated to Y and β (r_1 times and r_2 times, respectively) until the components of the command vector u_{lat}, i.e. δ_{a_c} and δ_{r_c}, are obtained; the following equations have resulted:

$$\dddot{Y} = a'_{61}\beta + a'_{62}p + a'_{63}r + a'_{64}\varphi + a'_{67}\delta_a + a'_{68}\delta_r - \frac{V_0 b_{11}}{T_a}\delta_{a_c} - \frac{V_0 b_{12}}{T_r}\delta_{r_c} + \left(a_{31} - a'_{11}\right)V_{vy} - a_{11}\widetilde{V}_{vy},$$
$$\ddot{\beta} = a'_{11}\beta + a'_{12}p + a'_{13}r + a'_{14}\varphi + a'_{17}\delta_a + a'_{18}\delta_r + \frac{b_{11}}{T_a}\delta_{a_c} + \frac{b_{12}}{T_r}\delta_{r_c} + \frac{a'_{11}}{V_0}V_{vy} + \frac{a_{11}}{V_0}\widetilde{V}_{vy}, \tag{15}$$

where $a'_{11} = a_{11}^2 + a_{12}a_{21} + a_{13}a_{31}$, $a'_{12} = a_{11}a_{12} + a_{12}a_{22} + a_{13}a_{32} + a_{14}$, $a'_{13} = a_{11}a_{13} + a_{12}a_{23} + a_{13}a_{33}$, $a'_{14} = a_{11}a_{14}$, $a'_{17} = a_{11}b_{11} + a_{12}b_{21} + a_{13}b_{31} - b_{11}/T_a$, $a'_{18} = a_{11}b_{12} + a_{12}b_{22} + a_{13}b_{32} - b_{12}/T_r$, $a'_{61} = V_0\left(a_{31} - a'_{11}\right)$, $a'_{62} = V_0\left(a_{32} - a'_{12}\right)$, $a'_{63} = V_0\left(a_{33} - a'_{13}\right)$, $a'_{64} = -V_0 a'_{14}$, $a'_{67} = V_0\left(b_{31} - a'_{17}\right)$, $a'_{68} = V_0\left(b_{32} - a'_{18}\right)$, $a'_{31} = a_{31} - a'_{11}$.

Thus, according to equations (15), the relative degrees are $r_1 = 3$ and $r_2 = 2$. The equations (15) may be combined in the equation of the vector $z_{lat}^{(r)} = \left[\dddot{Y} \;\; \ddot{\beta}\right]^T$, i.e.: $\boldsymbol{z}_{lat}^{(r)} = A_x \boldsymbol{x}_{lat} + B_u \overline{\boldsymbol{u}}_{lat} + G'_{lat}\tilde{\boldsymbol{u}}_{lat}$, where $\overline{\boldsymbol{u}}_{lat} = \left[\overline{\delta}_{a_c} \;\; \overline{\delta}_{r_c}\right]^T$, $\tilde{\boldsymbol{u}}_{lat} = \left[V_{vy} \;\; \widetilde{V}_{vy}\right]^T$, $A_x = \begin{bmatrix} a'_{61} & a'_{62} & a'_{63} & a'_{64} & 0 & 0 & a'_{67} & a'_{68} \\ a'_{11} & a'_{12} & a'_{13} & a'_{14} & 0 & 0 & a'_{17} & a'_{18} \end{bmatrix}$, $B_u = \begin{bmatrix} -\frac{V_0 b_{11}}{T_a} & -\frac{V_0 b_{12}}{T_r} \\ \frac{b_{11}}{T_a} & \frac{b_{12}}{T_r} \end{bmatrix}$, $G'_{lat} = \begin{bmatrix} a'_{31} & -a_{11} \\ -\frac{a'_{11}}{V_0} & \frac{a_{11}}{V_0} \end{bmatrix}$. The form of the control law $\overline{\boldsymbol{u}}_{lat}$ results from $\boldsymbol{z}_{lat}^{(r)} = A_x \boldsymbol{x}_{lat} + B_u \overline{\boldsymbol{u}}_{lat} + G'_{lat}\tilde{\boldsymbol{u}}_{lat}$, if one imposes the convergence of $z_{lat}^{(r)} = \left[\dddot{Y} \;\; \ddot{\beta}\right]^T$ to $\overline{z}_{lat}^{(r)} = \left[\overline{\dddot{Y}}\, \overline{\ddot{\beta}}\right]^T$ and the convergence of the system estimated state $(\widehat{\boldsymbol{x}}_{lat})$ to $\boldsymbol{x}_{lat}$; in these conditions, one gets [1]:

$$\overline{\boldsymbol{u}}_{lat} = B_u^{-1}\left(\overline{\boldsymbol{z}}_{lat}^{(r)} - A_x \widehat{\boldsymbol{x}}_{lat} - G'_{lat}\tilde{\boldsymbol{u}}_{lat}\right). \tag{16}$$

3.4. Design of the control law's second component (lateral-directional plane)

To obtain the second component of the command law $\boldsymbol{u}_{lat}$, the H-inf control is used; the state equation associated to aircraft dynamics in lateral-directional plane, the equations associated to $z_1 = Y$ and $z_2 = \beta$, as well as the equation of the output vector $\boldsymbol{y}_{lat}$, may be combined into the following equation:

$$\begin{bmatrix} \dot{\boldsymbol{x}}_{lat} \\ z_1 \\ z_2 \\ \boldsymbol{y}_{lat} \end{bmatrix} = \begin{bmatrix} A_{lat} & B_{lat} & G_{lat} & 0_{(8\times 7)} \\ C_{0lat} & D_{01lat} & 0_{(1\times 1)} & 0_{(1\times 7)} \\ C_{1lat} & D_{11lat} & 0_{(1\times 1)} & 0_{(1\times 7)} \\ C_{lat} & 0_{(7\times 2)} & 0_{(7\times 1)} & D_{22lat} \end{bmatrix} \begin{bmatrix} \boldsymbol{x}_{lat} \\ \boldsymbol{u}_{lat} \\ \tilde{\boldsymbol{u}}_{lat} \\ \boldsymbol{e}_{lat} \end{bmatrix}; \tag{17}$$

the matrices $A_{lat}, B_{lat}, G_{lat}$ have the forms (13) and $C_{0lat} = [0 \;\; 0 \;\; 0 \;\; 0 \;\; 0 \;\; 1 \;\; 0 \;\; 0]$, $C_{1lat} = [1 \;\; 0 \;\; 0 \;\; 0 \;\; 0 \;\; 0 \;\; 0 \;\; 0]$, $D_{01lat} = [c_1 \;\; 0]$, $D_{11lat} = [0 \;\; c_2]$; the matrix D_{22lat} has the form $D_{22\,lat} = I_7$ for the vector containing the sensor errors: $\boldsymbol{e}_{lat} = \left[e_Y \;\; e\dot{Y} \;\; e_\beta \;\; e_\phi \;\; e_p \;\; e_\psi \;\; e_r\right]^T$. It is known that the sensors (used to measure some important variables) have sometimes errors; for example, the most important errors of a gyro sensor are [1]: 1) the bias; 2) the scale factor; 3) the calibration error of the scale factor; 4) the noise of the sensor; 5) the sensibility to an acceleration applied along an arbitrary direction. The bias and the noise are the most severe for the control performance during landing. Usually, on aircraft, there are used gyros to measure the angular rates (e.g. p and r); by integration of these angular rates, one obtains the roll and yaw angles. Because on aircraft there are also transducers (sensors) for the attack angle and for the sideslip angle (β), in this chapter, one considered sensor errors for β, p, and r. Similar remarks can be done for the automatic landing subsystem in longitudinal plane. In the software validation of the two automatic landing subsystems, the authors will use some information from [1], but the values of the sensors' errors will be increased to analyze the robustness of the two ALS subsystems. Also, it is interesting to proof that, for the steady regime, the forms of $z_1 = Y$ and $z_2 = \beta$ are the same with the expressions in (17); the expansion of $z_{lat} = [z_1 \;\; z_2]^T$ as function of state (x_{lat}) and of the system command vector (u_{lat}) leads to the equations:

$$z_{lat} = \begin{bmatrix} z_1 \\ z_2 \end{bmatrix} = z_{lat}(x_{lat}, u_{lat}) \cong \underbrace{z_{lat}(x_{lat_0}, u_{lat_0})}_{z_{lat_0}} + \left(\frac{\partial z_{lat}}{\partial x_{lat}}\right)_{(x_{lat_0},\, 0)} \Delta x_{lat} + \left(\frac{\partial z_{lat}}{\partial u_{lat}}\right)_{(x_{lat_0},\, 0)} \Delta u_{lat} \cong z_{lat_0}$$

$$+ \underbrace{\begin{bmatrix} \frac{\partial z_1}{\partial x_1} & \cdots & \frac{\partial z_1}{\partial x_n} \\ \frac{\partial z_2}{\partial x_1} & \cdots & \frac{\partial z_2}{\partial x_n} \end{bmatrix}_{(x_{lat_0}, 0)}}_{\begin{bmatrix} C_{0lat} \\ C_{1lat} \end{bmatrix}} \Delta x_{lat} + \underbrace{\begin{bmatrix} \frac{\partial z_1}{\partial u_1} & \frac{\partial z_1}{\partial u_2} \\ \frac{\partial z_2}{\partial u_1} & \frac{\partial z_2}{\partial u_2} \end{bmatrix}_{(x_{lat_0},\, 0)}}_{\begin{bmatrix} D_{01lat} \\ D_{11lat} \end{bmatrix}} \Delta u_{lat} \Leftrightarrow \Delta z_{lat} \cong \begin{bmatrix} C_{0lat} \\ C_{1lat} \end{bmatrix} \Delta x_{lat}$$

$$+ \begin{bmatrix} D_{01lat} \\ D_{11lat} \end{bmatrix} \Delta u_{lat} \Leftrightarrow z_{lat} \cong \begin{bmatrix} C_{0lat} \\ C_{1lat} \end{bmatrix} x_{lat} + \begin{bmatrix} D_{01lat} \\ D_{11lat} \end{bmatrix} u_{lat} \cong \overline{C}_{lat} x_{lat} + \overline{D}_{lat} u_{lat},$$

with $C_{0lat} = \begin{bmatrix} \frac{\partial z_1}{\partial x_1} & \cdots & \frac{\partial z_1}{\partial x_n} \end{bmatrix}_{(x_{lat_0},\, 0)}$, $C_{1lat} = \begin{bmatrix} \frac{\partial z_2}{\partial x_1} & \cdots & \frac{\partial z_2}{\partial x_n} \end{bmatrix}_{(x_{lat_0},\, 0)}$; $x_i (i = \overline{1, n})$ are the system's states ($n = 8$), $D_{01lat} = \begin{bmatrix} \frac{\partial Y}{\partial \delta_{ac}} & \frac{\partial Y}{\partial \delta_{rc}} \end{bmatrix}_{(x_{lat_0}, 0)} = [c_1 \; 0]$, $D_{11lat} = \begin{bmatrix} \frac{\partial z_2}{\partial u_1} & \frac{\partial z_2}{\partial u_2} \end{bmatrix}_{(x_{lat_0}, 0)} = \begin{bmatrix} \frac{\partial \beta}{\partial \delta_{ac}} & \frac{\partial \beta}{\partial \delta_{rc}} \end{bmatrix}_{(x_{lat_0}, 0)} = [0 \; c_2]$, $\overline{C}_{lat} = \begin{bmatrix} C_{0lat} \\ C_{1lat} \end{bmatrix}$, $\overline{D}_{lat} = \begin{bmatrix} D_{01lat} \\ D_{11lat} \end{bmatrix}$. c_1 and c_2 have small positive values; in steady regime ($u_{lat} = 0$), one gets $z_1 = Y$ and $z_2 = \beta$.

The optimal control law in lateral-directional plane has the form [14]: $u_{\infty lat} = -K_{\infty lat}(\widehat{x}_{lat} - \overline{x}_{lat})$, $K_{\infty lat} = R_1^{-1} B_{lat}{}^T P_\infty$, $R_1 = \overline{D}_{lat}{}^T \overline{D}_{lat}$; $u_{\infty\, lat}$ must minimize the cost functional $J_{lat} = \frac{1}{2}\int_0^\infty z_{lat}{}^T z_{lat} dt =$ $= \frac{1}{2}\int_0^\infty \left[x_{lat}^T \underbrace{(\overline{C}_{lat}^T \overline{C}_{lat})}_{Q_1} x_{lat} + u_{\infty\, lat}^T \underbrace{(\overline{D}^T \overline{D})}_{R_1} u_{\infty lat} \right] dt$. The symmetric and positive defined matrix P_∞ is the stabilizing solution of the Riccati matriceal equation [1]:

$$A_{lat}^T P_\infty + P_\infty A_{lat} - P_\infty \left(B_{lat} R_1^{-1} B_{lat}^T - \mu_1^{-2} G_{lat} G_{lat}^T \right) P_\infty + Q_1 = 0. \tag{18}$$

The remarks regarding Q_1, R_1, and μ_1 remain the same; the controller gain matrix ($K_{\infty lat}$) has the general form $K_{\infty lat} = R_1^{-1} B_{lat}^T P_\infty$ which is typical for the optimal control theory. The optimal

http://dx.doi.org/10.5772/62666

control law $\boldsymbol{u}_{\infty lat}$ depends on $\Delta\widehat{\boldsymbol{x}}_{lat} = \widehat{\boldsymbol{x}}_{lat} - \overline{\boldsymbol{x}}_{lat}$, as one can see above. To obtain this signal, the observer presented above is again used; this time, one obtains the estimated state vector $(\widehat{\boldsymbol{x}}_{lat})$ and the signal $\Delta\widehat{\boldsymbol{x}}_{lat} = \widehat{\boldsymbol{x}}_{lat} - \overline{\boldsymbol{x}}_{lat}$; the equation of the observer is

$$\Delta\dot{\widehat{\boldsymbol{x}}}_{lat} = A_{lat}\Delta\widehat{\boldsymbol{x}}_{lat} + B_{lat}\boldsymbol{u}_{lat} + G_{lat}\tilde{\boldsymbol{u}}_{lat} + L_{\infty lat}\left(\Delta y_{lat} - C_{lat}\Delta\widehat{\boldsymbol{x}}_{lat}\right). \tag{19}$$

The observer gain matrix $L_{\infty lat}$ is calculated by using the formula: $L_{\infty lat} = P_{\infty}^{*} C_{lat}^{T}\left(D_{22lat}^{T} D_{22lat}\right)^{-1}$, with P_{∞}^{*}– the stabilizing solution of the Riccati matriceal equation [15]:

$$A_{lat}P_{\infty}^{*} + P_{\infty}^{*}A_{lat}^{T} - P_{\infty}^{*}\left(C_{lat}^{T}C_{lat} - \mu_2^{-2}\overline{C}_{lat}^{T}\overline{C}_{lat}\right)P_{\infty}^{*} + G_{lat}G_{lat}^{T} = 0; \tag{20}$$

μ_2 is a small positive scalar for which the Riccati equation (20) has a stabilizing solution; one used the same notations for the matrices Q_1, R_1, P_{∞}, and P_{∞}^{*} but their values are completely different from the ones in the case of aircraft motion in longitudinal plane.

4. Structure of the complete automatic landing system

To control all the variables in longitudinal plane, one also uses two reference models (**Figure 1a**) providing the desired altitude, velocity on the landing curve, and their derivatives up to relative degrees of the system [16]. Aircraft desired state $(\overline{\boldsymbol{x}}_{long})$ and the desired output vector $\left(\overline{\boldsymbol{y}}_{long}\right)$ are obtained by using the states of the reference models. The optimal control is calculated on-line by means of the error $\Delta\boldsymbol{x}_{long} = \hat{\boldsymbol{x}}_{long} - \overline{\boldsymbol{x}}_{long}$.

4.1. Block diagrams of the reference models

The two reference models (the former being a three order reference model, while the latter is a second order reference model) are also used for the calculation of the vector $\overline{\mathbf{Z}}$. The two reference models receive information from a block which models the geometry of landing in longitudinal plane; this block uses two equations—one for the glide slope phase and one for the flare phase. The equation associated to the glide slope phase ($H \geq \overline{H}_0$, $\overline{H}_0$– the altitude at which the glide slope phase ends and the second landing phase begins) is [10]:

$$\overline{H} = \left(X - X_{p_0}\right)\tan\left(\gamma_c\right), \tag{21}$$

where X is the covered distance, horizontally measured, X_{p_0}– describes the point where the horizontal axis intersects the glide slope, $\overline{H}$– the desired altitude, while γ_c is the aircraft desired slope angle. The seven components of the imposed vector $\overline{\mathbf{Z}}$ are: $\overline{H}$, $\overline{\dot{H}} = u \cdot \gamma_c$, $\overline{\ddot{H}} = 0$, $\overline{\dddot{H}} = 0$, $\overline{u} = u_0 \cong V_0$, $\overline{\dot{u}} = 0$, and $\overline{\ddot{u}} = 0$. The equation associated to the flare phase $\left(H < \overline{H}_0\right)$ is [10]:

$$\overline{H} = \overline{H}_0 \exp(-t/\tau), \tag{22}$$

with τ - the time constant that defines the exponential curvature (the flare phase); as a consequence, $\dot{\overline{H}} = -\frac{1}{\tau}\overline{H}$, $\ddot{\overline{H}} = \frac{1}{\tau^2}\overline{H}$, $\dddot{\overline{H}} = -\frac{1}{\tau^3}\overline{H}$, $\overline{u} = u_0 \cong V_0$, $\dot{\overline{u}} = 0$, $\ddot{\overline{u}} = 0$.. If the reference models in **Figure 1a** are used, the roles of the variables $\overline{H}$ and $\bar{u}$ from (21) and (22) are played by the variables H_c and u_c, respectively; the variables $\dddot{\overline{H}}$, $\ddot{\overline{H}}$, $\dot{\overline{H}}$, $\overline{H}$, $\ddot{\overline{u}}$, $\dot{\overline{u}}$, and $\bar{u}$ are provided by the reference models.

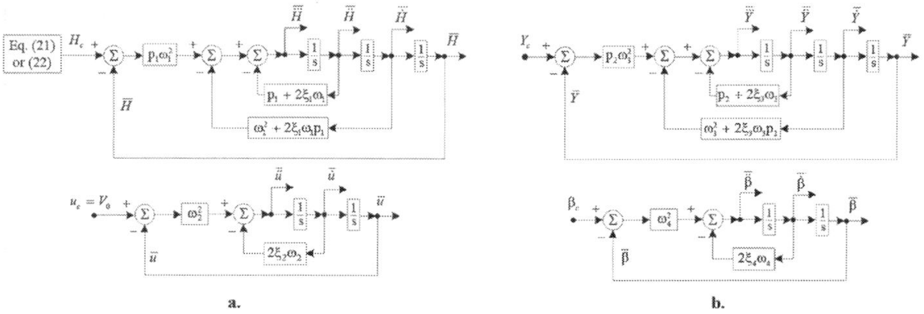

Figure 1. Block diagrams of the reference models.

Similar approach is used for aircraft motion in lateral-directional plane; the vectors $\overline{z}$ and $z_{lat}^{(r)}$ are calculated by means of other two reference models, the former being a three-order reference model (associated to Y), while the latter is a second-order reference model (associated to β) (**Figure 1b**) [1].

4.2. The block diagram of the new automatic landing system

The structure of the new ALS, using dynamic inversion and H-inf method, is presented in **Figure 2**; it consists of two subsystems—the first one controls aircraft motion in longitudinal plane, while the second one is for the control of aircraft motion in lateral-directional plane.

In longitudinal plane, to track the desired trajectory, one must control the aircraft speed (u) and its altitude (H). The landing requirements involve the aircraft descend to an altitude of 420 m above the ground in the same time with the reduction of its speed from the cruise value to the landing value (70 m/s); then, the speed should be maintained constant. In lateral-directional plane, the desired landing trajectory of aircraft mainly involves two variables' control: the aircraft lateral deviation with respect to the runway (Y) and the sideslip angle (β).

In longitudinal plane, the dynamic inversion and H-inf method must assure the convergences: $\Delta y_{long} \to 0\left(y_{long} = C_{long}x_{long} \to \overline{y}_{long} = C_{long}\overline{x}_{long}, x_{long} \to \overline{x}_{long}\right)$
$\Delta z_{long} \to 0\left(z = C_{long}^{'}x \to \overline{z} = C_{long}^{'}\overline{x}\right)$, $\Delta\widehat{x}_{long} \to 0\left(\widehat{x}_{long} \to x_{long} \to \overline{x}_{long}\right)$,
$u_{\infty long} \to 0$, $\overline{u}_{long} \to 0$, $u_{long} \to 0$; in lateral-directional plane, the following convergences should

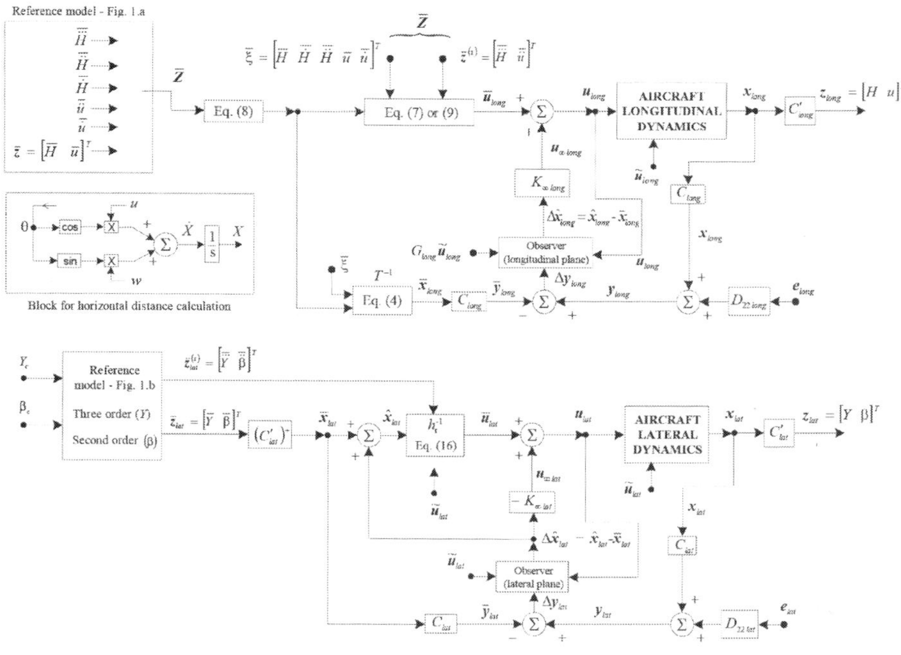

Figure 2. Structure of the new architecture for aircraft automatic control during landing.

be assured: $\Delta y_{lat} \to 0\left(y_{lat} = C_{lat}x_{lat} \to \overline{y}_{lat} = C_{lat}\overline{x}_{lat},\ x_{lat} \to \overline{x}_{lat}\right)$, $\Delta z_{lat} \to 0$ $\left(z = C^{'}_{lat}x \to \overline{z} = C^{'}_{lat}\overline{x}\right)$, $\Delta\widehat{x}_{lat} \to 0(\widehat{x}_{lat} \to x_{lat} \to \overline{x}_{lat})$, $u_{\infty lat} \to 0$, $\overline{u}_{lat} \to 0$, $u_{lat} \to 0$.

5. Numerical simulation results

5.1. Numerical simulation setup

In order to analyze the behaviour and the performances of the designed ALS, one considers a numerical example associated to the flight of a Boeing 747. The Matlab/Simulink environment is used for complex simulations; to obtain the time histories of the main variables describing the aircraft motion in longitudinal and lateral-directional planes, one software implemented the two optimal observers, the four reference models, and the two H-inf controllers.

For aircraft dynamics in lateral-directional plane, the values of the coefficients are [11]: a_{11} = −0.0013, a_{12} = 0, a_{13} = −1, a_{14} = 0.15, a_{21} = −1.33, a_{22} = −0.98, a_{23} = 0.33, a_{31} = 0.17, a_{32} = −0.17, a_{33} = −0.217, b_{11} = 0.001, b_{12} = 0.015, b_{21} = 0.23, b_{22} = 0.06, b_{31} = 0.026, b_{32} = −0.15, V_0 = 67 m/s, T_a = 0.7 s, $T_r = 0.1$s, $\mu_1 = 1$, $\mu_2 = 1$, $c_1 = c_2 = 0.01$, $\overline{Y} = 0$m, $\overline{\beta} = 0$ deg; the vector of sensor errors has been chosen as: e_{lat} = [0 m 0 m/s 1 deg 0 deg 1 deg/s 0 deg 1 deg/s]^T, the matrix G_{lat} has been obtained by means of the equation (13), while the system's initial state is

$x_{lat}(0) = [0.1\text{deg} \quad 0\text{deg/s} \quad -2\text{deg/s} \quad 0\text{deg} \quad 0.1\text{deg} \quad 25\text{m} \quad 0\text{deg} \quad 0\,\text{deg}]^T$; for the reference models, one has chosen: $p_2 = 25, \xi_3 = \xi_4 = 0.7, \omega_3 = \omega_4 = 2$ rad/s. To test the robustness of the new ALS (lateral-directional plane) with respect to the crosswind (lateral wind—V_{vy}), in simulations different values for $\tilde{u}_{lat} = V_{vy}$ between 2 and 10 m/s are considered. The values considered here for the sensors' errors (both planes—longitudinal and lateral-directional) are chosen very large because it is important to use strong disturbances instead of small ones when designing a robust ALS.

For aircraft dynamics in longitudinal plane, the values of the coefficients for Boeing 747 have been borrowed from [11]: $a_{11} = -0.021$, $a_{12} = 0.122$, $a_{14} = -0.322$, $a_{21} = -0.209$, $a_{22} = -0.53$, $a_{23} = 2.21$, $a_{31} = 0.017$, $a_{32} = -0.164$, $a_{33} = -0.412$, $a_{52} = -1$, $a_{54} = V_0 = 70$ m/s, $b_{11} = 0.01$, $b_{12} = 1$, $b_{21} = -0.064$, $b_{22} = -0.044$, $b_{31} = -0.378$, $b_{32} = 0.544$, $T_e = 0.3$ s, $T_T = 2$ s, $\bar{u} = V_0, V_{vx0} = 1$ m/s, $V_{vz0} = 1$ m/s $T_0 = 30$ s. The vector of sensor errors is $e_{long} = [0.2\text{ m } 0.2\text{ deg/s } 0.2\text{ m } 0\text{ m/s}^2\ 0.2\text{ deg } 0.1\text{ deg/s}]^T$, while, for the reference models, one has chosen: $p_1 = 25, \xi_1 = \xi_2 = 0.7$, $\omega_1 = \omega_2 = 2$ rad/s. For the first landing phase in longitudinal plane, the following values have been used: $\overline{H}_p = \overline{H}(0) = 420\text{m}, X(0) = 0, X_{p_0} = -\overline{H}_p/\tan(\gamma_c), \gamma_c = -2.5$ deg. The other components of vector $\overline{\xi}$ are provided by the reference models, $\eta(0) = [-4.2\text{ deg } -0.46\text{ deg/s}]^T$, $\mu_1 = 50$, $\mu_2 = 1$, while the initial value of the state is $x_{long}(0) = [72\text{ m/s} \quad -3.1\text{ m/s} \quad 0\text{ grd/s} \quad -0.6\text{ deg} \quad 420\text{ m} \quad 0\text{ deg} \quad 0\text{ deg}]^T$.

5.2. Results and discussion

In **Figure 3**, one represents the time characteristics for the flight direction control system (the second subsystem of the complete ALS in **Figure 2**); before the start of the two landing main stages in longitudinal plane, the pilot must cancel aircraft's lateral deviation with respect to the runway. The characteristics have been represented for the first ALS affected by crosswind ($V_{vy} = 2$ m/s) in the presence or in the absence of sensor errors (the sensors are used for the measurement of the states). The presence of the sensor errors is not visible—the curves with solid line (obtained in the absence of sensor errors) overlap almost perfectly over the curves plotted with dashed line (obtained in the presence of sensor errors).

The landing approach (the only landing phase which takes place in the lateral-directional plane) begins at the nominal speed of 67 m/s; the speed should be maintained constant. To test the robustness of the first designed ALS, in the simulations for lateral-directional plane, one has taken into consideration the crosswind, because low-altitude crosswind can be a serious threat to the safety of aircraft in landing. From sixth mini-graphic in **Figure 3** (achieved for $V_{vy} = 2$ m/s), one can see that the stationary value of Y (aircraft lateral deviation) is very close to zero; analyzing the Aviation Administration (FAA) accuracy requirements for Category III (best category) [17], one can remark that this error is very good; for best category, it must less than 4.1 m, for Category II precision standards, the error must be between 4.1 and 4.6 m, while Category I precision standards involve an error between 4.6 and 9.1 m. The H-inf control technique is ideal for handling plants affected by sensor errors, measurement noise, or other disturbances (e.g. crosswind). Because the convergence error of the sideslip angle is less than 0.01 deg, one can notice the convergence $\beta \to \beta_c = 0$ deg.

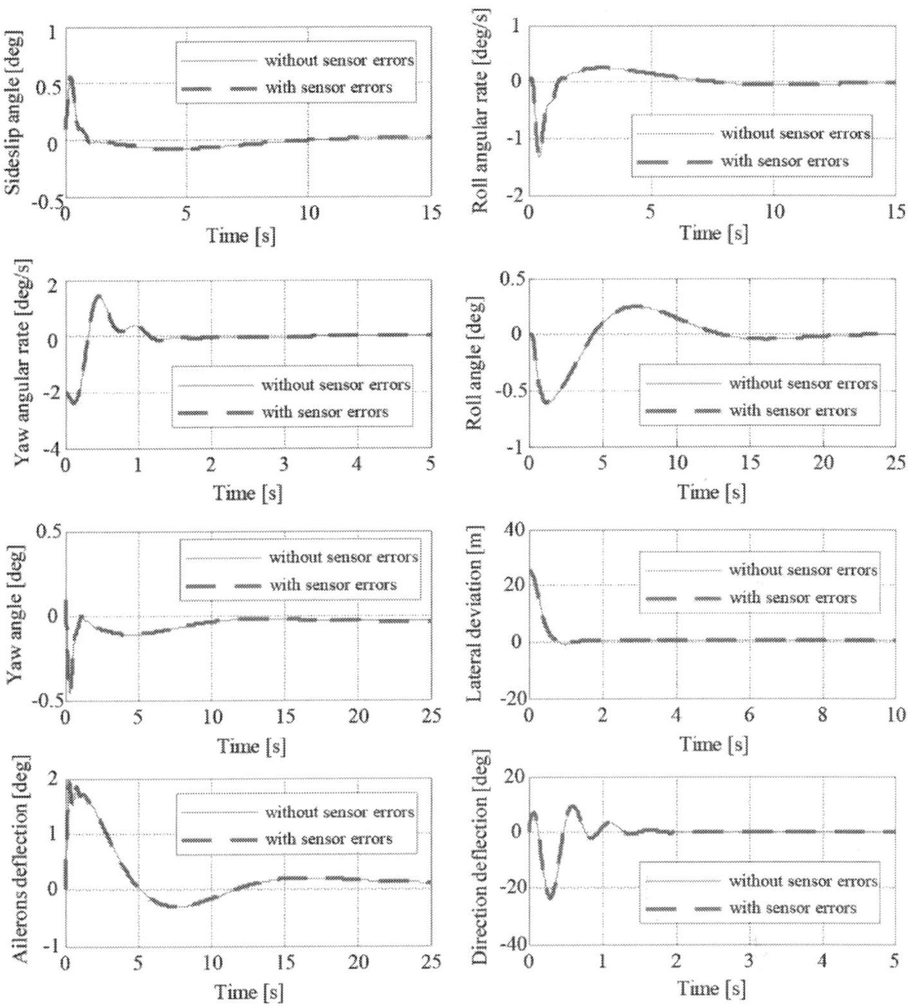

Figure 3. Time characteristics of the lateral-directional control subsystem.

In **Figures 4** and **5**, there are represented the time characteristics for the glide slope landing phase and flare landing phase, respectively; the characteristics have been represented for the ALS affected by wind shears in the presence or in the absence of sensor errors. The last four mini-graphics in **Figures 4** and **5** represent the differences between the real values of the speed (u), sink rate ($.H$), slope angle (γ), altitude (H) and the desired values of these variables: $u-\bar{u}$, $.H-.\overline{H}$, $\gamma-\gamma_c$, $H-\overline{H}$. As in the case of aircraft motion in lateral-directional plane, the sensor errors do not affect the landing. One may also remark in **Figures 4** and **5** that the slope

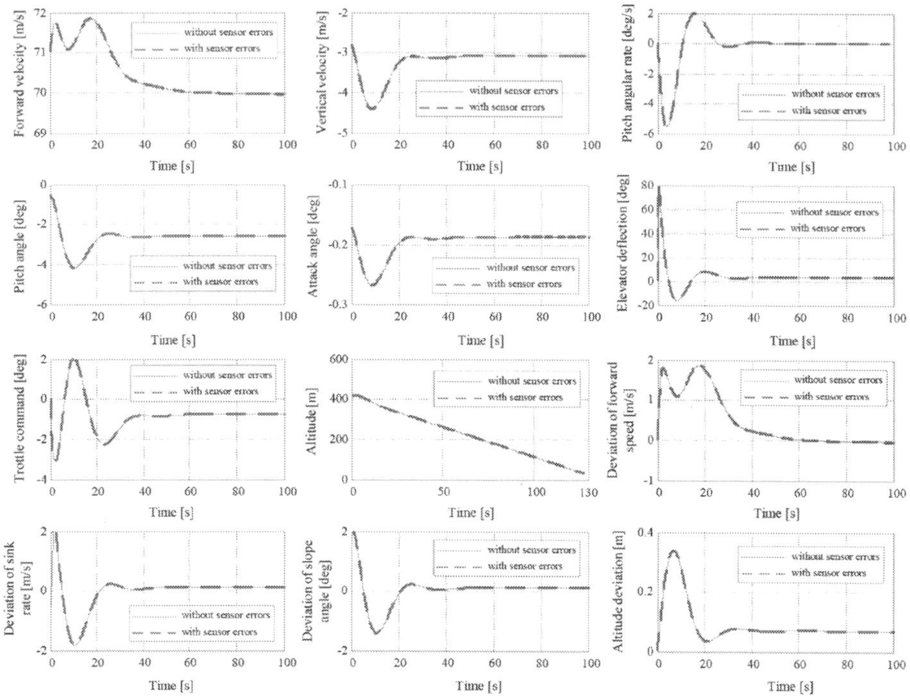

Figure 4. Time characteristics of ALS, for the glide slope phase, with or without sensor errors.

angle is in perfect accord with its desired values: −2.5 degrees during glide slope phase and 0 degrees during flare, respectively. During the glide slope phase, the aircraft describes a linear descendent trajectory (eighth graphic in **Figure 4**), while in the flare phase, it describes a parabolic trajectory (eighth graphic in **Figure 5**) with a null slope angle.

In longitudinal plane, to test the robustness of the new ALS, in all simulations, one has taken into consideration the wind shears. **Figures 4** and **5** prove that the altitude error (the difference between the desired path and the actual path) is less than 0.3 m during the first landing stage (longitudinal plane) and less than 0.2 m during the second landing stage (longitudinal plane). According to the Federal Aviation Administration (FAA) accuracy requirements for Category III [17], the resulted errors are very small; thus, according to FAA Category III accuracy requirements, the vertical error (altitude deviation with respect to its nominal value) must be less than 0.5 m, while the final altitude at the end of flare must be 0 m. The ALS designed in this chapter meets the requirement because the H-inf robust control technique has been used; this method can handle the plant with measurement noise (sensor errors) and wind shears.

5.3. Comparison with other works

The ALS designed in this chapter represents an improved version of the ALS designed in [11] and it differs from other similar ALSs from the specialty literature; first of all, our ALS is not

http://dx.doi.org/10.5772/62666

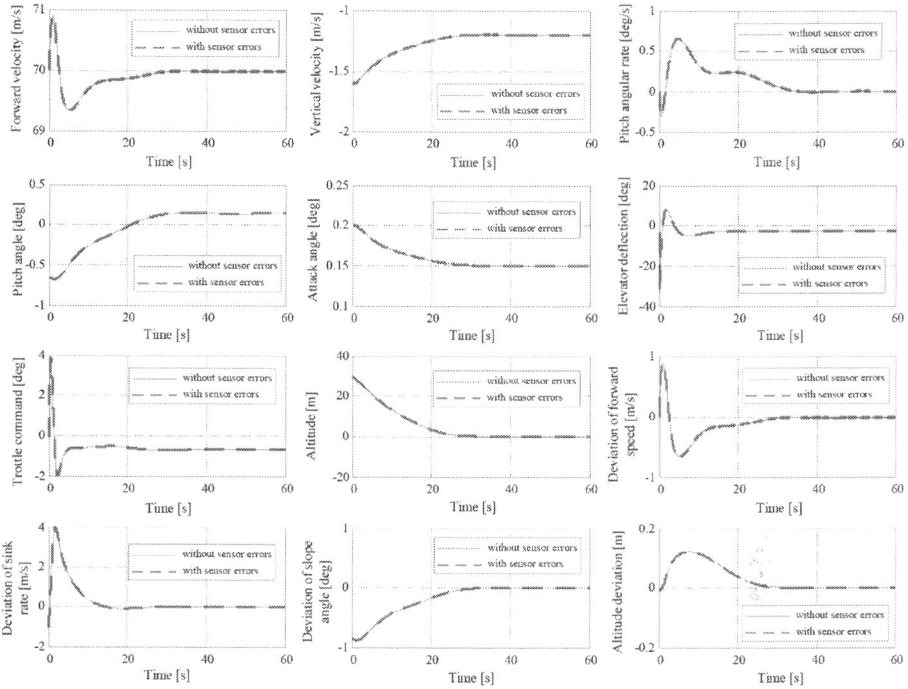

Figure 5. Time characteristics of ALS, for the flare phase, with or without sensor errors.

designed only for the longitudinal (vertical) plane but also for the lateral-directional plane; two subsystems have resulted, the new ALS being the mixture of these two automatic landing subsystems. Our new ALS has some additional elements with respect to the one presented in [11]: two optimal observers and four reference models which provide the desired altitude, velocity on the landing curve, their derivatives up to relative degrees of the system, the desired lateral deviation with respect to the runway, and the desired sideslip angle.

The results in this work have been compared to the ones obtained in [2] where the authors have designed a system which controls the lateral angular deviation of aircraft longitudinal axis with respect to the runway, by using a classical controller, a radio-navigation system, a system for the calculation of the distances between aircraft and the runway radio-markers, and an adaptive controller mainly used for the control of aircraft roll angle and its deviation with respect to the runway; the adaptive control system uses the dynamic inversion concept, a dynamic compensator, a neural network trained by the system's estimated error vector (signal provided by a linear observer), and a Pseudo Control Hedging block. The time regime period is better in our work (almost 15 seconds) but the lateral deviation's overshoot is larger; therefore, one can conclude that the neural networks-based adaptive controllers are more efficient than the conventional ones for aircraft landing in lateral-directional plane but their main disadvantage is that the neural networks require a priori training on normal and faulty operating data and these are enable only under limited conditions; on the other hand, the usage of Pseudo Control Hedging blocks (when the actuators are nonlinear) does not modify the final values of the variables. For the same aircraft type, same direction controller, and radio-navigation system but with a proportional-derivative type control after the roll angle and a proportional type control after $\Delta\psi$ [18], there have been obtained performance inferior to those obtained here by using the H-inf control, the dynamic inversion, optimal observers, and reference models.

The problem of landing in longitudinal plane has been also discussed in other papers, different types of ALSs being designed [9, 10]. If one makes a brief comparison between our ALS (longitudinal plane) and the ones based on an Instrumental Landing System or conventional/fuzzy control of flight altitude by using the system's state [9], one remarks that from the system transient regime period and overshoot's points of view, the ALS based on the H-inf technique and dynamic inversion works slightly better. Improvement of the performance was obtained by replacing the conventional controllers with fuzzy controllers [9], but those ALSs cannot be used for no-bounded exogenous signals or strongly nonlinear aircraft dynamics. Our new ALS uses the H-inf technique, this having the advantage over classical control techniques in that it has applicability to problems involving multivariate systems with cross-coupling between channels; the only disadvantage is related to the non-linear constraints which are generally not well-handled.

5.4. Current and future work

This chapter presents some of the work that has been carried out at Laboratory of Aerospace Engineering, University of Craiova. Till now, there have been designed and software implemented: 1) two new ALSs (longitudinal plane) using the Instrumental Landing System and the flight altitude's control by means of the state vector (the controllers of the ALSs are designed both with classical and fuzzy logic approaches); 2) a new ALS (longitudinal plane) using the dynamic inversion concept and PID controllers in conventional and fuzzy variants, taking into consideration the wind shears and sensor errors; 3) a new ALS (lateral-directional plane) which controls the lateral angular deviation of aircraft longitudinal axis with respect to the runway, by using a classical controller, a radio-navigation system, a system for the calculation of the distances between aircraft and the runway radio-markers, and an adaptive controller mainly used for the control of aircraft roll angle and its deviation with respect to the runway. Our future work will focus on the design of ALSs (mixtures between subsystems designed for the longitudinal and lateral-directional planes) putting together the dynamic inversion technique, dynamics compensators, feed-forward neural networks, and Pseudo Control Hedging blocks.

6. Conclusions

The purpose of this study was to design a robust ALS by using the H-inf and dynamic inversion techniques taking into consideration the sensor errors and other different disturbances; two landing subsystems have been designed, software implemented and validated; the first subsystem is useful for landing control in longitudinal plane, while the second one is

http://dx.doi.org/10.5772/62666

used in lateral-directional plane. After the separate design of the two subsystems, these have been combined to obtain a complete landing auto-pilot. The H-inf control technique handles the plant with measurement noise (sensor errors) and wind shears; the use of the dynamic inversion makes our control system more general and, therefore, it can be used both for the case when aircraft dynamics is nonlinear and for the case when the aircraft dynamics is linear; thus, this technique increases the generality character of our new ALS. Promising results have been obtained; these prove the robustness of the designed ALS even in the presence of disturbances and sensor errors.

Acknowledgements

This work is supported by the grant no. 89/1.10.2015 of the Romanian National Authority for Scientific Research and Innovation, CNCS – UEFISCDI, project code PN-II-RU-TE-2014-4-0849.

Author details

Romulus Lungu* and Mihai Lungu

*Address all correspondence to: romulus_lungu@yahoo.com

University of Craiova, Faculty of Electrical Engineering, Craiova, Romania

References

[1] Lungu R, Lungu M. Automatic control of aircraft in lateral-directional plane during landing. Asian Journal of Control. 2016; 18: 1–16.

[2] Lungu M, Lungu R. Automatic control of aircraft lateral-directional motion during landing using neural networks and radio-technical subsystems. Neurocomputing Journal. 2016; 171: 471–481.

[3] Singh S, Padhi R. Automatic path planning and control design for autonomous landing of UAVs using dynamic inversion. American Control Conference Riverfront, St. Louis, MO, 2009; p. 2409–2414.

[4] Wagner T, Valasek J. Digital autoland control laws using quantitative feedback theory and direct digital design. Journal of Guidance, Control, and Dynamics. 2007; 30: 1399–1413.

[5] Kumar V, Rana KP, Gupt V. Real-time performance evaluation of a fuzzy PI + fuzzy PD controller for liquid-level process. International Journal of Intelligent Control and Systems. 2008; 13: 89–96.

[6] Lau K, Lopez R, Onate E. Neural networks for optimal control of aircraft landing systems. Proceedings of the World Congress on Engineering. 2007; II: 904–911.

[7] Zhi L, Yong W. Intelligent landing of unmanned aerial vehicle using hierarchical fuzzy control. IEEE Aerospace Conference, 2012; p. 1–12.

[8] Ismail S, Pashilkar A, Ayyagari R, Sundararajan N. Improved autolanding controller for aircraft encountering unknown actuator failures. IEEE Symposium on Computational Intelligence for Security and Defense Applications (CISDA), 2013; p. 96–103.

[9] Lungu R, Lungu M, Grigorie TL. Automatic control of aircraft in longitudinal plane during landing. IEEE Transactions on Aerospace & Electronic Systems. 2013; 49: 1338–1350.

[10] Lungu R, Lungu M. Automatic landing control using H-inf control and dynamic inversion. Proceedings of the Institution of Mechanical Engineers Part G – Journal of Aerospace Engineering. 2014; 228: 2612–2626.

[11] Che J, Chen D. Automatic landing control using H-inf control and stable inversion. Proceedings of the 40th Conference on Decision and Control, Orlando, FL, 2001; p. 241–246.

[12] Yu GR. Nonlinear fly-by-throttle H-inf control using neural networks. Asian Journal of Control. 2001; 3: 163–169.

[13] Ochi Y, Kanai K. Automatic approach and landing for propulsion controlled aircraft by H_∞ control. IEEE International Conference on Control Applications, Hawaii, 1999; p. 997–1002.

[14] Stoica AM. Disturbance attenuation and its applications. Romanian Academy Publisher, Bucharest, 2004.

[15] Shue S, Agarwal RK. Design of automatic landing systems using mixed H_2/H_∞ control. Journal of Guidance, Control, and Dynamics. 1999; 22: 103–114.

[16] Lungu M. Sisteme de conducere a zborului [Flight control systems]. Sitech Publisher, Craiova 2008.

[17] Braff R, Powell JD, Dorfler J. Applications of GPS to air traffic control. Global Positioning System: Theory and Applications. 1996; II: 327–374.

[18] Lungu M, Lungu R, Grigorie L. Automatic command systems for the flight direction control during the landing process. Proceedings of International Symposium on Logistics and Industrial Informatics, Budapest, 25–27August 2011; p. 117–122.

Chapter 6

Adaptive Building Envelope: An Integral Approach to Indoor Environment Control in Buildings

Mitja Košir

Additional information is available at the end of the chapter

http://dx.doi.org/10.5772/64951

Abstract

The problem of energy consumption of buildings is complex and multidimensional, as it is a cross section of building envelope performance, indoor environmental conditions and user demands and preferences. In order to fulfil the EU goal stated in the 2020 climate and energy package and beyond, the implementation of high-performance buildings is crucial. Part of the solution is properly designed, flexible and adequately controlled building envelope that can contribute to reduced energy consumption and to increased occupancy comfort. In the presented chapter first, a structured treatment of the indoor environment formation is proposed that can be used in order to define appropriate fields of interventions when designing building automation systems. Furthermore, interaction between adaptive building envelope elements, indoor and exterior environment is discussed and elaborated. Second, the conventional and artificial intelligence control approaches used in building automation are discussed and commented, whereas advantages and disadvantages of each group are discussed. At the end, an example of building automation system designed on the principles of a holistic treatment of indoor environment in buildings is presented. The discussed system was designed at the Faculty of Civil and Geodetic Engineering using a combination of conventional and artificial intelligence control methods.

Keywords: building automation, building envelope, Indoor environment, daylight control, thermal control, ventilation control

1. Introduction

During the last decades, it has become obvious that the overall influence of human civilization has planetary consequences, which are most pronounced through climate change, resource depletion and energy shortage. The situation was additionally intensified with the onset of global economic crisis. One of crucial links in reducing environmental impacts is attaining higher energy efficiency and lower greenhouse gas emissions (GHGs) of the building sector. In the EU, buildings are responsible for roughly 40% of the EU's final energy consumption and GHG emissions [1]. Similar situation applies for the USA [2], with slightly different but nonetheless similar shares in other parts of the world as well (e.g. 28% in China, 42% in Brazil, 47% in Switzerland [3], and 53% in Singapore [4]). In fact, buildings are one of the largest global end users of energy, but they also have an extremely large untapped potential for energy savings. In the EU, this potential is estimated at 11,630 GWh (i.e. 1509 Mtoe) by 2050 [5]. Therefore, they are at the forefront of the EU's struggle to develop a low-carbon economy and reduce its dependency on imported energy while at the same time to limit its environmental impact.

The main focus of the EU's policy on energy and climate was stated in the 2020 Climate and Energy Package [6]. The goals stated in the aforementioned document were reduction of 20% in GHG emissions from the 1990 levels, 20% improvement in energy efficiency and supplying 20% of EU energy from renewable energy sources. The importance of buildings, especially the operational energy consumed by buildings during their life time, is highlighted through a series of EU Directives, of which the most crucial are the Energy Performance of Buildings Directive-recast (EPBD-r) [7] and the Energy Efficiency Directive (EED) [8]. The main objective of the EPBD-r is the formulation of national legislation of member states in which energy performance of buildings is prescribed, monitored and encouraged through multiple mechanisms for new developments as well as for renovation projects. The primary goal, put forward in the EPBD-r, is that by 2020 all newly constructed buildings in the EU will be nearly Zero-Energy Buildings (nZEB). In other words, this means that buildings should have very high energy performance and that the energy they consume for heating, cooling, lighting, ventilation and preparation of domestic hot water should be mostly from renewable energy sources produced on-site or nearby [7]. The exact implementation of minimum performance criteria for achieving nZEB is left to each member state, which is why they can vary and are often hard to directly compare [9]. For the renovation projects the nZEB criteria are not obligatory, as renovations have to be executed in a cost-effective manner considering the presumed costs of the renovation as well as savings resulting from the energy renovation through the expected life cycle of the building. Nevertheless, in some cases the nZEB criteria are also achievable for the renovation projects. From the practical viewpoint, the goal of nZEB can be achieved through conventional means of thermally insulating building envelopes, by proper overheating control and by providing energy-efficient heating, cooling and ventilating building services (HVAC) as well as through energy-efficient lighting systems. Proper design and coordination among different building elements and systems are crucial, as best results can be achieved through multidisciplinary integrated approach resulting in expected performance. In other words, building automation systems (BASs) can ensure proper functioning and coordination among different building elements and installed electrical and mechanical systems [10]. The result is lower energy consumption and thus better utilization of installed systems. The importance of BAS as well as monitoring and metering in buildings is also emphasized in the EPBD-r, which encourages member states to promote, where appropriate, the installation of active building control systems [7, 11]. To this end, a dedicated standard,

EN 15232 [12], was developed in the EPBD set of European standards, defining terminology and methods for determining the impact of BAS on the energy performance of buildings. The potential of BAS for reducing operational energy consumption in buildings is relatively substantial, as was shown by Rubinstein et al. [13] and Lee et al. [14] over a decade and a half ago. Nevertheless, the overall achievable energy savings with the implementation of BAS are still poorly understood due to its multidimensional nature connecting energy consumption, user comfort and level of implemented control [4, 15].

As we have seen, in regard to the implementation of automation in buildings, the EU legislation focuses only on the potential of attaining energy savings with the utilization of BAS. Consequentially, the influence on user comfort and well-being is disregarded, despite numerous studies showing that satisfaction of building users with the quality of indoor environment can have substantial impact on the energy consumption in buildings [3, 16, 17]. In fact, the influence of improved indoor environment in buildings has direct and indirect impact on building user health [18] and productivity [19, 20] and thus also on the greater socio-economic context of human society. In general, higher quality of indoor environment results in fewer instances of sick building syndrome (SBS), allergic reactions, asthma and communicable respiratory infections [17, 21, 22]. Inappropriate thermal conditions in buildings are the main cause of user discomfort [17] but have also been linked to cardiovascular problems if inhabitants are not exposed to regular fluctuations of indoor temperatures [23]. On the other hand, exposure to adequate levels of daylight is crucial for the regulation of human circadian rhythm [24] and has been linked to improved mood, reduced stress and fewer symptoms of seasonal affective disorder (SAD) [17] as well as higher productivity and better learning efficiency [19, 20]. All this is not surprising as in the developed world people spend more than 90% of their lives indoors [25], most of this in buildings, which is why the quality of indoor environment is probably the single most important environmental factor in human health. Hence, the design and performance of buildings are crucial for modern urbanized societies. Solutions such as smart buildings, high-performance buildings [26, 27] or active buildings [28] are a possible answer to the challenge posed to the designers by interconnectedness of energy efficiency, user well-being and comfort [17]. Such buildings, in contrast to the nZEB, put building users in the centre of the design process, while at the same time, they strive to be energy efficient, thus providing healthy and comfortable indoor environment with the lowest possible energy consumption and not the other way around [10]. Central to the design of high-performance buildings is the bioclimatic approach, which is focused on the users as well as energy efficiency of buildings [10, 15]. Crucial for the bioclimatic approach is the utilization of passive building features (i.e. passive solar architecture (PSA) features [29]), which enable appropriate utilization of climatic conditions to facilitate comfort and energy efficiency in buildings (**Figure 1**). Additionally, in high-performance buildings, Adaptive Building Envelope (ABE) elements (e.g. movable shading, automated natural ventilation) must be applied in order to enable adequate level of control and functionality of interactions between indoor and exterior environment. Building automation can be used to efficiently harmonize and regulate among PSA, ABE elements and HVAC systems (**Figure 1**) [30] to simultaneously achieve the goals of higher indoor comfort and lower energy consumption. Nonetheless the problem is extremely complex and non-linear and characterized by high noisiness of the processes that need to be addressed by BAS [4]; consequently appropriate control approaches have to be selected in order to achieve desirable results. It was shown by Dounis et al. [15] and Shaikh et al. [4] that in general advanced control methods like fuzzy logic and neural controllers are more suited for BAS applications than conventional controllers (e.g. on/off controllers). Thus, the trend in experimental and commercial applications of BAS is shifting towards widespread use of artificial intelligence-based controllers.

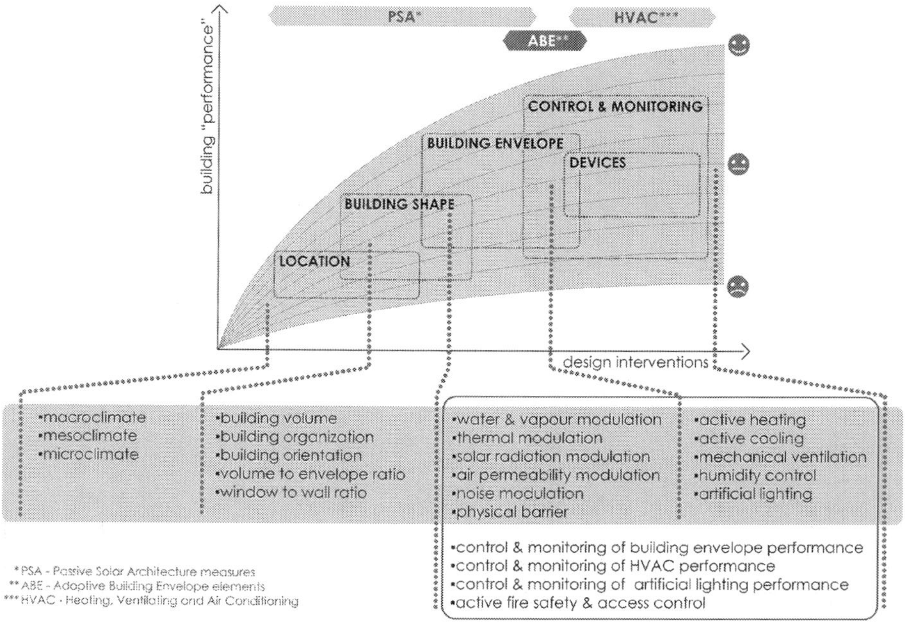

Figure 1. Conceptual representation of synergetic effects in the design of high-performance buildings that crucially influence the quality of the final outcome of a project.

Below the complexity of indoor environment automation via building-wide integration will be described. Special focus will be on indoor environment, ABE elements and user demands. The objective is to outline a broader picture and provide background information regarding the specifics, limitations and feasibility issues of implementing BAS. Basic characteristics of conventional and artificial intelligence controller-based BAS systems will be discussed, whereas special attention will be given to the advantages and drawbacks of each group. At the end, a simple experimental system for automated control of indoor environment implemented at the University of Ljubljana, Faculty of Civil and Geodetic Engineering (UL FGG), will be presented. Its structure and functioning will be described and thus illustrating the application of the presented holistic treatment of the indoor environment.

http://dx.doi.org/10.5772/64951

2. Indoor environment in buildings

Indoor environment is formulated with the creation of the building envelope—a separator that divides the interior from the exterior and thus creates an artificial human habitat. We perceive our surrounding environment on two distinct, but nonetheless interconnected, levels. One is dependent on the cultural and social predispositions, while the other is based on the physiological and psychological response of each individual. Culturally conditioned perception of the surrounding physical environment is strongly dependent on the individual upbringing and therefore connected to history and social environment [31]. It is determined by each individual's expectations, impressions, influences and wishes about the indoor environment; these are, of course, extremely subjective but nonetheless the result of individual's social context (e.g. society as a whole, family and friends). The psychophysiological response of the human body to the environmental impulses is on the other hand much easier to predict [32], although it still varies to some extent from one individual to another due to gender, age, health and fitness. Human sensory interpretation of surrounding environment starts with the environmental impulses received by our body's sensory system. From here, the information is passed to the brain that interprets these sensory impulses as properties of the environment.

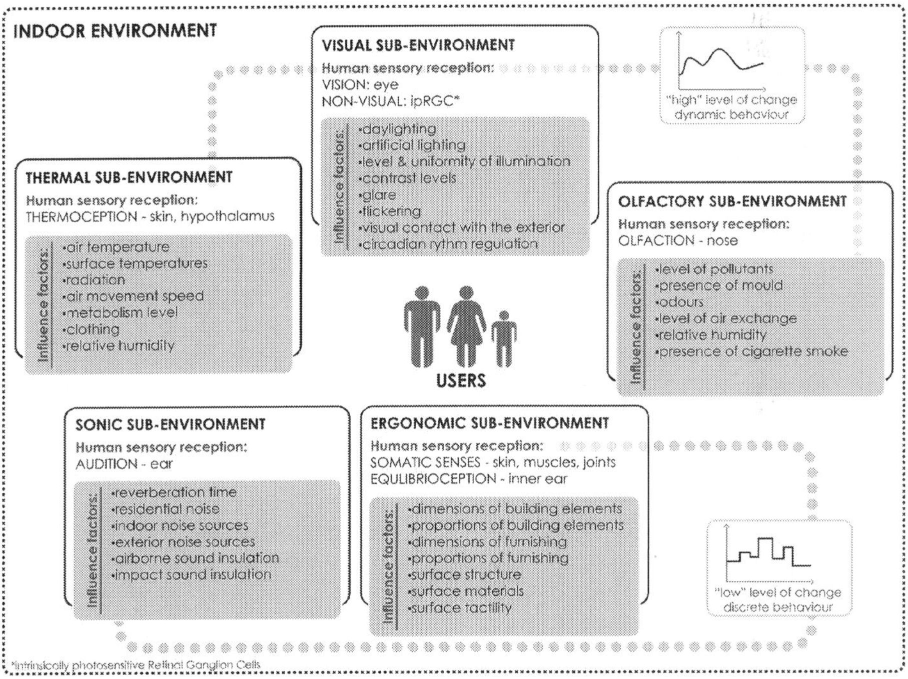

Figure 2. Indoor environment as a cross section of five sub-environments with corresponding human sensory reception system as well as major influential factors to be considered when designing indoor environments in buildings.

Sensory interpretation of the environment can therefore be reversely connected to a specific sense or group of senses (e.g. visual impulses can be linked to vision). This simple classification of different environmental impulses with human sensory reception system can be used to systematically structure the environmental influences on the building users according to the human psychophysiological response. Consequentially, five sub-environments can be defined: thermal, visual, olfactory, sonic and ergonomic environments (**Figure 2**). Together they form the wholeness of the indoor environment. The proposed classification can be implemented in the building design as well as in the implementation of BAS, thus defining the fields that are best suited to automated control in order to enhance the quality of indoor environment and subsequent user well-being and satisfaction. For each sub-environment, crucial influence factors can be identified. These factors govern to greater or lesser extent the human response to the environment and therefore the perception about its quality. Because some of the influence factors are interconnected and interdependent (e.g. daylighting and thermal comfort), an extremely complex picture of the indoor environment emerges [17, 33, 34].

The main problem of the proposed user-oriented approach in the design of BAS is its complexity and the number of possible interactions between the external environment, building envelope and indoor environment with the user-defined demands and wishes. In order to reduce the amount of considered influence factors, a selection according to the importance in regard to the user comfort should be executed. Additionally, it is also prudent to include in the design of BAS and ABE the control of only those influence factors that cannot be satisfactorily resolved by conventional building techniques. In this context, the ergonomic and, to some degree, the sonic sub-environments are less prone to unpredictable and highly dynamic changes. In other words, a large majority of comfort issues stemming from the dissatisfaction of users with aspects of sonic and ergonomic sub-environments can be solved on the level of building and/or interior furnishing design. It is true that some aspects of sonic sub-environment can also be actively controlled, like active noise cancelation systems [35] or automatically controlled movable absorbers to control room reverberation [33], but still such applications are relatively rare in comparison to other building automation issues. In comparison, the thermal, visual and olfactory sub-environment factors are characterized by extreme dynamics of change, high unpredictability and consequentially high risk for user dissatisfaction, having at the same time large energy savings potential [3, 4, 26]. Therefore, the issues connected to the control of thermal, visual and indoor air quality (IAQ) will be further discussed. This, of course, does not mean that during the design of BAS and ABE, sonic and ergonomic sub-environments should not be considered. Especially potential negative interactions, like in the case of automated natural ventilation, when opening the windows can cause the increase in the noise exposure of the occupants and consequential dissatisfaction with the indoor environment.

2.1. Thermal sub-environment

Indoor thermal sub-environment is predominantly the result of external macro- and micro-climatic characteristics of a building's location. The external seasonal and diurnal fluctuations in temperatures and solar radiation are the principal influences behind the formulation of internal thermal conditions, although the effects of external climate can be to some degree mitigated by building envelope design and HVAC systems [29, 31, 33]. In the majority of contemporary buildings, the predominant influence on indoor thermal sub-environment is the solar radiation [29] that drives the thermal environment of a building. Solar radiation is either beneficial as passive heat source during heating season or unwanted because it leads to overheating during cooling season. In addition to the influence of the solar radiation, the thermal sub-environment of a building is also dependent on the thermal exchange with the exterior (i.e. transmission and convection heat gains or losses) as well as on the building usage (i.e. indoor heat gains from appliances and metabolic heat of occupants). In some instances, when buildings have high occupancy rates and large amount of installed appliances (e.g. offices, hospitals), they become mostly dependent on the internally generated heat [33]. In such buildings, also called internal load-dominated buildings [29], the climatic conditions have far smaller influence on the overall formulation of the indoor thermal sub-environment.

Human thermal comfort in indoor environments can be linked to a multitude of influences, such as air temperature, humidity, mean radiant temperature, metabolic activity and clothing (**Figure 2**), but all these factors are linked to the human vasomotor control mechanism [34]. The vasomotor control mechanism, in relation to the surrounding thermal conditions, regulates the flow of blood in the skin and underlying tissue in order to maintain the deep-core body temperature approximately at 36.5°C. For the designers of buildings, HVAC systems and BAS, the main problem is how to correlate between influence factors that influence to larger or lesser degree the vasomotor control response and therefore human satisfaction with specific thermal sub-environment. Many measurement systems of indoor thermal sub-environment parameters have been proposed during the last decades [34], with the most complex being the PMV index [36] proposed by Fanger in the 1970s. The PMV index links indoor air temperature, humidity, air movement, mean radiant temperature, metabolic rate and clothing factor to the human thermal sensation. Although the PMV index is an extremely useful tool, it has its limits [37] and poses in connection to the automation of building additional problems from the practical standpoint, as it is difficult to acquire appropriate data (especially mean radiant temperature, metabolic rate and clothing factor), although there have been successful applications in BMS (see [15, 38]). Alternatively, less complex indicators of indoor thermal sub-environment can be utilized. One of them is the idea of thermal neutrality that links the trend of change in external temperatures to the indoor temperatures deemed acceptable by a large number of people [39]. Thermal neutrality inherently includes the influence of seasonal thermal adaptation of users and is therefore linked to certain locale as well as culture. In the end, even just a simple measurement of dry bulb air temperature can be used for BMS applications [30] if a building has a relatively uniform radiant environment and limited indoor air movement (e.g. no draft due to ventilation system or insufficiently air sealed envelope).

2.2. Visual sub-environment

Adequate performance of visual tasks during activities in buildings is one of key occupant demands. Therefore, proper formulation of visual indoor sub-environment (**Figure 2**) is crucial in building design. It can be split into visual and non-visual effects of light on the human body, with daylighting as crucial element, as it is preferred by users over artificial illumination [17], as well as necessary for the regulation of biological processes [40, 41]. While artificial illumination is inevitable for the functioning of modern societies, it is no substitute for daylighting, as exposure to natural light is central to the biological functioning of our bodies [40]. The spectral composition and direction (i.e. light from the side as well as from the top) of daylight are decisive for the activation of intrinsically photosensitive retinal ganglion (iPRG) cells and consequential regulation of human circadian rhythm [24, 41] and have to this day for all practical reasons still not been matched by artificial lighting. In addition to the circadian regulation, daylight is also crucial in the process of synthetization of vitamin D and resulting in better absorption of calcium in human bodies, therefore reducing the risk of osteoporosis and rickets [42]. The beneficial influence of daylight goes even further, as studies have shown that schoolchildren in classrooms with adequate daylight had 20% better results in mathematical tests and were by 26% better in reading abilities in comparison with those that were in non-day-lit classrooms [19]. Similar results have also been found for office environments [20]. Other studies have also shown that there is a link between daylight and sales in shops [42]. In regard to the visual performance, daylight is highly valued by building users, so much even that they are willing to tolerate higher levels of visual discomfort from daylight than in the case of artificial illumination. For the majority of visual tasks performed in buildings, the most important criterion is the amount and uniformity of horizontal illuminance measured on the working plane [24, 33]. On the other hand, the most common problem connected to the use of daylight in working and living environments is the occurrence of glare due to the influence of direct sunlight and/or placement of high luminance objects in the field of view [34, 41]. As daylight in buildings is provided through the building envelope, the design as well as the control of transparent parts (i.e. windows, skylights and shading devices) is essential for indoor visual comfort of users. Especially, the level of shading control is crucial because it influences the aspects of visual (i.e. glare, illuminance levels and view) as well as of the thermal sub-environment (i.e. overheating and passive heating control). In the end, all modern buildings have a need for artificial illumination in order to facilitate adequate visual conditions in times when daylight is not available. The coordination between daylight and artificial illumination is vital for the reduction in electrical energy consumption, as control and coordination over daylight and lights can result in savings in the range from 30 to 60% [43]. Visual sub-environment parameters in buildings are probably the hardest to adequately regulate using BAS [30] but at the same time promise the largest long-term social and healthcare dividends [17].

2.3. Olfactory sub-environment

The indoor atmospheric conditions in buildings as a whole are very poorly understood and many times neglected, despite strong indications of multiple links between IAQ, occupant health and comfort [21, 22]. The influence factors governing the formation of the olfactory sub-environment can be divided into two groups: the sensible factors which can be perceived by the human olfactory sensory system (e.g. stale air) and the nonsensible factors in the form of harmful chemicals undetectable to humans (e.g. radon gas) [44, 45]. The sources of harmful substances in the indoor air are mostly the materials used in the building elements, furnishing, improperly designed and maintained ventilation systems and external natural and artificial sources. Because the influence of chemicals and their combinations on the humans are poorly understood [45], the most prudent cause of action is to remove all known and potentially harmful substances from the indoor environment. Presuming that all such sources have been removed from the indoor environment, we can conclude that the primary sources of dissatisfaction with the IAQ are organic substances present in the air [22] and occupant metabolic by-products [44] (**Figure 2**). Exemption to this presumption are indoor environments where the removal of hazardous chemicals is impossible (e.g. industrial environments dealing with toxic substances) or where the contaminant is present in the external environment [46] and is therefore the result of the location of a building. In order to maintain adequate levels of IAQ in buildings, ventilation is used either in the form of natural, mechanical or combined ventilation that periodically exchanges indoor air with external fresh air. The level of air exchange and the method [19] of ventilation (natural or mechanical) have been shown to drastically influence the occurrence of the SBS symptoms (e.g. asthma, respiratory inflammation and headache), allergic reactions and communicable respiratory infections. On the basis of available studies, Sundell et al. [22] conclude that SBS symptoms are drastically reduced if the ventilation air flow rate is higher than 25 l/s per person. This ventilation air flow rate is higher than the minimum required values in many standards and guidelines [22, 44], which causes a concern in regard to the contemporary buildings that are designed to be energy efficient and therefore often use minimum ventilation rates in order to conserve energy [10], thus neglecting occupant comfort. From the standpoint of BAS design, the most practical control strategy is demand-side ventilation, either mechanical or natural, controlled according to the CO_2 concentration [30] in the indoor air. Although humans cannot sense the presence of CO_2, it can be reliably used [44] as an indicator of air quality, where values above 2000 ppm should be avoided, as at such levels the majority of users already report problems with concentration and occurrence of headaches. Regarding the method of ventilation, studies on user comfort show a slight preference towards natural ventilation [17, 19], although it negatively influences energy use. Therefore, for better performance of naturally ventilated buildings, BAS can be used to coordinate between heating, cooling and natural ventilation [30].

3. Adaptive building envelope

Indoor environments in buildings are at the same time separated from and connected to the external natural environment via building envelopes, which enable the exchange of energy (e.g. heat), materials (e.g. air) and information (e.g. view) between the two [31]. Therefore, building envelope is an interface that connects the two dynamic and unpredictable environments. Traditionally, the function of building envelope was seen as a separator, limiting the influence of undesired external climatic conditions on the indoor environmental conditions. However, such interpretation is insufficient, as the interaction between the two environments is equal in importance, if not even more important [47]. This duality of demands represents a problem for the design of building envelopes. As static solutions (i.e. conventional PSA) are not flexible enough to provide adequate level of flexibility demanded from modern high-performance buildings (**Figure 1**). To facilitate higher level of functionality, ABE elements (**Figure 1**) are used in order to enable dynamic and flexible interaction between interior and exterior. In the future, the whole building envelope might become adaptable and/or morphable [48], like in the case of hypothetical "polyvalent wall" proposed by Mike Davis [27], which would combine the benefits of opaque building elements with the functionality of the transparent envelope and integrate them with the HVAC systems. However, due to the limitations of current technology, building envelopes of today must be divided into two distinct types: transparent and opaque envelopes (**Figure 3**). For the most part, the ABE elements and technologies are focused on the transparent envelope, which is characterized by high level of energy, matter and information exchange (**Figure 3**) and therefore presents the most dynamic part of a building. On the level of realization, this mostly means the application of movable shading elements, automated natural ventilation, electrochromic glazing, smart windows [49], light deflectors, shading elements with integrated solar collectors [50] or PVs, etc. Although ABE elements are featured in modern high-performance buildings, the usage of adaptable envelope elements in buildings is nothing new. A very good example of ABE application in traditional architecture is the Japanese house, which exhibits high level of envelope adaptability due to its movable "shoji" screens and "amado" shutters. The main difference between traditional and modern ABE systems is in the level of control, where traditional solutions relied on manual control with high margins of error, while modern ABE elements must be automated to satisfy the increasingly high demands of users regarding accuracy. Automation of ABEs also enables increased energy efficiency because it eliminates or reduces the energy wasted due to unwanted user behaviour, like keeping lights on and blinds down during daytime or leaving windows open while the air condition is active [3, 17]. Therefore, some sort of automation is inherently present in the ABEs of high-performance buildings, while the best results can only be achieved with building-wide integration, via BAS, of all systems (i.e. ABE, HVAC and lighting), crucial for providing acceptable indoor conditions.

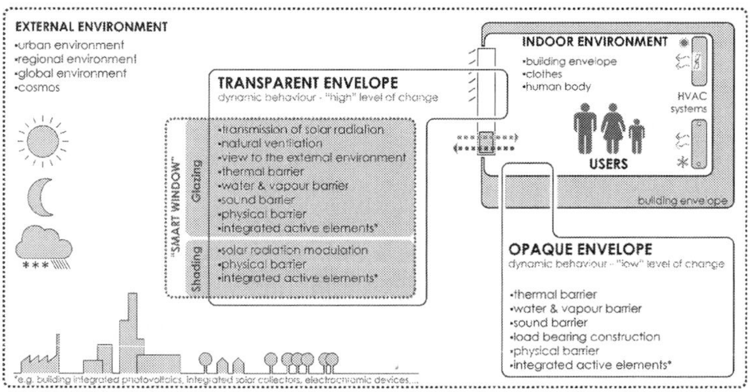

Figure 3. Building envelope as an interface between external and indoor environment and corresponding primary functions of the transparent and the opaque part.

4. Control approaches for BAS

The history of building automation and the development of smart buildings are closely tied to the advances in modern telecommunications and computer technologies. The first implementations of "building intelligence" can be traced back to the early 1980s in Japan and the USA, where oversupply of office spaces pushed developers to provide advanced telecommunication services in order to attract tenants. Automation in such buildings was primarily focused on the provision of information technology, although rudimentary automation of building services such as HVAC was also implemented [35]. The limitations of such a narrow view of building intelligence soon became apparent, as it became evident that smart buildings are much more than just telecommunications. The importance of responsiveness to environmental as well as spatial and business change was shown to be of extreme importance. Therefore, the focus shifted from technological centered solutions to the all-around building performance [35], including the performance and comfort of occupants [17] as a central part of high-performance buildings. In this context the automation of building elements and systems became a central point of research and development due to its large potential to affect user comfort, energy consumption [14, 26] and thus also increased productivity. Despite this, the field of BAS implementation was, and still is, predominantly driven by the application of existing technologies [51] and far less by the introduction of advanced control techniques, although there are signs of shifting trends [4], predominantly due to the nature of the problem characterized by high unpredictability, complex models, noisiness of the system and non-universal solutions.

Controller type	Mathematical model necessary	Suitable for complex BAS	Adaptable (i.e. learning)	Complexity	User interaction
Conventional approaches					
on/off	No	No	No	Low	No
PID	No	Yes*	No	Low	No
Optimal, predictive and adaptive control	Yes	Yes	**	High	No
Artificial intelligence approaches					
FLC	No	Yes	No	Low	Yes
ANN	No	Yes	Yes	Medium	Yes
ANFIS	No	Yes	Yes	Medium	Yes
MPC	Yes	Yes	No	High	No
MACS	***	Yes	***	Medium	***

*Generally poor performance in cases of non-linear and noisy systems.
**YES for adaptive control.
***Depending on the used control approach.

Table 1. Comparison of major advantages and drawbacks of described conventional and AI controllers.

The problem of automated control of indoor environment and ABE systems is characterized by relatively large complexity. With the integration of HVAC and lighting, the complexity of the controlled system is additionally increased and is further complicated by the unpredictability of external weather conditions and user behaviour. All this poses a challenge to the control system designer as the choice of control type determines to some degree the success of the implemented BAS. The majority of BASs are centralized and to some degree integrated with the building systems as well as the building itself. The focus was traditionally on achieving minimum energy consumption, although, as shown herein, it has shifted to user comfort with minimum possible energy consumption [10, 17]. Various building control approaches can be used in order to control the performance of a building. Although the type of controller can be arbitrary, it has been shown [15] that at least to some level the choice is influenced by the complexity of the implemented automation. In other words, it could be claimed that what is being controlled also determines the type of a controller, which can roughly be categorized into conventional and artificial intelligence (AI) approaches. The following overview of the two groups of controllers is a general introduction outlining and comparing the basic features (**Table 1**), while a more in-depth state of the art can be found in Refs. [4, 15, 17].

4.1. Conventional approaches

The conventional control approaches to building automation originate primarily from industrial applications and were the first to be studied and used for BAS. The primary concern was mostly the control over energy consumption and indoor temperatures, although user comfort can also be controlled using conventional approaches. This group primarily includes on/off (i.e. thermostats) and PI (i.e. proportional-integrative) and PID (i.e. proportional-integrative-derivative) controllers [52]. The simple on/off controller is the most rudimental controller that was and still is used in indoor temperature regulation. An inherent problem of such an approach is the inevitable overshot of the regulated value and consequential wastage of energy as well as possible user dissatisfaction. In general, such control performs poorly and is incapable of achieving optimal control of indoor environment [4], especially in situations where complex systems like daylighting and ABE elements are to be satisfactorily regulated. Nonetheless, building automation using on/off controllers can be a suitable solution when the overshot is not a problem, like in the case of indoor temperature regulation where due to a large thermal capacity of buildings and consequential long oscillatory periods of indoor temperatures occupants can adapt to the temperatures if they are kept within reasonable margin around the set-pot value (e.g. ±2 K). An improvement over the on/off controllers can be achieved with the application of PI and PID controllers, which are closed-loop controllers with constant parameters with no direct knowledge of the system that is controlled. In general, their application in the control of industrial process is successful and widespread. In BAS applications, they perform adequately in cases of linear systems and when the controlled process is relatively stable and without extensive noise (e.g. ventilation and HVAC systems) and disturbances from the environment. Otherwise, they have been shown, like in the case of work presented by Li et al. [53], to perform relatively poorly due to problems stemming from their inability to perform in noisy and non-linear systems that are characteristic for certain aspects of building automation (e.g. daylighting). Using PID controllers in cascade configurations and incorporating feed-forward controllers [54] can enhance their performance in BAS. Successful implementation of PID control in building automation was also achieved by hybrid systems using PID controllers in conjunction with AI control approaches [30, 55]. In the end, improper gain selections can cause PID controllers to become unstable. They are also harder to optimally set up in cases of highly dynamic systems, which can result in slower transient response and larger overshot than in comparable AI control techniques, as it was demonstrated by Menghal and Jaya Laxmi [56].

As an alternative to PID and on/off controllers, the designers of BAS turned to the use of optimal, predictive and adaptive controllers [15, 54, 57]. These controllers are not "black-box" controllers as in the case of PID and on/off controllers. Thus, they require a mathematical model of a building, as in the case of optimal and adaptive controllers, or a model of future disturbances (e.g. the impact of solar radiation), as in the case of predictive controllers. The need for such a model presents an obstacle in the case of BAS application, as building thermal and visual behaviour models are extremely complicated and non-linear. Furthermore, each model differs from building to building due to specifics in their geometry, construction type, location, etc., practically making each controller solution unique. Although the application of mathematical model in case of BAS is achievable in some instances, like for thermal control, as it was shown by Škrjanc et al. [58], it is hard to achieve and therefore uneconomical in other cases like daylighting, as demonstrated by Logar et al. [59]. Additionally, the usage of optimal, predictive and adaptive controllers is further limited by the notion that user interaction with the controller settings is limited and that such controllers are highly susceptible to noise due to parameter estimations [15]. Despite the above-stated shortcomings, it must be stressed that experimental systems have shown very good results [60], although practical implementations are almost non-existent due to extremely complicated application [4]. More importantly, the adaptive controllers in conjunction with fuzzy logic (adaptive neural fuzzy-inference system—ANFIS) are considered as one of the most promising approaches to building automation [15].

4.2. Artificial intelligence approaches

The study of alternative approaches to building automation gained ground in the 1990s, as the limitations of conventional controllers for the application in BAS became evident. The focus shifted to AI approaches that include among others fuzzy logic controllers (FLCs) [55, 61], artificial neural network controllers (ANNs) [62], adaptive fuzzy neural network controllers (ANFISs) [63], model-based predictive control (MPC) [64] and multi-agent control systems (MACSs) [58]. All these control approaches have gained in popularity with researchers as well as in practical applications, because they have certain advantages over the conventional control techniques and are at least in some cases better suited for the implementation in BAS. In fact, according to a survey conducted by Shaikh et al. [4], MPC, MACS and FLC are the most frequently employed control approaches in BAS, followed by the on/off conventional control systems. The FLCs have been successfully applied to many control problems like process automation and robotics and are especially suited to control systems where there is no detailed mathematical model of the process or where the development of such a model would be uneconomical. FLC controllers can successfully cope with imprecise data as a consequence of unknown model or imprecisions from gathered sensor data [65, 66]. Their main advantage is the use of linguistic variables with which descriptive expressions can be mathematically modelled [65] and expert knowledge can thus be used transparently and more intuitively in order to control the system actuators. Nonetheless, it has to be mentioned that the application of expert knowledge for the setting of FLC can also present a problem as such tuning process does not guarantee optimal performance due to trial and error approach and the subjectivity of the "expert". The problem can be surpassed by the application of adaptive techniques applied in ANFIS, by computer simulation-based optimization [67] and by using tuning techniques like genetic algorithms applied by Guillemin and Molteni [68] for a self-tuning FLC-based BAS. Because fuzzy systems have the ability to map non-linear building system characteristics by applying if-then statements that pair each combination of input variables to the desired output parameter, they are suitable for the control of highly non-linear and complex functions. FLCs have also been used in hybrid systems along with conventional PID controllers [30, 55, 65], effectively utilizing the advantages of conventional and AI control. Fuzzy logic has been successfully applied to control ABE elements and HVAC systems as well as to energy management and comfort control in buildings with promising results [4, 61, 65], comparable to or outperforming conventional approaches. A study by Ulpiani et al. focused on the comparison of thermal performance of an energy-efficient building controlled by on/off, PID and FLC-based BAS and demonstrated that FLC outperformed both conventional techniques by achieving up to 67% lower energy consumption with simultaneous higher average thermal comfort index [69].

In a similar manner to FLC, ANN and ANFIS, controllers can be used for building automation as they are based on an artificial system of neurons mimicking the human brain and its learning abilities [62]. The main advantage of ANN controllers is the possibility of the controller to perform self-tuning and therefore learn and adapt to changes in the building environment without expert knowledge from a system operator. Such tuning process can be executed if and when sufficient data about controlled system behaviour are available and the controller is trained by a training algorithm [70]. A generic scheme of an ANN model is composed of an input layer and a hidden layer, both with multiple neurons and a single-neuron output layer. In order to achieve adequate functioning of the ANN controller, usually a training phase is conducted, which is used to adopt a learning algorithm with pre-prepared data sets [63, 70]. For the ANFIS controllers, the ANN structure utilizing artificial neurons is introduced to the fuzzy logic control system where the nodes in the hidden layer of the ANN perform the purpose of membership functions and fuzzy rules. Another method to building automation that has gained in popularity in recent decades is the MPC which utilizes a model of a controlled system to predict future development. Therefore, the control actions of an MPC BAS are gained by optimizing the objective functions in regard to predicted future functioning of the system [64]. This is a great advantage in automation of buildings where thermal inertia, unpredictability in occupancy schedules, variations in energy prices and weather forecasts can be taken into account to perform an optimization in accordance with predicted future developments. Although such control approach is based on the principles of conventional control techniques (i.e. predictive control), it is listed in the literature mostly under AI approaches (e.g.

[4]) and is usually used in conjunction with AI controllers. While MPC controllers have been proven to outperform other methods, the computational costs and the complexity of the building model can be considerable and therefore impose a limitation to the application of MPC, as highlighted by Afram and Janabi-Sharifi [71]. However, the benefits in potential energy savings and enhanced indoor comfort can be substantial. Because BASs have grown in complexity, the resulting controllers can become extremely complex, which results in a system that is inflexible and hard to design as well as to modify. To solve this problem, MACS can be used by splitting the whole problem of the indoor control in buildings into smaller manageable controller-agents [15]. These are used to perform a certain operation and are then guided by the coordinator-agent to the optimal solution. A MACS-based BAS can utilize multiple control approaches (e.g. FLC, ANN) to solve specific control tasks [58, 72]. These are coordinated and optimized by a set of rules that can be actively changed through a learning process.

4.3. BMS application example

Integral control system of indoor environment (ICsIE) is an experimental BAS implemented in an occupied office of the main building of the UL FGG. The office has two work places, a

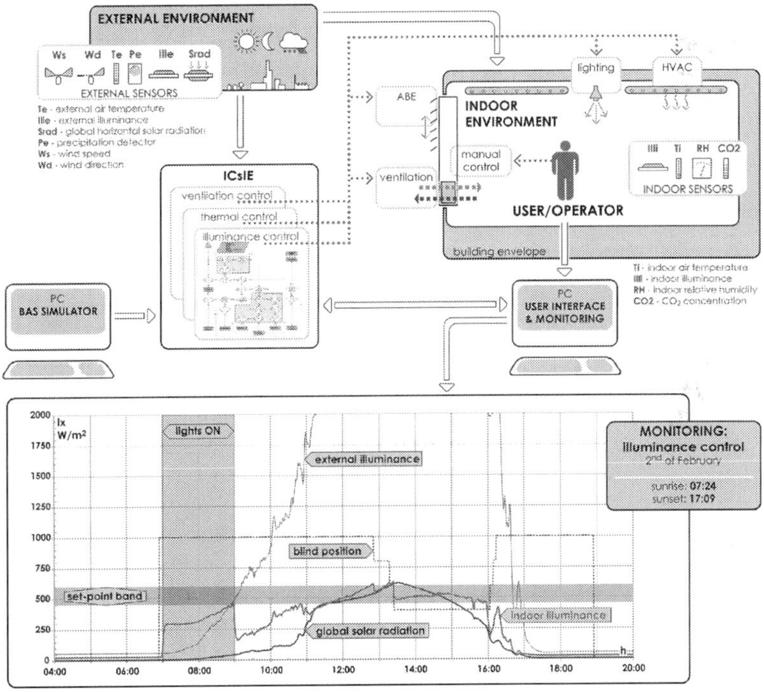

Figure 4. Conceptual representation of the ICsIE structure, presenting the sensor array, control level, user interface, utilized actuators and monitoring of performance. The diagram in the bottom of the figure presents the performance of the visual control loop on a typical late winter day.

floor area of approximately 40 m^2 (i.e. occupancy of 0.05 persons/m^2) and a large western-oriented window with 11.40 m^2 of glazing. The transparent part of the external envelope of the office is a typical double-glazed window with aluminium frames segmented into six individual units. Each segment is equipped with external motorized louvres that enable the adaptive changing of optical characteristics of the transparent envelope (i.e. shading and daylight regulation). One of the six window segments can be opened and is therefore motorized and utilized for automated natural ventilation and nighttime cooling of the office. In addition to the ABE elements of the building envelope, the office is equipped with a heating and cooling system comprising of 12 ceiling-mounted low-temperature radiative panels connected to the building's heating and cooling plant. When daylight is insufficient, the office can be illuminated by six ceiling-suspended, typical office fluorescent luminaries. The conceptual diagram of the ICsIE with the sensors, process level, supervision and data acquisition level as well as with the installed actuators is presented in **Figure 4**. The installed sensors are used to monitor indoor (i.e. temperature, illuminance, relative humidity and CO_2 concentration) and exterior (i.e. direct solar radiation, illuminance, temperature, wind speed and direction and precipitation) environmental parameters necessary for the control of the installed actuators in order to regulate indoor thermal, visual and olfactory sub-environment parameters. In the case of visual sub-environment, the controlled parameters are the working plane horizontal illuminance and the vertical eye level illuminance. The vertical illuminance is used to measure the potential non-visual effects on the occupants [24] as well as an indicator of possible glare which can occur during the evening hours because of the low sun elevation. For the control and assessment of thermal conditions in the office, a simple measurement of the internal dry bulb temperature is used in connection to the control of solar heat gains controlled by the external louvres, while for the ventilation of the office, the CO_2 concentration is the decisive parameter.

The BAS is designed around an industrial programmable controller that executes the necessary operations according to the desired set points inputted by the user/operator through dedicated interface software installed on a PC (**Figure 4**). The controller is divided into three control loops: the illuminance, thermal and ventilation loop. Although the three loops are treated individually, the interaction between them is regulated according to the priority set by the operator. The system can either be in thermal or visual priority. In either case, the IAQ is always a priority action, meaning that the ventilation is regulated according to the CO_2 concentration in the office. Switching between thermal and visual priority is not automated as there is no occupant detection system installed in the ICsIE. Therefore, the system operator defines the state of the system either manually or by defining the schedules that determine the operation of the systems. Typically, this means that during office hours the system is in visual priority, while during weekends, holidays and during nighttime, it switches to thermal priority. In the end this means that during visual priority the louvres are not available as an actuator to the thermal regulation loop, while in the opposite situation, the indoor illuminance is ignored. All control loops are designed similarly but with different levels of complexity, as illuminance and thermal control algorithms are far more complex than the ventilation one [30]. Hierarchically speaking, in all three control loops, activation of the ABE elements has priority over the HVAC and lighting system, in order to utilize the bioclimatic potential of the building before using mechanical or electrical systems. The user interface and the monitoring of BMS functioning are executed in the SCADA Factory Link (Supervisory Control and Data Acquisition and Human Machine Interface) environment, which enables the control over the functioning of the system as well as the storage and analysis of the recorded data and corresponding system responses.

4.3.1. Controller structure and setup

The ICsIE is executed as a hybrid control system combining conventional and AI control approaches. A conventional PI controller is used in a cascade configuration with the FLC controller in case of visual and thermal control loop, while the ventilation is controlled only by a simple on/off controller. Such configuration was proven successful in a pilot experimental system executed at UL FGG [55]. The FLCs of the ICsIE were developed using the IDR BLOK [73] software package advanced process control algorithms for fuzzy logic controllers, applying a fuzzy-inference system in the Takagi-Sugeno form that returns a crisp value as an output. For the visual control FLC, the input variables are the set-point value (ST_{ill}) and the error variable (ER_i), which is determined as a difference between measured value of indoor illuminance and the ST_{ill} set by the operator. The ST_{ill} is defined in the range between 0 and 1400, while the ER_i is set between −300 and 300, where 0 corresponds to measured illuminance being equal to the ST_{ill}. The output of the corresponding fuzzy decision matrix is defined in the range between 0 and 100, where the value of 100 corresponds to completely closed and value 0 to retracted louvres. The output crisp value of the FLC is communicated to the auxiliary PI controller that executes the necessary modifications of actuators in respect to their current position. The possible actions executed by the ICsIE are the retraction or extension of louvres, change of blade inclination in 30° increments from horizontal (i.e. blades open – 0°) to vertical (i.e. blades closed – 90°) position, or the activation of lights. The number of possible louvre positions is determined by the responsiveness of the actuator, where the actuator motor

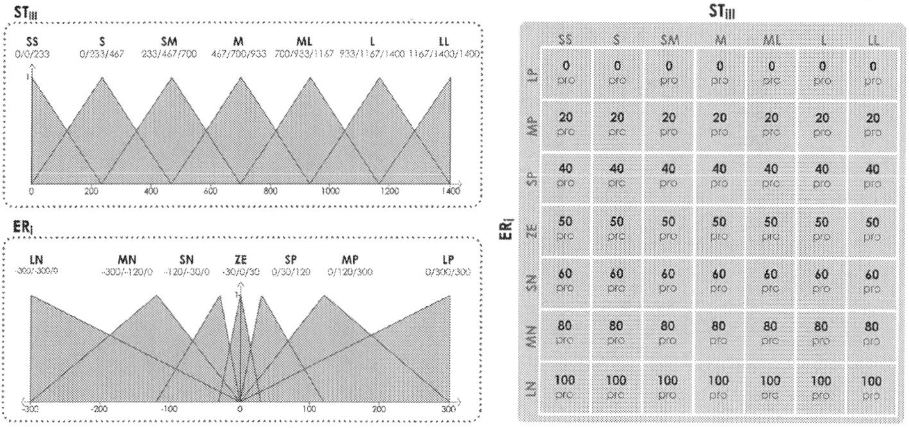

Figure 5. Membership functions ER_i and ST_{ill} and the corresponding decision matrix of the visual control FLC of the ICsIE.

enables the setting of the blade inclination only in the completely extended state. Although the blades of the shading device can be set at an arbitrary angle, the 30° increment was chosen as a compromise between flexibility and accuracy of the mechanical drive of the louvres. If the ST_{ill} is not reached even if all of the louvres are retracted, the system activates artificial illumination using a simple on/off controller. The lights can be activated only if all of the louvres are retracted, the system is in visual priority and the indoor measured illuminance is lower than ST_{ill}. The membership functions and the decision matrix of the visual FLC are presented in **Figure 5**.

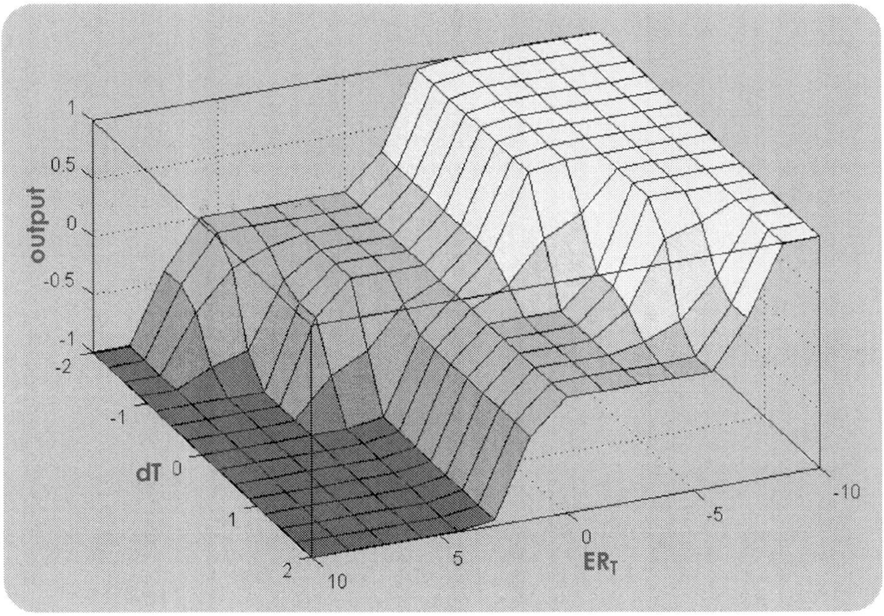

Figure 6. The input-output characteristics of the thermal control FLC of the ICsIE.

Similar structure of FLC as in visual control is also implemented in the case of thermal control loop, where the two input variables to the fuzzy controller are the indoor temperature derivative (d_T) and the error (ER_T) determined by the difference between set point (ST_T) and measured indoor dry bulb temperature. As in the case of visual control, the Takagi-Sugeno fuzzy-inference system was used applying triangular membership functions of the input variables. The if-then rules of the decision matrix are determined using AND logical operator, while for the de-fuzzification of the output variable, the weighted average is used. The input-output characteristic of the thermal controller is presented in **Figure 6**, where it can be seen that the output values are defined between −1 and 1. The output value of 0 means that the office is in "free run", meaning that neither heating nor cooling is needed. If the output value is −1, the ICsIE is in cooling mode, while in case of 1, the system is in heating mode. In both cases firstly, the possibility of using passive measures (i.e. shading and natural ventilation) is checked. The output actions are the movement of louvres (if the system is in thermal priority) and activation of active heating or cooling via the ceiling-mounted radiative panels. In case of cooling, an additional output is available in the form of convective cooling using natural ventilation, which is enabled during times when the external temperatures are lower than indoor ST_T value (e.g. during nighttime). Before activating active heating or cooling, the system has to determine whether the heating or cooling plant is active. This is determined by activating the heating/cooling circulation pump and measuring the cooling or heating medium temperature for a short period of time (i.e. 5 min). If the medium is of an appropriate temperature, active cooling or heating can be used. In the opposite case, the BAS disables the circulation pump in order to prevent damage. Therefore, it has to rely solely on the passive measures. The implementation of the described protocol was necessary as there is no communication between heating and cooling plant of UL FGG building and the ICsIE, since the plant is controlled manually by the building caretaker. Additionally, the operator can override the system and manually set whether the ICsIE is in cooling or heating mode. This can be done on-line for each day or it can be determined through schedules, where a winter (i.e. heating) or summer (i.e. cooling) season can be defined, while during the transitional period (i.e. spring and autumn), the system decides whether heating or cooling is necessary. The user demands regarding indoor thermal (i.e. indoor temperature) and visual (i.e. indoor work plane horizontal illuminance) comfort parameters are not crisp values, but rather a range of values around a set point that define the acceptable deviation around the target value. Therefore, in the ICsIE, the operator defines a range of values that are acceptable (e.g. ST_{ill}-50 lx and ST_{ill} + 100 lx), and if the indoor measured value is in the defined dead band, the system does not modify the actuator states. This limits the number of actuator movements that can be potentially annoying to the occupants and it reflects the comfort definitions in the standards and regulations [36, 44]. In contrast to the visual and thermal control, the ventilation controller of the ICsIE is a simple on/off controller designed to open or close the automated window in correlation to a maximum allowed CO_2 concentration (ST_{CO2}). The window is opened when the ST_{CO2} value (e.g. 1000 ppm) is reached and it closes when the indoor concentration is reduced by a defined value d_{CO2} (e.g. 200 ppm). As already mentioned, the ventilation control is always in priority mode and is suspended only in case of detected precipitation in order to prevent rain and snow from entering the building.

The visual control of the ICsIE was developed using experiments and expert knowledge [55]. Although there are better and more objective methods to tune the FLC [15], the trial and error approach was chosen as there were substantial data available on the functioning and setup of a FLC for a previous BAS system developed at UL FGG and presented by Trobec Lah et al. [66] and Kristl et al. [55]. The final implemented version of the visual FLC configuration was based on consecutive testing in real-time conditions of selected 12 controller setups from the previous experimental BAS controller. The functioning of each was evaluated and compared and the best performing controller was then fine-tuned and used as an ICsIE visual FLC. In contrast, the configuration of the thermal FLC was determined through simulations on a mathematical model based on energy balance equations simulated in the Matlab/Simulink environment. The thermal model presented and developed by Škrjanc et al. [65] was used to define the thermal FLC setup using trial and error method supported by data gathered from the aforementioned experimental BAS system. Such approach was relatively time consuming, especially in the case of illuminance control, where trial and error tests were conducted in real time using real BAS. Thus, the need for a quicker and easier way to set the FLC rules was identified. Therefore, a BMS simulator (**Figure 4**) was developed mirroring the functioning of the control system as well as the thermal and visual response of the controlled indoor environment. The simulator was developed using Matlab/Simulink and Dymola/Modelica environments and enables the operator to quickly test different controller alternatives using real weather input files. Thermal simulations integrated into the simulator are based on the abovementioned model developed by Škrjanc et al., while the visual model was developed as a black-box model on the basis of data gathered through the functioning of the ICsIE as presented by Tomažič et al. [67] and Logar et al. [59]. Although the simulator is not vital to the performance of the ICsIE, it is still a useful tool as it enables fast testing and tuning of new FLC setups.

4.3.2. Performance of the ICsIE

The ICsIE has been in almost continuous operation since 2009. Although at the beginning of the operation, there were certain problems with the functioning of the actuators, the overall performance can be described as successful. The ICsIE was able to fulfil its primary objective in controlling the indoor user comfort parameters in desirable limits and consequentially improving the comfort levels in the office. In case of visual environment of the office, the system was able to regulate the indoor illuminance by controlling the shading devices and therefore daylight penetration. If external conditions were favorable (i.e. adequate levels of external illuminance), the indoor daylight conditions were successfully managed only by relatively few movements of the shading device (typically less than five movements per hour). An example of indoor visual environment control can be seen in **Figure 4**, where indoor illuminance control on the 2nd of February is presented. If the time period from 11:30 to 16:00 is observed, it can be seen that the ICsIE was capable of guiding the indoor work plane illuminance in the desired set-point band defined in the range from 450 to 600 lx. When the upper limit of the set-point band was reached, the system extended a louvre. During the considered day, only three louvres were necessary in order to control the indoor illuminance (**Figure 4**). In the evening (after 16:00), when the sun was setting, the external illuminance was quickly decreasing and with it also the indoor illuminance. The ICsIE tried to compensate this by successively retracting the louvres, but this was inadequate. Lights were not activated as the system was already in the off-work mode when the automated activation of lights was disabled. During morning hours, the system switched from thermal to visual priority at 7:00. A few minutes prior to that, all louvres were retracted, thus enabling daylighting. Nonetheless, during the morning hours, the external illuminance was too low to provide adequate daylighting and consequentially the ICsIE activated the office lights, which were on, until the occupants manually disabled them at 9:00 (**Figure 4**). In the instance of thermal regulation, the ICsIE was also able to guide indoor temperatures around the defined ST_T with acceptable typical deviations not exceeding ±1.5 K. On the other hand, the indoor thermal comfort was still inadequate during certain days of the cooling season, when in case of high external temperatures and high levels of solar radiation

http://dx.doi.org/10.5772/64951

during afternoon the office overheated despite shading and active cooling. The reason for inadequate thermal conditions is not in the functioning of the BAS but in the building itself. The office in question is oriented to the west and therefore exposed to high levels of solar radiation during evening. Additionally, the external building envelope has high thermal transmission (external wall U value is 1.29 W/m^2K; window U value is 2.9 W/m^2K) and is therefore susceptible to overheating. The effectiveness of passive cooling with nighttime ventilation was also demonstrated, as 4–5 K reduction in temperatures was achievable with its use. The effect of the ICsIE on the reduction in energy use of the office cannot be objectively evaluated because there is no comparable reference office in the UL FGG building to compare its performance. Despite this it can be at least speculated, in accordance with the work conducted by Firlag et al. [49], Ulpiani et al. [69] and the EN 15232 [12] standard, that even some basic automatization of building performance and systems results in measurable energy savings.

5. Conclusion

The challenges posed to the building industry by the need to reduce energy consumption and GHG emissions of buildings, while at the same time striving to increase occupancy comfort, are extremely complex. They cannot be solved only by conventional architectural measures, especially in cases of high-performance buildings where high standards of user comfort are demanded with simultaneous energy efficiency. A viable solution to increase the performance of future buildings is the application of BAS-controlled ABE. The potential of BAS for increasing energy efficiency of buildings was also recognized by the EU in the EPBD-r [7]. Additionally, Firlag et al. [49] demonstrated through simulations the influence of BAS on energy performance, where it was shown that manual control of window shades has almost no impact on the reduction in energy consumption, while even the most rudimental type of automated controller can achieve a reduction in a range from 11 to 13%. Although the application of AI control methods in building automation does not guarantee better performance in comparison to conventional approaches, it can still be concluded from the extensive body of work presented in the paper that AI techniques are at least better suited, if not a priori more efficient. Comparison between FLC and conventional control in the example of energy-efficient building, conducted by Ulpiani et al. [69], demonstrated that FLC-based BAS can outperform other controllers with 31.4–67.8% lower energy consumption. Through the paper the importance of occupant comfort was highlighted and supported by overview of the subject of indoor comfort and its influence on overall performance of the building and its occupants. Even though the influence of indoor comfort can be hard to evaluate and even harder to automatically control, especially in the case of highly changeable parameters such as daylighting, an example of such BAS was presented through the case of the ICsIE developed at UL FGG. The presented system was focused on the control of indoor thermal-visual and air quality conditions of an occupied office. On the level of applied control techniques, a combination of FLC and PI controllers was used, while for natural ventilation control, a simple on/off controller was applied. The indoor temperature, horizontal illuminance and CO_2 concentration were used as controlled variables, while other comfort parameters (e.g. mean radiant temperature, glare) were omitted due to the complexity issues. The results presented confirmed the ability of the system to satisfactorily control the indoor environmental conditions. Especially in the case of the illuminance control, the executed controller was successful as it was capable to control the indoor daylighting with relatively few actuator movements and it reduced the activation of lights, thus optimizing daylight usage [24]. The main shortcoming of the ICsIE identified through its design and testing is the process of controller tuning. Especially in the case of FLC setup, the applied trial and error method was time consuming, and even though substantial data on the functioning of a similar system [55, 65, 66] were available, the process was lengthy and prone to mistakes. Therefore, a more objective and faster process would enable easier adaptability of the system to other situations and buildings.

Author details

Mitja Košir

Address all correspondence to: mitja.kosir@fgg.uni-lj.si

Faculty of Civil and Geodetic Engineering, University of Ljubljana, Ljubljana, Slovenia

References

[1] European Union. EU Energy in Figures – Statistical pocketbook 2015. Luxembourg: Publications Office of the European Union; 2015. 264 p.

[2] U.S. Department of Energy. Energy Efficiency Trends in Residential and Commercial Buildings. McGraw-Hill Construction for the U.S. Department of Energy, Office of Energy Efficiency and Renewable Energy; 2010. 51 p.

[3] O. T. Masoso, L. J. Grobler. The dark side of occupants' behaviour on building energy use. Energy and Buildings. 2010;42(2):173-177. DOI: 10.1016/j.enbuild.2009.08.009

[4] P. H. Shaikh, N. B. M. Nor, P. Nallagownden, I. Elamvazuthi, T. Ibrahim. A review on optimized control systems for building energy and comfort management of smart sustainable buildings. Renewable and Sustainable Energy Reviews. 2014;37:409-429. DOI: 10.1016/j.rser.2014.03.027

[5] V. Marinakis, H. Doukas, C. Karakosta, J. Psarras. An integrated system for buildings' energy-efficient automation: application in the tertiary sector. Applied Energy. 2013;101:6-14. DOI: 10.1016/j.apenergy.2012.05.032

[6] Commission of the European Communities. Communication from the Commission to the European Parliament, the Council, the European Economic and Social Committee

and the Committee of the Regions: 20 20 by 2020, Europe's climate change opportunity, COM(2008) 30 final. Brussels: Commission of the European Communities; 2008. 12 p.

[7] Directive 2010/31/EU of the European Parliament and of the Council of the May 2010 on the energy performance of buildings (recast). Official Journal of the European Union. 2010;153:13-35.

[8] Directive 2012/27/EU of the European Parliament and of the Council of 25 October 2012 on energy efficiency, amending Directives 2009/125/EC and 2010/30/EU and repealing Directives 2004/8/EC and 2006/32/EC. Official Journal of the European Union. 2012;315:1-55.

[9] B. Atanasiu, editor. Principles for nearly zero-energy buildings: Paving the way for effective implementation of policy requirements. Brussels: Buildings Performance Institute Europe (BPIE); 2011. 99 p.

[10] A. Krainer. Passivhaus contra bioclimatic design, Dedicated to em. Univ. Prof. Dr. Ing. habil. Dr.h.c. mult. Karl Gertis on the occasion of his 70th birthday. Bauphysik. 2008;30(6):393-404.

[11] M. G. Ippolito, E. Riva Saseverino, G. Zizzo. Impact of building automation control systems and technical building management systems on the energy performance class of residential buildings: an Italian case study. Energy and Buildings. 2014;69:33-40. DOI: 10.1016/j.enbuild.2013.10.025

[12] European Committee for Standardisation. EN 15232: Energy Performance of Buildings —Impact of Building Automation, Controls and Building Management, 2nd edition. Brussels: European Committee for Standardisation; 2012. 84 p.

[13] F. Rubinstein, J. Jennings, D. Avery, S. Blanc. Preliminary results from an advanced lighting controls testbed. In: 1998 Conference Proceedings, IESNA Annual Conference; 10–12 August; San Antonio, Texas. Illuminating Engineering Society of North America; 1999.

[14] S. E. Lee, L. D. DiBartolomeo, E. S. Selkowitz. Thermal and daylighting performance of an automated venetian blind and lighting system in a full-scale private office. Energy and Buildings. 1998;29(1):47-63. DOI: 10.1016/S0378-7788(98)00035-8

[15] A. I. Dounis, C. Caraiscos. Advanced control system engineering for energy and comfort management in building environment—a review. Renewable and Sustainable Energy Reviews. 2009;13(6-7):1246-1261. DOI: 10.1016/j.rser.2008.09.015

[16] V. Fabi, R. V. Andersen, S. Corgnati, B. W. Olesen. Occupants' window opening behaviour: a literature review of factors influencing occupant behaviour and models. Building and Environment. 2012;58:188-198. DOI: 10.1016/j.buildenv.2012.07.009

[17] J. K. Day, D. E. Gunderson. Understanding high performance buildings: The link between occupant knowledge of passive design systems, corresponding behaviours,

occupant comfort and environmental satisfaction. Building and Environment. 2015;84:114-124. DOI: 10.1016/j.buildenv.2014.11.003

[18] P. Sobocki, B. Jönsson, J. Angst, C. Rehnberg. Cost of depression in Europe. Journal of Mental Health Policy and Economics. 2006;9(2):87-98.

[19] L. Heschong. Windows and Classrooms: A Study of Student Performance and the Indoor Environment. Fair Oaks: Heschong Mahone Group, Inc. for California Energy Commission; 2003. 111 p.

[20] L. Heschong. Windows and Offices: A Study of Office Worker Performance and the Indoor Environment. Fair Oaks: Heschong Mahone Group, Inc. for California Energy Commission; 2003. 143 p.

[21] W. J. Fisk. Health and productivity gains from better indoor environments and their relationship with building energy efficiency. Annual Review of Energy and the Environment. 2000;25:537-566. DOI: 10.1146/annurev.energy.25.1.537

[22] J. Sundell, H. Levin, W. W. Nazaroff, W. S. Cain, W. J. Fisk, D. T. Grimsrud, F. Gyntelberg, Y. Li, A. K. Persily, A. C. Pickering, J. M. Samet, J. D. Spangler, S. T. Taylor, C. J. Weschler. Ventilation rates and health: multidisciplinary review of the scientific literature. Indoor Air. 2011;21(3):191-204. DOI: 10.1111/j.1600-0668.2010.00703.x

[23] J. L. Stoops. A possible connection between thermal comfort and health. Report Number: LBNL-55134. Lawrence Berkley National Laboratory, 2004. https://publications.lbl.gov/islandora/object/ir%3A123164 (accessed: 26.1.2016).

[24] M. Košir, A. Krainer, M. Dovjak, Ž. Kristl. Automatically controlled daylight for visual and non-visual effects. Light Research and Technology. 2011;43(4):439-455. DOI: 10.1177/1477153511406520

[25] G. H. Evans, J. M. McCoy. When buildings don't work: the role of architecture in human health. Journal of Environmental Psychology. 1998;43(1):85-94. DOI: 10.1006/jevp.1998.0089

[26] E. Lee, S. Selkowitz, V. Bazjanac, V. Inkarojrit, C. Kohler. High-Performance Commercial Building Facades. Berkley, California: Lawrence Berkeley National Laboratory; 2002. 133 p. DOI: http://escholarship.org/uc/item/7d30b3rd

[27] K. Daniels. Low Tech, Light Tech, High Tech. Basel: Birkhäuser; 2000. 238 p.

[28] Active House Alliance. Active House – The Guidelines. Brussels: Active House Alliance, http://www.activehouse.info/about-active-house/active-house-radar/guidelines (accessed: 26.1.2016); 2015. 87 p.

[29] D. Y. Goswami, editor. Passive Solar Architecture Pocket Reference. Freiburg: International Solar Energy Society; 2009. 90 p.

[30] M. Košir, A. Krainer, Ž. Kristl. Integral control system of indoor environment in continuously occupied spaces. Automation in Construction. 2012;21:199-209. DOI: 10.1016/j.autcon.2011.06.004

[31] A. Krainer. SUSTAINABLE? ARCHITECTURE, bioclimatic architecture, on line teaching package. Ljubljana: SARA – Sustainable Architecture Applied to Replicable Public Access Buildings, http://kske.fgg.uni-lj.si/sara/SARA%20teachnig%20pack%20www.pdf (accessed: 12.11.2015); 2008. 174 p.

[32] H. R. Schiffman. Sensation and Perception: An Integrated Approach. 5th ed. Hoboken, New Jersey: John Wiley & Sons; 2001. 608 p.

[33] S. V. Szokolay. Introduction to Architectural Science: The Basis of Sustainable Design. 3rd ed. London: Taylor & Francis Ltd.; 2014. 392 p.

[34] J. Pohl. Building Science: Concepts and Application. Oxford: John Wiley & Sons; 2011. 271 p.

[35] A. Harrison, E. Loe, J. Read, editors. Intelligent Buildings in South East Asia. London: E & FN Spon; 1998. 183 p.

[36] International Organization for Standardization. ISO 7730: Ergonomics of the Thermal Environment — Analytical Determination and Interpretation of Thermal Comfort using Calculation of the PMV and PPD Indices and Local Thermal Comfort Criteria. Geneva: International Organization for Standardization; 2005.

[37] S. ter Mors, J. L. M. Hensen, M. G. L. C. Loomans, A. C. Boerstra. Adaptive thermal comfort in primary school classrooms: Creating and validating PMV-based comfort charts. Building and Environment. 2011;46:2454-2461. DOI: 10.1016/j.buildenv.2011.05.025

[38] D. Kolokotsa, K. Niachou, V. Geros, K. Kalaitzakis, G. S. Stavrakakis, M. Santamouris. Implementation of an integrated indoor environment and energy management system. Energy and Buildings. 2005;37(1):93-99.

[39] F. Nicol, S. Roaf. Pioneering new indoor temperature standards: the Pakistan project. Energy and Buildings. 1996;23(3):169–174. DOI: 10.1016/0378-7788(95)00941-8

[40] L. Wulund, A. B. Reddy. A brief history of circadian time: the emergence of redox oscillations as a novel component of biological rhythms. Perspectives in Science. 2015;6:27-37. DOI: 10.1016/j.pisc.2015.08.002

[41] M. Boubekri. Daylighting, Architecture and Health: Building Design Strategies. Boston: Elsevier/Architectural Press; 2008. 144 p.

[42] D. G. Ander. Daylighting: Performance and Design. 2nd ed. Hoboken: John Wiley & Sons; 2003. 336 p.

[43] D. H. W. Li, T. N. T. Lam, S. L. Wong. Lighting and energy performance for an office using high frequency dimming controls. Energy Conversion Management. 2006;47(9–10):1133-1145. DOI: 10.1016/j.enconman.2005.06.016

[44] European Committee for Standardisation. CR 1752 Ventilation for Buildings – Design Criteria for the Indoor Environment. Brussels: European Committee for Standardisation; 1999. 74 p.

[45] World Health Organization. Air Quality Guidelines for Europe. 2nd ed. Copenhagen: World Health Organization, Regional Office for Europe; 2000. 288 p.

[46] European Environment Agency. EEA Report No. 4/2012: Air Quality in Europe – 2012 Report. Luxembourg: Office for Official Publications of the European Union; 2012. 104 p.

[47] A. Deplazes, editor. Constructing Architecture: Materials, Processes, Structures. A Handbook. 3rd ed. Basel: Birkhäuser Verlag ; 2013. 555 p.

[48] A. E. Del Grosso, P. Basso. Adaptive building skin structures. Smart Materials and Structures. 2010;19(12): 1–12. DOI: http://dx.doi.org/10.1088/0964-1726/19/12/124011

[49] S. Firlag, M. Yazdanian, C. Curcija, C. Kohler, S. Vidanovic, R. Hart, S. Czarnecki. Control algorithms for dynamic windows for residential buildings. Energy and Buildings. 2015;109:157-173. DOI: 10.1016/j.enbuild.2015.09.069

[50] M. Košir, Ž. Kristl, B. Orel, A. Krainer. Shading device integrated solar collector for better utilization of renewable solar energy in buildings. In: Renewable Energy 2010: Advanced Technology Paths to Global Sustainability: Joint with 4th International Solar Energy Society Conference, Asia Pacific Region; 27 June–2 July 2010; Yokohama, Japan. Yokohama: International Solar Energy Society; 2010.

[51] J. A. Clarke, J. Cockroft, S. Conner, J. W. Hand, N. J. Kelly, R. Moore, T. O'Brien, P. Strachan. Simulation-assisted control in building energy management systems. Energy and Buildings. 2002;34(9):933-940. DOI: 10.1016/S0378-7788(02)00068-3

[52] A. I. Dounis, M. Bruant, M. Santamouris, G. Guarracino, P. Michel. Comparison of conventional and fuzzy control of indoor air quality in buildings. Journal of Intelligent and Fuzzy Systems. 1996;4(2):131-140. DOI: 10.3233/IFS-1996-4205

[53] Y. Li,K. H. Ang, G. C. Y. Chong. PID control system analysis and design: problems, remedies, and future directions. IEEE Control Systems Magazine. 2006;26(1):32-41. DOI: 10.1109/MCS.2006.1580152

[54] T. Y. Chen. Real-time predictive supervisory operation of building thermal systems with thermal mass. Energy and Buildings. 2001;33(2):141-150. DOI: 10.1016/S0378-7788(00)00078-5

[55] Ž. Kristl, M. Košir, M. Trobec Lah, A. Krainer. Fuzzy control system for thermal and visual comfort in building. Renewable Energy. 2008;33(4):694-702. DOI: 10.1016/j.renene.2007.03.020

[56] P. M. Menghal, A. Jaya Laxmi. Comparative Analysis for Various Artificial Intelligence Techniques Applied to Induction Motor Drive. In: Procedia of Fifth International Conference on Control, Communication and Power Engineering, CCPE; 21–22 February 2014; Chennai, India. Elsevier; 2014. p. 533-545.

[57] M. Zaheer-uddin, G. R. Zheng. Optimal control of time-scheduled heating, ventilating and air conditioning processes in buildings. Energy Conversion and Management. 2000;41(1):49-60. DOI: 10.1016/S0196-8904(99)00094-1

[58] H. Hagras, I. Packharn, Y. Vanderstockt, N. McNulty, A. Vadher, F. Doctor. An intelligent agent based approach for energy management in commercial buildings. In: IEEE International Conference on Fuzzy Systems, 2008. FUZZ-IEEE 2008. (IEEE World Congress on Computational Intelligence); 1–6 June 2008; Hong Kong. Hong Kong: IEEE; 2008. p. 156-162. DOI: 10.1109/FUZZY.2008.4630359

[59] V. Logar, Ž. Kristl, I. Škrjanc. Using a fuzzy black-box model to estimate the indoor illuminance in buildings. Energy and Buildings. 2014;70:343-351. DOI: 10.1016/j.enbuild.2013.11.082

[60] D. Kolokotsa, A. Pouliezos, G. Stavrakakis, C. Lazos . Predictive control techniques for energy and indoor environmental quality management in buildings. Building and Environment. 2009;44(9):1850-1863. DOI: 10.1016/j.buildenv.2008.12.007

[61] D. Kolokotsa, D. Tsiavos, G. S. Stavrakakis, K. Kalaitzakis, E. Antonidakis. Advanced fuzzy logic controllers design and evaluation for buildings' occupants thermal–visual comfort and indoor air quality satisfaction. Energy and Buildings. 2001;33(6):531-543. DOI: 10.1016/S0378-7788(00)00098-0

[62] J. W. Moon, J.-J. Kim. ANN-based thermal control models for residential buildings. Building and Environment. 2010;45(7):1612-1625. DOI: 10.1016/j.buildenv.2010.01.009

[63] T. Kazanasmaz, M. Günaydin, S. Binol. Artificial neural networks to predict daylight illuminance in office buildings. Building and Environment. 2009;44(8):1751-1757. DOI: 10.1016/j.buildenv.2008.11.012

[64] F. Ascione, N. Bianco, C. De Stasio, G. M. Mauro, G. P. Vanoli. Simulation-based model predictive control by the multi-objective optimization of building energy performance and thermal comfort. Energy and Buildings. 2016;111(1):131-144. DOI: 10.1016/j.enbuild.2015.11.033

[65] I. Škrjanc, B. Zupančič, B. Furlan, A. Krainer. Theoretical and experimental FUZZY modelling of building thermal dynamic response. Building and Environment. 2001;36(9):1023-1038. DOI: 10.1016/S0360-1323(00)00053-6

[66] M. Trobec Lah, B. Zupančič, J. Peternelj, A. Krainer. Daylight illuminance control with fuzzy logic. Solar Energy. 2006;80(3):307-321. DOI: 10.1016/j.solener.2005.02.002

[67] S. Tomažič, V. Logar, Ž. Kristl, A. Krainer, I. Škrjanc, M. Košir. Indoor-environment simulator for control design purposes. Building and Environment. 2013;70:60-72. DOI: 10.1016/j.buildenv.2013.08.026

[68] A. Guillemin, S. Molteni. An energy-efficient controller for shading devices self-adapting to the user wishes. Building and Environment. 2002;37(11):1091-1097. DOI: 10.1016/S0360-1323(01)00113-5

[69] G. Ulpiani, M. Borgognoni, A. Romagnoli, C. Di Perna. Comparing the performance of on/off, PID and fuzzy controllers applied to the heating system of an energy-efficient building. Energy and Buildings. 2016;116:1-17. DOI: 10.1016/j.enbuild.2015.12.027

[70] V. Kumar, P. Gaur, A.P. Mittal. ANN based self tuned PID like adaptive controller design for high performance PMSM position control. Expert Systems with Applications. 2014;41(17):7995–8002. DOI: 10.1016/j.eswa.2014.06.040

[71] A. Afram, F. Janabi-Sharifi. Theory and applications of HVAC control systems – a review of model predictive control (MPC). Building and Environment. 2014;72:343-355. DOI: 10.1016/j.buildenv.2013.11.016

[72] H. Hagras, V. Callaghan, M. Colley, G. Clarke. A hierarchical fuzzy-genetic multi-agent architecture for intelligent buildings online learning, adaptation and control. Information Sciences. 2003;150(1–2):33-57. DOI: 10.1016/S0020-0255(02)00368-7

[73] INEA. IDR BLOK [Internet]. 2011. Available from: http://www.inea.si/en/products/idr-blok/ [Accessed: 15.2.2016]

Chapter 7

Automatic Prompt Gamma-Ray Analysis System: Automation of an Existing Large-Scale Analytical Device

Takahito Osawa

Additional information is available at the end of the chapter

http://dx.doi.org/10.5772/64650

Abstract

The prompt gamma-ray analysis (PGA) system installed in the Japan Research Reactor-3 (JRR-3) was automated between 2012 and 2013. This automation is a good example of a large-scale old analytical device automated in a nuclear facility. This automatic system has several useful functions, such as automatic sample exchange and analysis, automatic helium gas flow control and flow channel switching function, automatic neutron recording system, and fail-safe function using Machine Vision, and the Internet. The analysis system was automated using a vertical revolute joint robot, control programs, and data acquisition devices. The main control software named AutoPGA was developed using LabVIEW and the program can control all functions of the automatic system, capable of analyzing up to 14 samples automatically. In the automation, the core of the PGA system was not modified and the extremely low background level of gamma rays was maintained well; however, the efficiency of routine measurements dramatically increased. Because the instruments used in the automatic PGA system are not unique, the basic design of the system can be easily applied to other large-scale analytical devices.

Keywords: analytical equipment, LabVIEW, revolute joint robot, Machine Vision

1. Introduction

Recently, many laboratory-scale analytical devices have been automated because most users are not analysis experts; hence, simple operation is generally very attractive for consumers. In particular, many instruments used in biology and medicine are highly automated and user-friendly. Users can execute the analysis by a mere push of a button. State-of-the art instruments can automatically analyze the data and produce sophisticated reports. In general, users never conduct the complex data analysis themselves. For example, modern X-ray diffraction systems can automatically output the structural analysis results of macromolecules using online databases for materials. Routine analysis will become easier in the future owing to the evolution of robotics, information technology, and artificial intelligence. Most laboratory-scale analytical devices will be automated in the near future.

On the other hand, most large-scale analytical devices, for example, instruments installed in accelerators, nuclear reactors, and synchrotron radiation facilities, are not presently automated because they are built for specific scientific purposes and most users are experts in their respective fields. Thus, user interface is typically neglected and overall operation of instruments is complex. Because substituting a large-scale device with a new one is difficult, existing large-scale devices tend to be used longer than small devices. Further, such large instruments are not commercially available, unlike the laboratory-scale analytical devices listed in a product catalogue and they are developed for specific purposes. Therefore, automation of such devices is preferable; however, automation is not easy because many of them are old and not designed for automation. The automation of such devices, that is, those requiring complex and manual operation, is slowly but surely progressing. In this study, one example of automation of a large-scale analytical device installed in a nuclear reactor is provided.

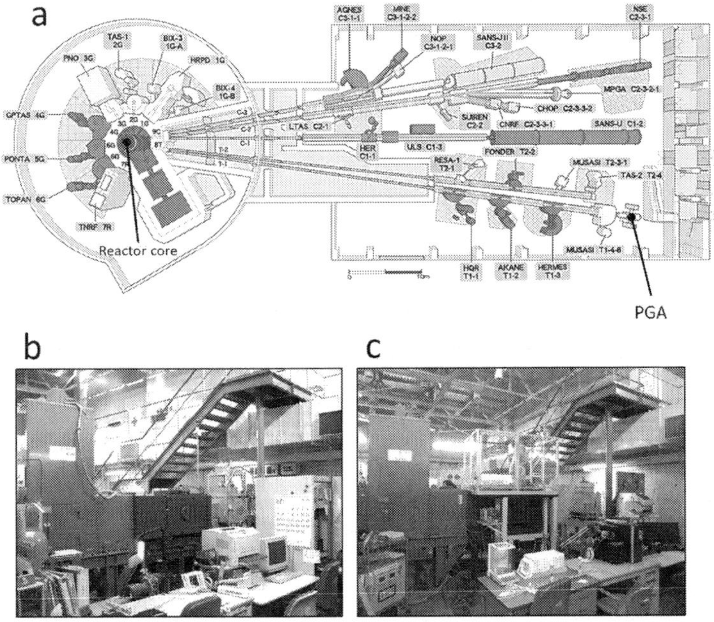

Figure 1. The location of PGA in JRR-3 (a). The PGA is at the end of the thermal neutron beam line (T1) in the guide hall. Two photographs taken in 2010 (b) and 2016 (c) show the difference before and after the automation upgrade. A revolute joint robot is set up at the side of the shielding body after the upgrade.

Before describing the automation, the analytical device will be explained. Prompt gamma-ray activation analysis is a convenient and nondestructive method to determine the concentrations of many elements in bulk samples that requires the use of a neutron beam, which is generated by a nuclear reactor or an accelerator. The gamma rays emitted from target atoms are recorded within 10^{-14} s after the neutron capture reaction. PGA is widely used in agriculture, earth and planetary sciences, materials science, environmental science, and archeology [1–5] because of its high sensitivity for specific light elements, such as boron, hydrogen, and chlorine. Because the atomic nucleus emits prompt gamma rays with specific energies when it reacts with a neutron, concentrations of elements can be determined by detecting the emitted gamma rays using a germanium detector.

The PGA system installed in the Japan Research Reactor-3 (JRR-3) was constructed in 1992 [6]. The system has achieved a very low gamma-ray background level, but it is outdated because no notable improvements have been made since its construction. In addition, the PGA system was considerably damaged by the Great East Japan Earthquake on March 11, 2011. The automatic system for PGA was developed to update the old analytical system and improve its measurement efficiency [7]. The development was conducted between 2012 and 2013 after the system was repaired following the earthquake. The location of PGA in the JRR-3 and a comparison of the system outline before and after the upgrade are shown in **Figure 1**.

The basic strategy for the automation of the existing analytical equipment is listed below. Please note that a field-programmable gate array (FPGA) and programmable logic controller (PLC) are intentionally not used in the automatic system.

1. The inside of the shielding bodies of the analytical system is not modified because the measurement system is highly sophisticated and has very low background level. This property is also very important in other large-scale devices because special devices cannot be completely modified, as it is vital to maintain their original function and performance. Therefore, adding automatic functions without remodeling the core of the device is important. In addition, strict restrictions on the type and position of the sensors used as components for the automatic system exist, in particular when the sensors are used in an environment with intense quantum beams and radiation. For example, metallic components should not be exposed to neutron beams because metallic elements will be activated.

2. The samples can be exchanged by using a six-axis vertical revolute joint robot, and thus the automatic measurements are performed. The industrial robot is indispensable to establish the automatic system for an existing analytical device because of its high flexibility and multiple uses. However, limitations are placed on where the robot is set up; for example, environment with high radiation, high humidity, and high temperature environments should be avoided for smooth robot operation. Particularly, high-intensity gamma rays, X-rays, and other quantum beams can cause the electronic robot equipment to malfunction. The proposed device is a solution to these problems.

3. The integrated control program (AutoPGA) is based on LabVIEW. Although there are various choices in the development environment to design the control program, LabVIEW is one of the best software choices because of its graphical programming language,

numerous add-ons, and its support of various hardware [8–11]. The considerably complex system developed in this work can be formulated based on using LabVIEW and NI hardware.

4. The existing measurement program (Spectrum Navigator) and an old system are used according to the users' needs because the program is widely used in the gamma-ray and X-ray analysis [12–15]. To satisfy the demand, two computers and four programs, namely, Auto PGA, a communication program (PGA-Talk), Spectrum Navigator, and a robot control program, are developed. A new measurement program is not developed because many experienced users want to use existing measurement programs.

5. The helium gas flow and flow channel are automatically controlled in the automatic system. The Teflon sample box used for the passage of neutron beams is well shielded and purged by pure helium gas to reduce the background level because the neutron cross section of helium is very small. Therefore, a large amount of helium gas is used in the activation analysis and the decrease in the consumption of helium gas is critical to the improvement of the PGA. This study improves the trade-off between the consumption of helium gas and background by using a highly sophisticated control program.

6. Neutron flux and neutron scattering are monitored and automatically recorded using a counter/timer board. Before the upgrade, these two parameters were recorded by a thermal printer and an X-Y recorder, respectively. The condition of the measurement device should be recorded to improve the accuracy of the analysis because the neutron flux is directly related to the sensitivity of the target elements. Thus, an automatic recording system for these parameters improves the quality of measurements. In addition, the recording system is the only method to directly check the condition of the white neutron beam of the facility and the activity of the nuclear reactor. Although such a data acquisition system is typical, the shift from an analog device to digital device must be smooth.

7. The system implements network functions. Because most modern equipment support network functions, connecting an old device to the network for more convenience and adding remote control or remote supervision. Particularly, the remote supervision through the Internet reduces the exposure dose in the case of analytical devices installed in a radiation control area. The new PGA system automatically sends e-mails and tweets.

8. Machine Vision, an imaging-based automatic inspection technology, is widely used in many fields, for example, the manufacturing industry and agriculture [16–21]. This technology is implemented to improve the fail-safe function in the PGA system. Image recognition is one of the most effective technologies to construct an automated system, and this function can be easily used by a LabVIEW add-on. Advanced and complicated sensing can be enabled through a USB camera. In particular, Machine Vision is available to devices in which a contact sensor cannot be used, for example, inside a chamber directly irradiated by gamma rays, X-rays, or a neutron beam. Image recognition technology overcomes this difficulty by setting up a small camera outside the beam path where typical sensors cannot withstand severe conditions.

http://dx.doi.org/10.5772/64650

The above-described strategies can be applied not only to PGA, a special analytical device, but also to other equipment. In this chapter, automation of large-scale experimental devices is explained by referring to the development of the automatic PGA system in JRR-3.

2. System outline

Images of the automatic PGA system are shown in **Figure 2**. The new automatic PGA system is mainly composed of two personal computers (PC1 and PC2), four programs, a six-axis vertical revolute joint robot (Mitsubishi RV-3SD), and data acquisition devices. The PGA system ensures low background noise without greatly modifying the interior of the shielding body. The installation of the device inside the PGA would increase the background level, and the electronic equipment would malfunction almost instantly owing to the intense neutron beam and gamma rays. However, in this study, most of the devices and systems outside the shielding body were considerably improved.

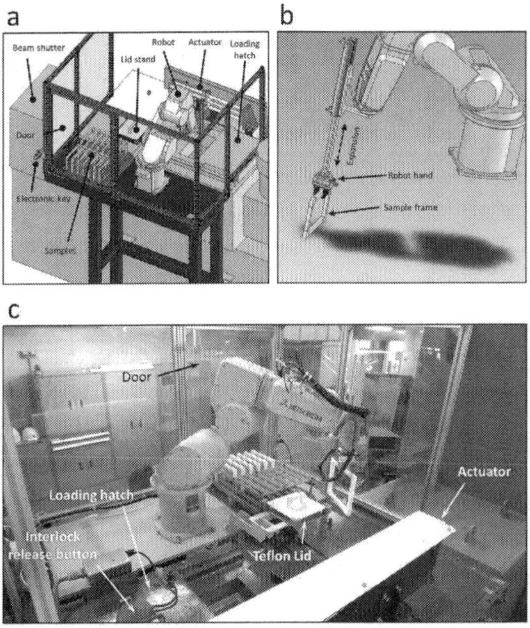

Figure 2. 3D images of the automatic PGA system (a), the robot hand (b), and a photograph of the vertical revolute joint robot (c). The robot is enclosed with acrylic fiber boards to avoid human intervention.

The automated PGA is shown in **Figure 3**. The core function of the new system is an automatic sample exchanging and measurement system, with several automatic control functions integrated into the system. Each function of the reformed system is detailed in the following sections.

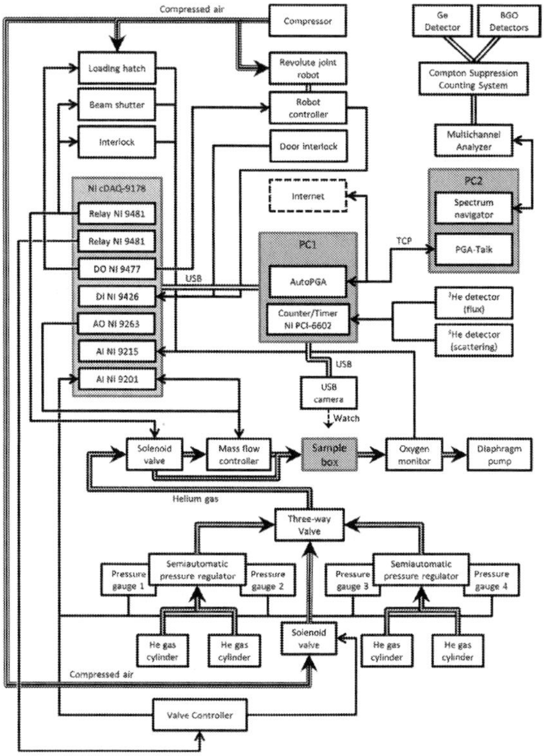

Figure 3. Connection diagram of the automated PGA system. The AutoPGA program installed in PC1 controls all the functions of the complex automation system and PC2 conducts prompt gamma-ray analysis using the existing measurement program and multichannel analyzer.

3. Software

The integrated PGA control program (AutoPGA) was developed by using the LabVIEW Developer Suite. The program runs on the Microsoft Windows operating system and is designed to easily control all functions of the PGA system with a user-friendly interface. **Figure 4a** shows the main screen of the program. The program is composed of seven screens, including the main screen, the neutron monitor screen, the helium flow control screen, the input/output signal screen, the Machine Vision screen, the logging and communication screen, and the error message screen. Switching between screens is accomplished by selecting the appropriate tab. Users other than administrators generally open only the main screen, and end users of the PGA use only selected functions included in the other screens. On the other hand, administrators can control all functions of the complex system by entering their password. When an administrator logs on the program, all the hidden control buttons become visible and available. This security function prevents the system from malfunctioning and mishandling by end users. Because most large-scale devices in research institutes are shared or used by many end users, the system architect should establish foolproof mechanisms in the control program.

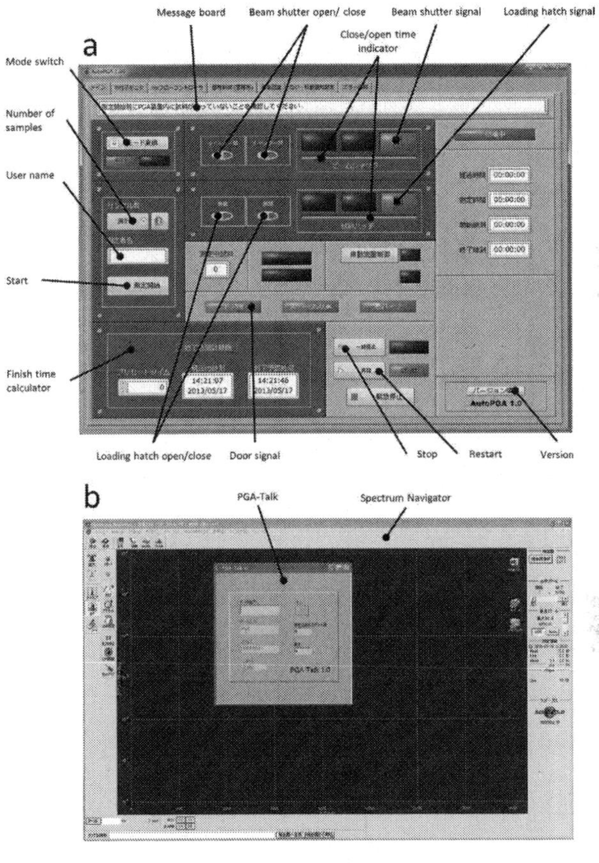

Figure 4. Screenshot of the main screen of the AutoPGA (a) and PGA-Talk called by the Spectrum Navigator (b). Only the Japanese version is available in the present stage. End users can control the functions of the PGA system by using only the main panel of the AutoPGA. When the automatic analysis is started, the mode switch button is pressed and the mode is switched into automatic mode, and the open/close buttons of the beam shutter and loading hatch are invalidated. The PGA-Talk is called by the Spectrum Navigator when a measurement is finished.

4. Automatic analysis system

The automatic measurement sequence is that of the conventional manual measurement method. Samples are sealed in Teflon filters using an electrothermal sealer and hung on the center of Teflon frames with two Teflon strings. In the automatic PGA system, 14 samples are placed onto a sample stand beside the robot. Each sample frame is selected and introduced into the Teflon sample box that is purged with helium gas using the revolute joint robot.

The robot hand's design is important in the automation. There are many types of robot hands and the appropriate design should be adopted, keeping the purpose in mind. The robot hand of the automatic PGA system can not only grasp the sample frame but also expand and contract with compressed air (**Figure 2b**). This expansion mechanism is necessary while inserting the sample frame into the Teflon sample box because the height of the neutron beam at its center, which corresponds to the position of the center of the sample frame, is 20 cm lesser than the height of the trestle on which the robot is mounted. Although customization of the robot may be necessary for some existing devices (as the devices cannot be modified), the customization is unnecessary in most cases. There are several types of industrial robots, such as vertical-type robot, horizontal-type robot, ceiling-mounted-type robot, parallel link robot, and orthogonal robot. A vertical-type robot (RV-3SD) by Mitsubishi was selected in this study because of its reasonable price, high performance, and flexibility. When a robot is installed into an existing system, the designer must carefully consider the installation location because of the many physical restrictions. Since the shielding bodies, which are composed of iron plates and lead, cannot be modified in the case of the PGA system, there are naturally restrictions on the location of the robot. In addition, the heavy loading hatch that opens when the sample is inserted into the sample box was not automated before the improvement. The interference between the robot and the shielding bodies was carefully checked by 3D simulations using the data of the operation range of the robot, and an appropriate small robot was selected for the PGA system. Many system designers tend to choose robots manufactured by FANUC but they are virtually the same as the Mitsubishi robot. The robot was set up on the side of the shielding body and was controlled by a robot controller (Mitsubishi CR1D-700). A robot controller memorizes the operating positions of the robot and the coordinate data are taught and corrected during the trial operation. A sequence program written in MELFA BASIC V was uploaded to the robot controller through a universal serial bus (USB) port, and the controller was connected to a digital output module (NI 9477) and digital input module (NI 9426). These digital modules were controlled by AutoPGA through the USB (**Figure 3**).

Opening and closing the loading hatch was enabled by an actuator, which moves using compressed air and air valves controlled by a 24 V digital output signal from the digital output module (NI 9477). This module can be controlled by AutoPGA. Because there is an interlock system and the loading hatch cannot open when the neutron beam shutter is open, the interlock system was modified to be externally controlled by the computer. The physical interlock on the loading hatch was operated by a single-pole single-throw relay (NI 9481), and the relay also controlled the opening and closing of the neutron beam shutter. The lock of the hatch can be unlocked by an open signal from the relay but the lock is never unlocked when the beam shutter is opened. The fail-safe mechanism is important to prevent radiation hazards.

Another interlock mechanism was installed in the door, which was used to place the samples on the sample stand. When the electronic key was removed and the door was open, the servomechanism of the revolute joint robot was shut down and the alarm beeped. When the door was closed and the electronic key was connected, the AutoPGA sent the reset signal to the robot controller using NI 9477 and the alarm stopped. Thus, the user does not need to directly operate the reset switch of the robot controller. In addition, the door cannot be opened when the electric key is connected, thus protecting the user from the powerful robot.

The AutoPGA program developed by LabVIEW is installed in PC1 and controls the entire series of analytical operations. The user inputs a user name and the number of samples on the main screen and then clicks the start button. Then a voice message is played and AutoPGA automatically starts the servomechanism of the robot and initiates the sequence program. It then closes the neutron beam shutter, releases the interlock, and opens the loading hatch. The robot begins operation and the Teflon lid on the sample box is removed and placed on a stand. The robot selects the sample frame, introduces it into the sample box, and places the lid on the sample box. The loading hatch is closed, the neutron shutter is opened, and the measurement begins. The sample exchange requires approximately 40 s. The sequence flow of the automatic sample exchange and measurement is shown in **Figure 5**.

An existing measurement program (SEIKO EG & G Spectrum Navigator) is installed in PC2 and is used in the gamma-ray measurements. In the automatic analysis, a batch-processing mode is used, which calls the communication program (PGA-Talk, **Figure 4b**) after each measurement. PGA-Talk, also designed using LabVIEW, sends a signal to PC1 through the transmission control protocol (TCP) and the AutoPGA recognizes the completion of the gamma-ray recording and begins the sample exchange. When the sample exchange is complete, the AutoPGA sends a signal to PC2 through TCP and PGA-Talk automatically shuts down. Spectrum Navigator then begins the measurement of the next sample. Upon completing the measurement of the last sample, AutoPGA sends an end signal to the robot controller, and the robot removes the last sample from the sample box. The loading hatch and neutron beam shutter are closed, an end message appears as a popup window, and a voice message is played informing the user of the end of the measurement.

The AutoPGA program communicates with the robot controller using the 24 V digital output/input modules (NI 9477 and NI 9426) installed in the NI cDAQ-9178. The AutoPGA sends a set of digital signals, including the sample number expressed as 4-bit data, the start signal, the last sample signal, the operation permission signal, and the robot control signals. The AutoPGA can control all functions of the revolute joint robot when the permission signal for the operation of the robot is on. However, a user cannot control the robot in the user mode; this is only possible in the administrator mode.

Users can manually measure their samples when the AutoPGA analysis mode is switched to the manual mode to compare the effectiveness of measurement with that achieved before the upgrade. The neutron beam shutter and the loading hatch can be opened and closed by the four switches of the AutoPGA program (**Figure 4**), and the users can manually perform the sample exchange when the loading hatch is opened. On the other hand, users can control the hatch without the AutoPGA and the computer; state-of-the-art buttons with organic EL display are used as open/close buttons to control the air valves directly connected to the actuator.

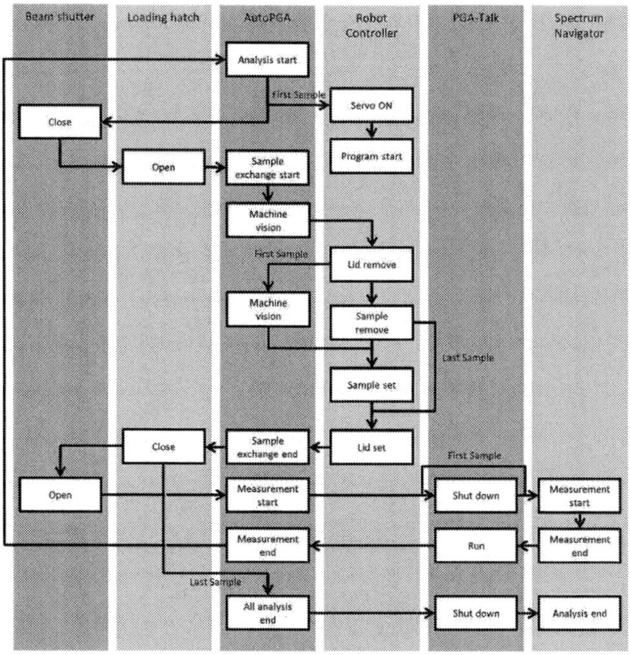

Figure 5. Flow chart of the sequence of the automated prompt gamma-ray analysis. The automatic sample exchange and automatic gamma-ray recording are enabled by the functional linkage among the beam shutter, loading hatch, AutoPGA, robot controller, PGA-Talk, and Spectrum Navigator.

5. Helium gas flow control and neutron recording systems

Before the automation, the Teflon sample box was purged with pure helium gas during the measurement, but the mass flow of helium was controlled manually. Therefore, in this upgrade, an automatic mass flow control system was developed and integrated into the AutoPGA program. The helium gas flow control panel in the AutoPGA is shown in **Figure 6a**. Helium gas flows into the sample box through a tube connected by a joint, and the small amount of air in the box is aspirated using a small diaphragm pump through another tube connected to the bottom of the sample box. An oxygen monitor (JKO-O2LJD2) is installed upstream of the pump, and the partial pressure of oxygen in the air in the box can be recorded by the monitor (**Figure 3**). The AutoPGA reads the partial pressure of oxygen through the analog voltage input (NI 9215) and automatically controls the mass flow controller (Azbil MQV0010) through the analog voltage output (NI 9263). The mass flow is also recorded by the analog voltage input module (NI 9201). When the loading hatch is opened, the flow volume is zero, and when the hatch is closed, the box is rapidly purged. The concentration of oxygen (%) and the settings for the flow volume and current flow volume are always displayed on AutoPGA program screen. The mass flow of helium is maintained between 1 L/min and 10 L/min using three parameters: the minimum flow, upper threshold, and lower threshold. If the oxygen pressure is higher than the upper threshold, the mass flow is set at a maximum of 10 L/min, whereas if the oxygen pressure is lower than the lower threshold, the mass flow is set at a minimum of 1 L/min. The helium mass flow continuously fluctuates between the upper and lower thresholds. This system efficiently reduces helium gas consumption and contributes to the decrease in the background noise level for the gamma-ray analysis.

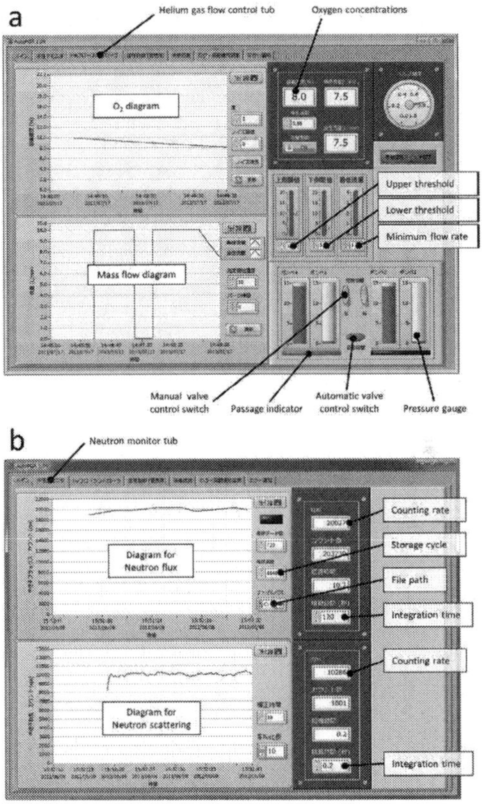

Figure 6. Helium gas flow control panel (a) and neutron monitor panel (b) of the AutoPGA program.

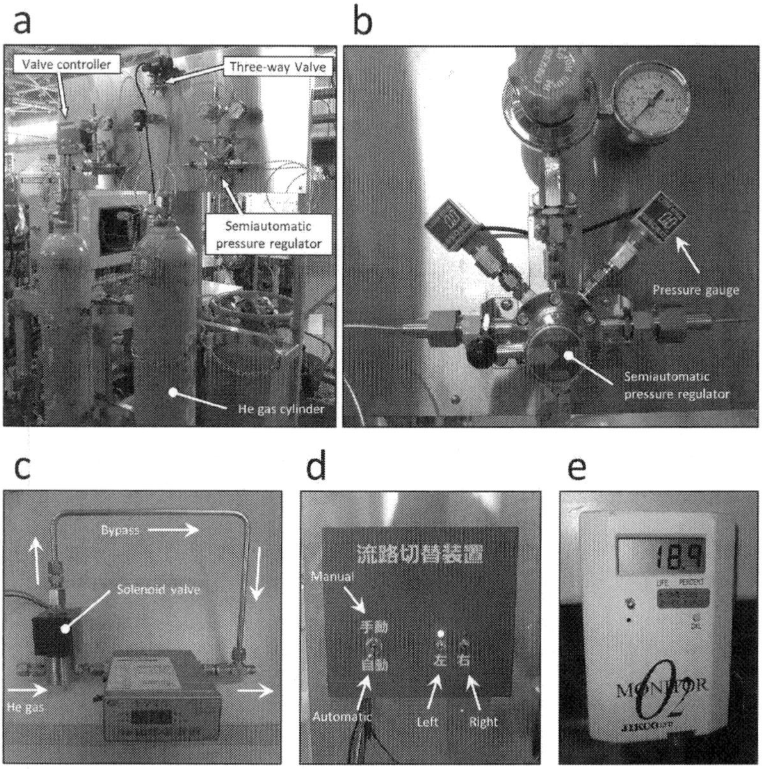

Figure 7. Equipment of the helium gas flow control system. Gas cylinder holder (a), pressure gauges connected with a semiautomatic pressure regulator (b), mass flow controller (c), valve controller (d), and oxygen monitor (e).

The automatic gas flow control system also has an automatic flow switching function (**Figure 7**). A special stainless steel gas cylinder holder is equipped with two semiautomatic pressure regulators (Yamato TN-50B) and four digital pressure gauges (Nagano Keiki GC31) with an analog output of 1–5 V DC. Two gas cylinders can be connected to a semiautomatic pressure regulator and the regulator automatically switches the flow channel; when the right side flow channel is selected and the right side cylinder empties, the regulator automatically switches to the left side channel. The two pressure regulators are connected through a three-way valve operated with compressed air through a solenoid valve. The valve is controlled by AutoPGA according to the pressure data from the digital pressure gauges. When the automatic passage switching system is activated, the user does not need to check the regulators and the valve because an appropriate channel is automatically selected. When the empty cylinder is replaced with a full one, no operations of the valve and control program are required. However, the user can skip the automatic mass flow control system and manually control the mass flow using the pressure regulator. When the user exits the AutoPGA program, the switch

http://dx.doi.org/10.5772/64650

of the solenoid valve upstream of the mass flow controller is automatically turned off and the helium gas flows into the bypass tube (**Figure 7c**). When the user opens the AutoPGA program, the switch of the solenoid valve is automatically turned on again. When the valve controller is switched to the manual mode (**Figure 7d**), even if the AutoPGA is running, the function of the automatic flow channel switching is nullified and the user can select the flow channel manually.

Two neutron helium-3 detectors are installed in the PGA; one is for the neutron flux and the other is for the neutron scattering. Prior to this study, the neutron flux and neutron scattering were recorded using a thermal printer and an X-Y recorder, respectively, and the pen for the recorder is no longer for sale. This old system was updated in this study using a counter/timer (NI PCI-6602) installed in the PCI bus of PC1. The neutron flux data are continuously recorded and automatically saved in Excel sheet daily by the AutoPGA. The neutron scattering is also monitored, and the data are used to check the degree of purging of the helium gas in the sample box. The neutron monitor panel in the AutoPGA is shown in **Figure 6b**.

It is important to monitor the flux of the neutron beam to evaluate the operation of the nuclear reactor and the accuracy of the measurement. Previously, the flux of the neutron beam was checked every morning before the start of operation but the shifting of the neutron flux during the day could not be estimated. The new system can continually record the state of the neutron beam and the measurement, thus improving the accuracy even when rapid changes in neutron flux occur. The daily neutron flux fluctuation was observed to be approximately 2.5% in an operation cycle (26 days). If the same fluctuation occurs hourly, the accuracy of the measurement may improve by 2.5%.

6. Machine Vision

Machine Vision is one of the most important technologies in modern automation systems and is used in many automatic manufacturing systems. Machine Vision offers many advantages; one of them is that contact-type sensors can be replaced by cameras. As aforementioned, the technology is well suited for nuclear reactors because contact-type sensors cannot be used inside shielding bodies where materials are exposed to high-intensity neutron beams and gamma rays.

AutoPGA provides imaging-based automatic inspection that is used to enhance the fault tolerance of robot operation. Images are acquired by a USB camera placed above the loading hatch. Note that the camera is not a sophisticated industrial camera but a cheap commercial product. Screenshots of the Machine Vision panel of AutoPGA are shown in **Figure 8**. Although there are many automatic inspection methods, edge line detection is used in the PGA system because of it is very simple and consistent. Color inspection cannot be used in this case because the Teflon lid and sample frame, the objects to be detected by Machine Vision, are in the Teflon sample box and there is no clear difference in color between the white objects and the white box. In edge detection, the detection area is set in advance, as shown in **Figure 8c**. When the Teflon lid is in the normal position, the Machine Vision inspection system can detect the two horizontal edge lines of the handle of the lid (**Figure 8c**). However, when the Teflon lid is not in the normal position, the Machine Vision system cannot detect the horizontal edge lines and the robot stops. AutoPGA simultaneously displays an alert window to prevent the robot from malfunctioning. If the lid is set in the normal position, the robot operates normally and removes the lid according to the procedure of the automatic analysis shown in **Figure 5**.

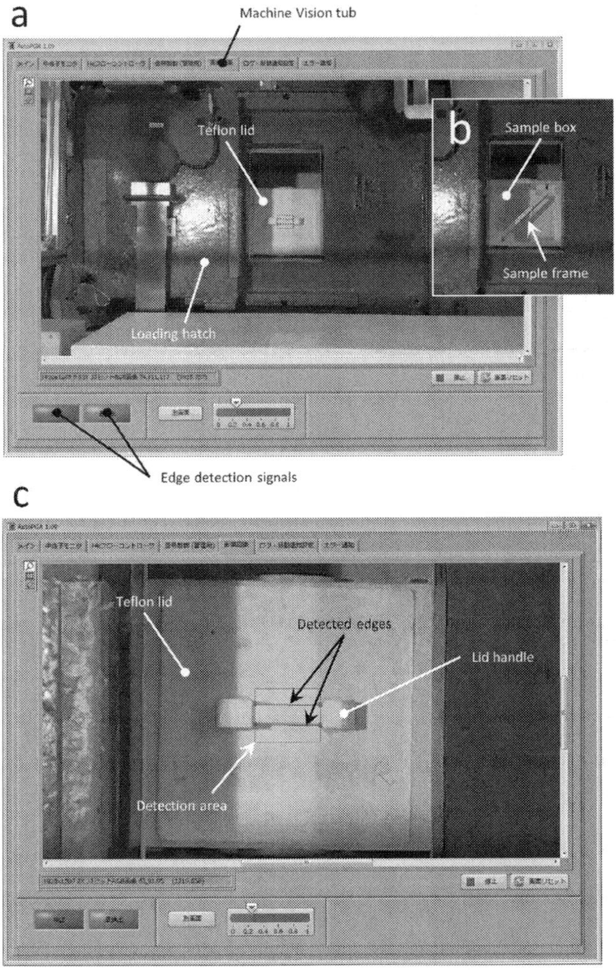

Figure 8. Machine Vision used in the AutoPGA program. Screenshots of the Machine Vision tub when the Teflon lid is on the sample box (a), the lid is removed and the sample frame is inserted into the sample box (b), and a magnified image of the Teflon lid (c). The square and two lines in (c) denote the detection area of the image inspection and the detected edges of the lid handle, respectively.

Similarly, the sample frame in the sample box can be detected by the system as two edge lines inclined by 45° (**Figure 8b**). The presence of a frame in the sample box at the beginning of the automatic analysis implies that a previous user forgot to remove the last sample during manual analysis and AutoPGA displays an alert window and stops the robot.

7. Logging, Internet, error, and memory release functions

AutoPGA uses several other functions, for example, logging, Internet, error, and memory release functions. All events in the automatic system including such as the start of the analysis, the exchange of samples, the end of the analysis, and error warnings are logged on a panel of the AutoPGA program. The users can easily confirm the operational conditions by using the time series log and the log information is automatically e-mailed to the administrator through the e-mail function of LabVIEW. In addition, the same information is automatically tweeted; therefore, all users can remotely know the condition of the PGA.

Automatic memory release is a characteristic function of AutoPGA and it can automatically deallocate the memory resource associated with the program using processHandles.dll. The function regularly specifies its own process ID and release memory area regularly. The most severe problem of the complex control program developed by LabVIEW is memory leak. This function is a coping process to solve the problem of memory leak because the AutoPGA program is large and resource hungry. Further, although this program has been debugged for a long time and performs stably, the memory release function has not been modified.

8. Conclusion

The archaic PGA system installed in the JRR-3 of JAEA a quarter of a century ago was totally revamped, and a new automated PGA system was developed using a revolute joint robot and original software. The main control program AutoPGA developed using LabVIEW can control the entire analysis system automatically. The important points of the improvements are given below.

i. The automation of existing large-scale analytical equipment is achieved by using an industrial robot and in-house programs without modifications inside shielding bodies. The core of the analytical system is thus perfectly preserved even after the automation and the high performance of the analytical system is maintained. The basic design concept of the automation can be applied to other large-scale analytical devices.

ii. The existing measurement program, Spectrum Navigator, is still used to minimize users' discomfort. The automatic analysis system is realized by an elaborate system design in which the communication program (PGA-Talk) operates jointly with the measurement program. PGA-Talk is called by the batch-processing mode of Spectrum Navigator in the system, but this might not be used in other measurement programs. If an existing program cannot use the batch-processing mode, the system designer should either develop a new measurement program or develop another program that calls the existing measurement program. If there is no demand by end users, a new measurement program that is integrated with the control program should be designed.

iii. An automated helium gas flow control system with automatic flow channel switching function was developed using a mass flow controller and two semiautomatic pressure regulators. This system can execute all the steps of gas regulation except the exchange of the empty gas cylinder; therefore, the burden on the operator is lesser and the consumption of helium gas decreases. This unique system can be applied to most devices using high-pressure gas cylinders.

iv. Machine Vision can be implemented by using a cheap USB camera easily available to consumers and improves the safe operation of the revolute joint robot. Thus, it can be used even if one has insufficient funds for automation, as it does not require high economic investment. In particular, it is useful for cases where the user requires neither high speed nor high sensitivity. In addition, despite the simplicity of the edge detection method, it is capable of detecting the lid and sample frame.

In summary, the strategies for the automation of PGA can be applied to other large-scale experimental devices without significant cost. Most of the hardware and software used are easily accessible. An extremely cheap, small computer, such as Raspberry Pi, may facilitate automation efforts and many large-scale devices may be automated in a similar manner in the future.

Author details

Takahito Osawa

Address all correspondence to: osawa.takahito@jaea.go.jp

Quantum Beam Science Center, Japan Atomic Energy Agency, Tokai-mura, Ibaraki, Japan

References

[1] Saito T, Tanoi K, Matsue H, Iikura H, Hamada Y, Seyama S, Masuda S, Nakanishi TM. Application of prompt gamma-ray analysis and instrumental neutron activation analysis to identify the beef production distinct. Journal of Radioanalytical and Nuclear Chemistry. 2008;278(2):409-413. DOI: 10.1007/s10967-008-0810-8

[2] Tanoi K, Matsue H, Iikura H, Saito T, Hayashi Y, Hamada Y, Nishiyama H, Kobayashi NI, Nakanishi TM. Element profiles of onion producing districts in Japan, as determined using INAA and PGA. Journal of Radioanalytical and Nuclear Chemistry. 2009;278(2):375-379. DOI: 10.1007/s10967-008-0803-7

[3] Ebihara M, Oura Y. Chemical characterization of the extraterrestrial material returned by future space mission: an application of nuclear activation methods. Advances in Space Research. 2004;34(11):2305-2310. DOI:10.1016/j.asr.2004.06.004

[4] Osawa T, Hatsukawa Y, Appel PWU, Matsue H. Mercury and gold concentrations of highly polluted environmental samples determined using prompt gamma-ray analysis and instrument neutron activation analysis. Nuclear Instruments and Methods in Physics Research Section B. 2011;269(8):717-720. DOI: 10.1016/j.nimb.2011.01.129

[5] Yoshida S, Yamahana K, Matsue H, Murata I. Nondestructive analysis of the Ancient Egyptian vitreous relics by neutron. Progress in Nuclear Science and Technology. 2011;1:259-262. DOI: 10.15669/pnst.1.259

[6] Yonezawa C, Wood AKH, Hoshi M, Ito Y, Tachikawa E. The characteristics of the prompt gamma-ray analyzing system at the neutron beam guides of JRR-3M. Nuclear Instruments and Methods in Physics Research Section A. 1993;329(1-2):207-216. DOI: 10.1016/0168-9002(93)90938-E

[7] Osawa T. Development of an automatic prompt gamma-ray activation analysis system. Journal of Radioanalytical and Nuclear Chemistry. 2015;303:1141-1146. DOI: 10.1007/s10967-014-3436-z

[8] Zaytsev SM, Popov AM, Zorov NB, Labutin TA. Measurement system for high-sensitivity LIBS analysis using ICCD camera in LabVIEW environment. Journal of Instrumentation. 2014;9:P06010. DOI: 10.1088/1748-0221/9/06/P06010

[9] Novak P, Navarik J, Pechousek J, Prochazka V, Machala L, Tucek J. Development of fast pulse processing algorithm for nuclear detectors and its utilization in LabVIEW-based Mössbauer spectrometer. Journal of Instrumentation. 2014;9:T01001. DOI: 10.1088/1748-0221/9/01/T01001

[10] Wrobel P, Czyzycki M, Furman L, Kolasinski K, Lankosz M, Mrenca A, Samek L, Wegrzynek D. LabVIEW control software for scanning micro-beam X-ray fluorescence spectrometer. Talanta. 2012;93:186-192. DOI: 10.1016/j.talanta.2012.02.010

[11] Osawa T, Kobayashi M, Konno T, Egashira M, Okazaki R, Miura YN, Nagao K. Temperature control system for laser heating: Application for minute asteroidal materials. Measurement. 2014;50:229-235. DOI: 10.1016/j.measurement.2013.12.044

[12] Miura T., Matsue H, Kuroiwa T, Chiba K. Precise determination of Cr and Co in certified reference material of silicon nitride by neutron activation analysis using internal standardization. Analytical Sciences. 2009;25:881-885. DOI: 10.2116/analsci.25.881

[13] Shozygawa K, Nogawa N, Matsuo M. Deposition of fission and activation products after the Fukushima Dai-ichi nuclear power plant accident. Environmental Pollution. 2012;163:243-247. DOI: 10.1016/j.envpol.2012.01.001

[14] Hasegawa S, Wakamatsu S, Ohara T, Itano Y, Saitoh K, Hayasaki M, Kobayashi S. Vertical profiles of ultrafine to supermicron particles measured by aircraft over Osaka metropolitan area in Japan. Atmospheric Environment. 2007;41(4):717-729. DOI : 10.1016/j.atmosenv.2006.09.031

[15] Mizuno K, Konishi T, Oikawa M, Iso H, Ishikawa T, Imaseki H, Uesaka M. Uptake of CDDP-containing polymeric micelles by cells using particle induced X-ray emission. Journal of Radiation Research. 2011;52(2):193-198. DOI: 10.1269/jrr.10074

[16] Kurada S, Bradley C. A review of machine vision sensors for tool condition monitoring. Computers in Industry. 1997;34(1):55-72. DOI: 10.1016/S0166-3615(96)00075-9

[17] Chen YR, Chao K, Kim MS. Machine vision technology for agricultural applications. Computers and Electronics in Agriculture. 2002;36(2-3):173-191. DOI: 10.1016/S0168-1699(02)00100-X

[18] Cubero S, Aleixos N, Moltó E, Gómez-Sanchis J, Blasco J. Advances in machine vision applications for automatic inspection and quality evaluation of fruits and vegetables. Food and Bioprocess Technology. 2011;4(4):487-504.

[19] Aldrich C, Marais C, Shean BJ, Cilliers JJ. Online monitoring and control of froth flotation systems with machine vision: A review. International Journal of Mineral Processing. 2010;96(1-4):1-13. DOI: 10.1016/j.minpro.2010.04.005

[20] Sun TH, Tseng CC, Chen MS. Electric contacts inspection using machine vision. Image and Vision Computing. 2010;28(6):890-901. DOI: 10.1016/j.imavis.2009.11.006

[21] Li D, Yang W, Wang S. Classification of foreign fibers in cotton lint using machine vision and multi-class support vector machine. Computers and Electronics in Agriculture. 2010;74(2):274-279. DOI: 10.1016/j.compag.2010.09.002

Chapter 8

Fuzzy PD Controller in NAO System's Platform

Edgar Omar López-Caudana and
César Daniel González Gutiérrez

Additional information is available at the end of the chapter

http://dx.doi.org/10.5772/63979

Abstract

Humanoid robotic platforms rarely achieve the desire trajectory because of the deviation generated during the robot walking. This problem is due to different circumstances such as robot manufacturing, wear and tear of mechanic parts, or variations of floor flatness. Currently, one of the humanoid robots on the market is the robotic platform developed by Aldebaran Robotics called NAO robot, and it is used for different purposes where the robot needs to navigate into controlled spaces. NAO presents the issue of deviation during walking; therefore, a Fuzzy PD Controller is developed and implemented for this platform to reduce the orientation error and to ensure reliability during navigation. Inertial sensors are used to get the orientation reference and for feedback of the closed-loop control. Consequently, a robust control was implemented and tested in different conditions of floor and velocity during the robot's navigation such as robot races and maze resolution. Experimental results show that fuzzy controller achieves significant improvements in the trajectories of NAO.

Keywords: NAO, Fuzzy Controller, Biped walking, trajectory, robot

1. Introduction

Currently, robotics is an area with many challenges such as stabilization, communications, manipulation, path planning, vision, and so on. The challenge becomes even more problematic when robots are designed for being autonomous with the task of interacting with the world independent of the environment. Humanoid robots are one of the different structures that exist, and it is a bio-inspired development. The idea of designing artificial intelligence entities is almost as old as humanity [1], and its origins focus on the creations of robots with human capabilities. Al-Jazari designed a humanoid structure as he wrote in the text "The Science of Ingenious

Mechanisms" in the thirteenth century [2]. In 1495, Leonardo da Vinci designed and built a mechanical structure that looks like an armored knight, and his work was inspired in the researches and achievements reached by the Greek culture [3].

Due to the advances in digital computation in the second half of the twentieth century, researches had the opportunity to introduce significant computation into robots for sensing, control, and actuation. The achievements were developed around 1970 by Kato and Vukobratovic researches [1] after the revolutionary advances in technologies in the field of legged robots. Then, the first robot that integrates capabilities of sensing, locomotion, and manipulation was WABOT-1, developed by Ichiro Kato et al. at Waseda University of Japan [4]. After that, the research group of Ichiro Kato developed WABOT-2, a robot which could read notes and play piano. In 1986, Honda began a research group about humanoid robotics, and in 1996, Honda introduced robot P2 which was followed by P3 in 1997 and by Asimo in 2002 [3]. In the world, many universities and research centers keep developing different humanoid robots. Aldebaran Robotics are working with NAO, Romeo, and Pepper robots, ASIMO is developed by Honda, MIT is working on Atlas and NASA's Valkyrie, QRIO by Sony, and HRP by Kawada [1].

Unlike industrial robots that operate in fixed environments, humanoid robots must operate under various and changeable environmental conditions and complete a wide range of tasks, with the characteristic of being autonomous [5]. The previous conditions stand different issues to solve such as locomotion, manipulation, artificial vision, cognition, and communication. Bipedal walking is one of the research issues in humanoid robots because it allows robots to interact and to move through the environment in which they are involved. Currently, one of the most used control methods to solve this problem is the zero-moment point (ZMP) and it sits within the support polygon of the robot's foot to ensure that the foot remains planted on the ground, assuming that friction is high enough to avoid slipping [1]. This algorithm was proposed by Vukobratovic and Stepanenko in 1972 [1]. Reaction mass pendulum (RMP) is a multibody inverted pendulum model, and it is inspired in human walking model [6].

The two previous algorithms are used to achieve bipedal walking; however, they need more algorithm layers to complete the full control of the robot for following trajectories. The most common algorithms are modulated playback, mathematical synthesis, passive dynamic walking, and physics-based heuristics [7]. Kastsian et al. [8] maximize the speed of a compass-like biped robot for a passive dynamic walking through applying the normal vector method. Yilmaz et al. in [9] used a natural ZMP reference trajectory and Fourier series approximation-based method which was proposed for a straight walk for the robot SURALP. Kurazume et al. [10] use a method for generating a straight-legged walking pattern for a biped robot using up-and-down motion of an upper body.

NAO is a robot developed by Aldebaran Robotics, and its locomotion is based on a dynamic model of the linear inverse pendulum inspired by work of Kajita and Tani [11] and is solved using quadratic programming [12]. The developed locomotion allows users for controlling the displacement of the robot in x, y, and z according to its body or global frame. One can generate motions through assigning values to lineal velocities or defining position targets. However, the robot is incapable of achieving with precision those targets, and it always has deviations on its trajectory. Aldebaran proposed a method called *ALVisualCompass* to correct this problem based on artificial vision. Nevertheless, it consumes a lot of computational resources and the algorithm is dependent of the fact that at least part of the reference image is visible while the compass is running. This robot has different sensors such an accelerometer and a gyroscope which can be used to solve this issue. In this chapter, a PD fuzzy controller is proposed to eliminate this problem using inertial sensors and the implemented locomotion infrastructure in the platform.

2. Fuzzy PD controller

2.1. Mamdani Fuzzy Inference System

In 1965, Lotfi Asker Zadeh proposed the bases of a new logic system in his paper *Fuzzy Sets* [13]. Fuzzy logic was created to emulate the human logic and take decisions despite of the inaccurate received information from the environment. It is a system based on linguistic variables depicted by experts; for example, when humans describe the temperature of a day, they used words such as "hot," "cold," "too hot," and so on. In 1975, Ebrahim Mamdani et al. used the fundaments of fuzzy logic to create fuzzy logic controller for a steam engine and boiler combination in his paper "An experiment in linguistic synthesis with a fuzzy logic controller" [14]. Mamdani Fuzzy Inference System has three stages: fuzzification, inference system, and defuzzification.

Fuzzification process consists in mapping a crisp value into the membership functions along the discursive universe to get a fuzzy value [15]. **Figure 1** depicts the whole process, where the line is the crisp value (input to the system), and it is evaluated in the membership function. The value of that function is called a fuzzy value.

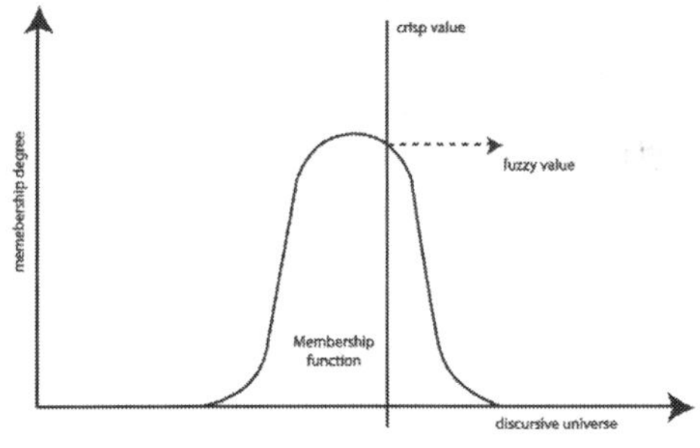

Figure 1. Fuzzification process.

The inference system performs the reasoning mechanism based on the rule if-then. This step has three components: a rule base, which contains the fuzzy rules of the system; a database, which contains all the membership functions of each input and output [15], and the last component is the reasoning component that executes the inference system. The next expression depicts the reasoning mechanism:

If x is A, then y is B

Some examples are "If pressure is high, then volume is small" and "If a tomato is red, then it is ripe."

Finally, defuzzification consists in extract a crisp value from the output fuzzy sets. In general, there are five methods for defuzzification: centroid of area, bisector of area, mean of maximum, smallest of maximum, and largest of maximum [15]. **Figure 2** depicts the complete Mamdani Fuzzy Inference System.

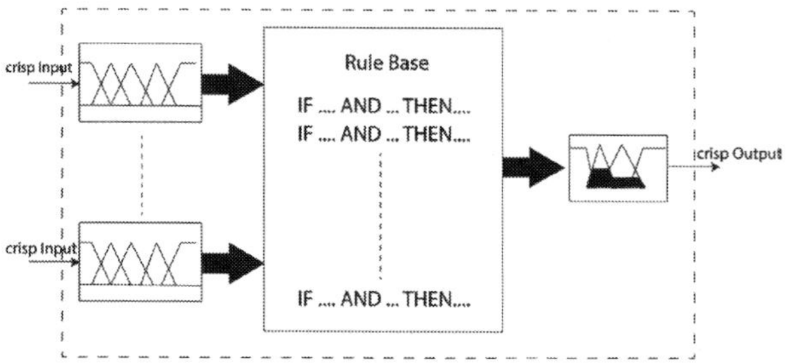

Figure 2. Mamdani Fuzzy Inference System.

2.2. Fuzzy PD controller

A classical closed-loop control system is depicted in **Figure 3**. The reference is compared with the actual value of the system to get a difference. The error is the input to the implemented control system, which response is the input to the model of the plant. One of the most used controllers is the PD controller, and its equation is described as follows:

$$u(t) = K_p e(t) + K_d \dot{e}(t)$$

where $e(t) = r(t) - y(y)$

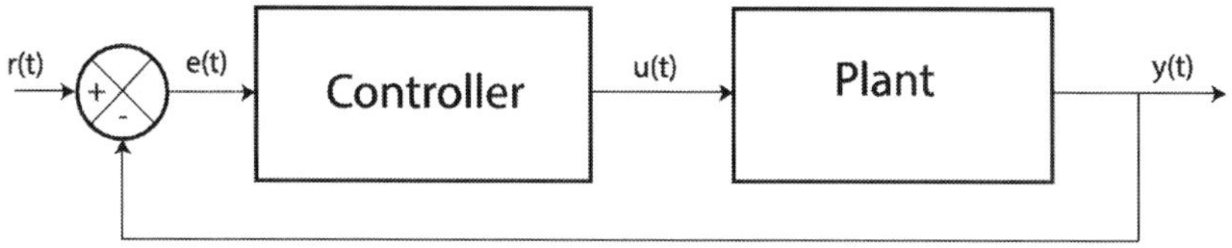

Figure 3. Basic control system.

In **Figure 4**, a step response with the desired value is shown. The different pointed marks are conditions that can be described with linguistic variables. For example, the pointed dots in

Figure 4 can be described as "A value with positive error and negative derivative of error for dot 1," "A value with negative error and zero derivative of error for dot 3," "A value with zero error and zero derivative of error for dot 7," and so on. For each condition, the controller varies its output and can be described as "positive," "negative," "zero," and so on.

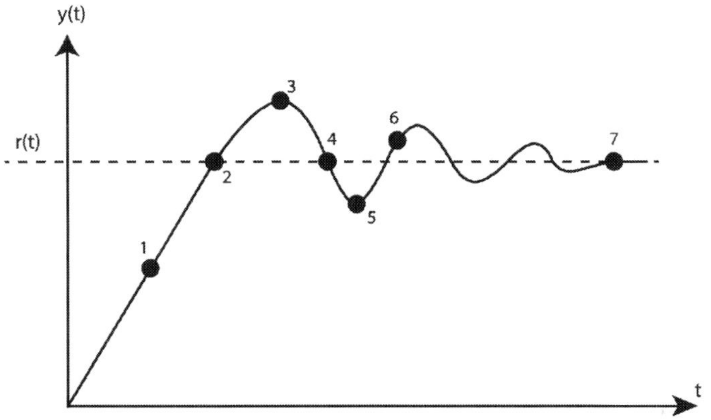

Figure 4. Step response.

For the above-mentioned examples, a fuzzy PD controller can be implemented with two inputs (error and derivative of the error), where each input must have n-membership functions that represent the linguistic variables. **Figure 5** depicts the final design of a fuzzy PD control system.

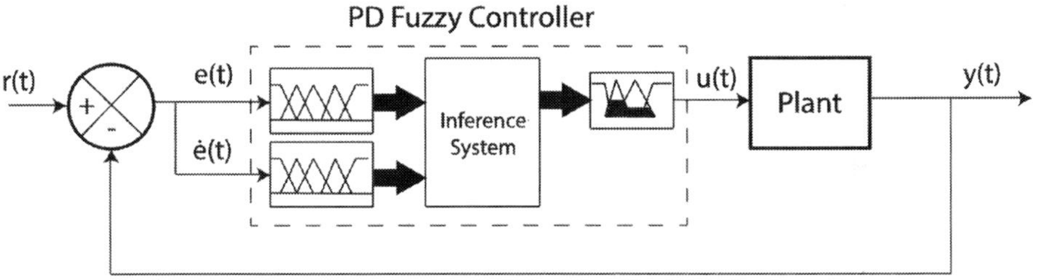

Figure 5. Fuzzy PD control system.

2.3. Robot environment

Bipedal walking robots have different challenges depending on the environment in which they are enrolled. The kind of soil in which robots walk affects directly in the dynamics of the robot due to the friction forces that are generated during motions. If the soil coefficient friction is enough high, the robot could not walk and also will demand high consumption in motors; on the other hand, if the biped robot walk over soil with low coefficient friction, it could slide and fall down. Also, when the soil presents impurities such as small rocks, fissures, mud and so on, the robot stabilization can be affected and also its trajectory. Another issue is the mechanical deterioration, the engines of the motors that allow to move robot articulations will present a wear depending on the manufacturing material, and then, the mathematical model of the robot will be affected. In addition, there could be external forces that may change or eliminated bipedal walking.

NAO is a humanoid robot created in 2006 by Aldebaran Robotics in France. This robot has 25 degrees of freedom (DOF) and has a height of 58 cm. It also contains inertial sensors such as accelerometer and gyroscope, ultrasonic sensors, capacitive touch sensor, bumpers, infrared sensors, and cameras. This robot is used for competitions, presentations, teaching, social assistant, and exhibitions. **Figure 6** shows the NAO robot structure.

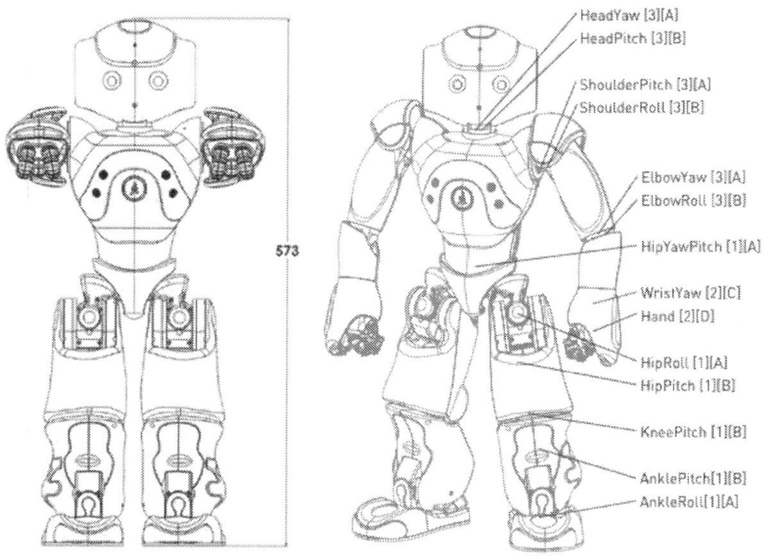

Figure 6. NAO robot and locations engine (pictures taken from *Aldebaran Robotic: NAO Documentation*).

According Aldebaran, NAO System presents nest characteristics:

- 25 Degrees of Freedom (Degrees of Freedom)
- Stepped omnidirectional
- Two grasping hands
- ATOM Z530 CPU 1.6 GHz

- Flash Memory SDRAM 256 MB/2 GB
- Inertia sensor with two-axis gyroscope and 3-axis accelerometer.
- 1x RJ45 Ethernet port—10/100/1000 Base T and Wi-Fi IEEE 802.11b/g
- 2x video cameras (960p @ 30fps), better sensitivity in VGA. View—239° horizontal, vertical view of 68°. HD resolution.
- Object recognition
- Detection and Face Recognition

Text to Speech:

Two speakers and multilanguage voice synthesis (Spanish and English Preloaded)

Four microphones and voice recognition multilanguage (Spanish and English preloaded)

Supports multiple programming languages.

It has special programming and simulation software.

According to degrees of freedom of the Robot

Head: 2 DOF

Arms: 5 DOF

Pelvis: 1 DOF

Legs: 5 DOF

Hands: 1 DOF

Image Engine 2.27 Locations

Battery:

Type: Lithium-Ion

Voltage: 21.6/2.15 Ah

Maximum load voltage: 2 A

Charging time: 5 h

Battery life: 60 min (using principal)

90 min (normal use)

Mother board:

- Processor: Intel ATOM Z530
- Cache memory: 512 KB

- Clock speed: 1.6 GHz
- Ram memory: 1 GB
- Flash memory: 2 GB
- Wireless: IEEE 802.11b/g/n

Camera:

- Model: MT9M114
- Resolution: 1.22 MP
- Pixels: 1288 × 968
- Number of images: 30 images per second

Engines:

- Motor Type 1:
- Model: 22NT82212P
- No load speed: 8300 rpm ± 10%
- Load speed: mNm 68 ± 8%
- Continuous torque: 16.1 mNm max

Motor Type 2:

- Model: 17N88208E
- No load speed: 8400 rpm ± 12%
- Load speed: 9.4 mNm ± 8%
- Continuous Torque: 4.9 mNm max
- Motor Type 3:
- Model: 16GT83210E
- No-load speed: 10,700 rpm ± 10%
- Load speed: 14.3 mNm ± 8%
- Continuous torque: 6.2 mNm max

As mentioned before, robots present a wide range of issues depending on the environment. NAO robot also presents these problems. The robot includes different locomotion methods to control the robot based on a mathematical model of the inverse pendulum. One can set a target velocity on x-, y-, and z-axis or even in positions to follow a trajectory. However, the robot exposes often deviations of the generated trajectories.

Some work on NAO robots and motion analysis can be reviewed in [16], where a report on omnidirectional walk engine focused on use of robot soccer is done; or in [17], where some kind of control strategy which contains a controller using quantitative feedback theory is used to establish a control method. Both cases show different environments in order to get better movement control methods, but our proposal is made of a PD fuzzy controller. In [18], we can observe how a neural network or fuzzy logic techniques can be utilized to achieve basic behavioral functions necessary to mobile robotics system, as we show in next section in our proposal.

2.4. Proposed solution

NAO has two three-axis inertial sensors. Accelerometer provides measurements in range of ±2g, while gyroscope can measure angular velocities in range of ±500°/s. It is important to have reliable values to perform control techniques implementation and can obtain by using potentiality of accelerometer and gyroscope data. According to Higgins [19], a complementary filter can be used to acquire an accurate angle position. **Figure 7** shows the body framework, and it illustrates the way the robot can follow different trajectories applying lineal velocity on x-axis and adjusting the path by applying turns (z angular velocities) in z-axis [20].

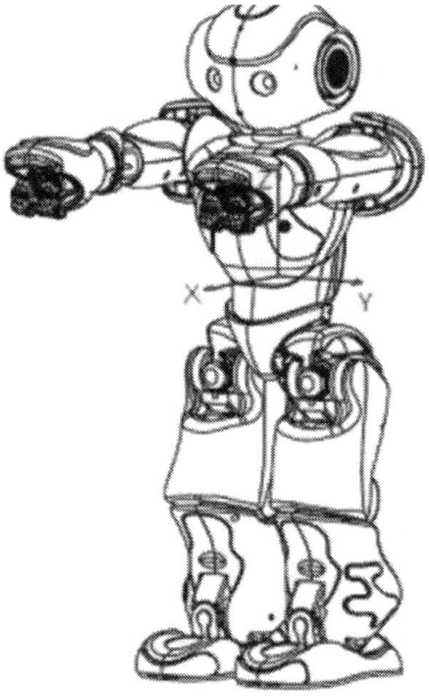

Figure 7. NAO robot body frame (picture taken from *Aldebaran Robotics: NAO Documentation*).

In this section, two controllers are proposed. The first proposed PD fuzzy controller was designed with the aim of following a given angle reference respect to z-axis. **Figure 8** shows the whole process to build a fuzzy PD controller. According to that, the first step requires to define the system type. Multiple input–single output is presented for this controller due to the error, derivative of the error, and the z angular velocity output. The next step consists in selecting the discursive universe for each input and output. Discursive universe is selected according to the characteristics of the variable and the expert. To achieve that, the expert must know the robot behavior. Therefore, NAO was configured to display the error and its derivative with respect an initial reference in console. After getting a set of values, error and derivate ranges were defined. The error range goes from –40° to 40° and the normalized derivate error

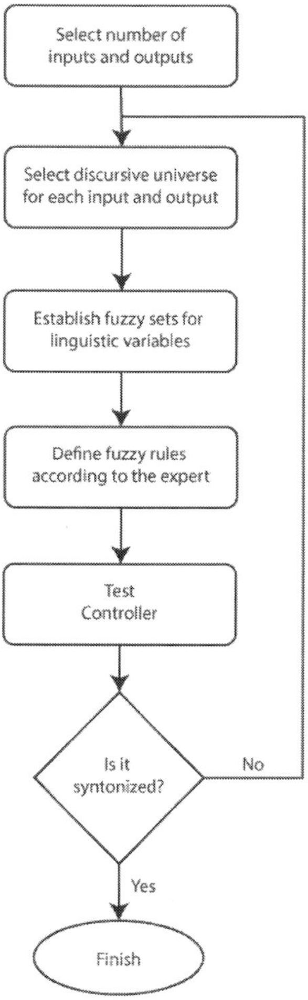

Figure 8. Flow chart for tuning Fuzzy Controller.

goes from -1 to 1. Similarly, the robot was programmed to make turns around its axis in a range of a normalized velocity. A first proposed discursive universe for the output was settled from -0.4 to 0.4.

Once the discursive universe is established, a number of fuzzy sets must be defined to describe linguistic variables. The error input (**Figure 9**) has five membership functions labeled as VERY NEGATIVE (VN), NEGATIVE (N), ZERO (Z), POSITIVE (P), and VERY POSITIVE (VP), and its discursive universe goes from -0.6981 to 0.6981 (in radians). Second input (derivative of the error (**Figure 10**)) is designed with three membership functions labeled as NEGATIVE (N), ZERO (Z), and POSITIVE (P), and the discursive universe was defined from -1 to 1 with the intention to be normalized. Finally, the output (**Figure 11**) has five membership functions labeled as VERY RIGHT (VR), RIGHT (R), ZERO (Z), LEFT (L), and VERY LEFT (VL) which describe the direction and magnitude of z velocity.

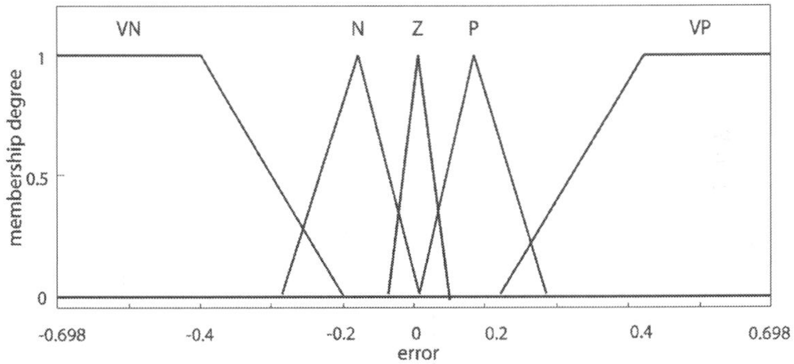

Figure 9. Membership functions of error input from controller 1.

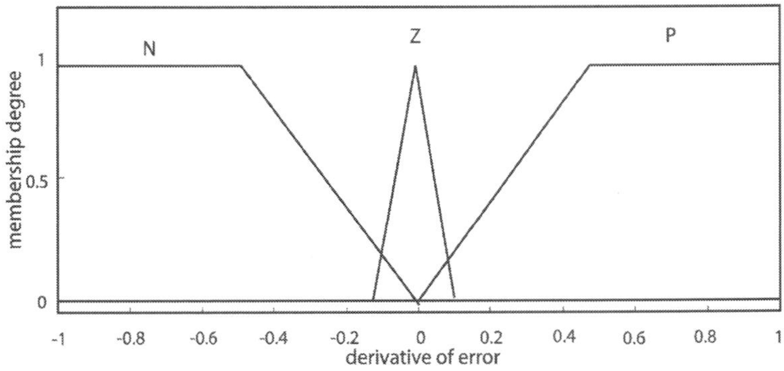

Figure 10. Membership functions of the derivative of error input from controller 1.

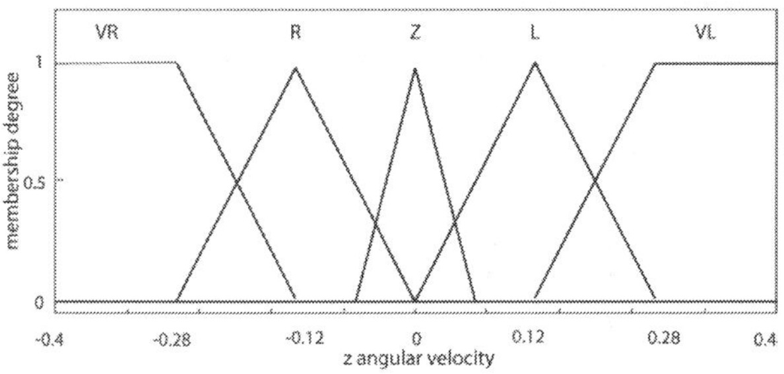

Figure 11. Membership functions of z angular velocity output.

Table 1 shows inference system that the PD fuzzy controller used, the first row encloses fuzzy sets of derivative of the error, and the first column contains the fuzzy sets of the error. The rest of the table spaces corresponds to the output decision.

$e\backslash\dot{e}$	**N**	**Z**	**P**
VN	VL	VL	VL
N	L	L	L
Z	R	Z	L
P	R	R	R
VP	VR	VR	VR

Table 1. Fuzzy rules for controller 1.

Figure 12 shows the response of the system when the PD controller is applied. The response presents oscillations around the desired value. Then, according to **Figure 8**, a change must be

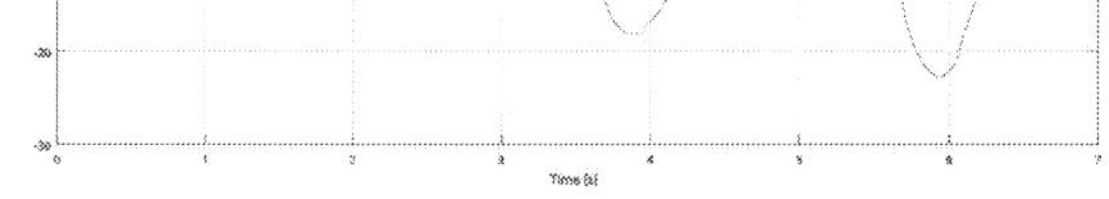

Figure 12. Output response of the first designed controller.

applied in membership functions, rules, or discursive universe. In agreement with the response, the evaluation of the inference system is correct, because when the current moves away from the reference, the controller tries to correct the error. However, the applied correction is more than necessary. For instance, the modification must be done in the output discursive universe or the output fuzzy sets.

After repeating the process, the final output for defuzzification is presented in **Figure 13**. As shown, the main change against **Figure 11** was the discursive universe. The output range was reduced to eliminate the oscillations in the response and the results are shown in Section 3.

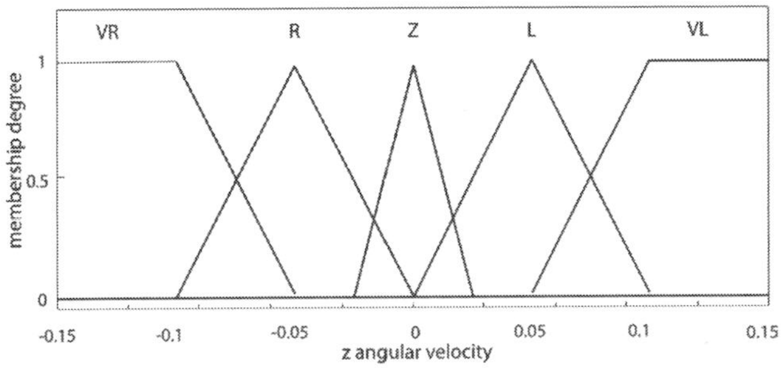

Figure 13. Membership functions of z angular velocity output for controller 1.

The second controller has the task to perform turns around its own z-axis; therefore, any force in x and y was applied. The structure and the design process of the PD fuzzy controller was the same as the first controller. The characteristics of the numbers of membership functions in each input and output and the inference system were preserved. The parameters that changed in this design was the discursive universe: the error input is established from $-\pi/2$ to $\pi/2$, the derivative of the error goes from -1 to 1, and the output goes from -0.3 to 0.3, as shown in **Figure 14**, to achieve bigger changes in reference and reduce the settled time.

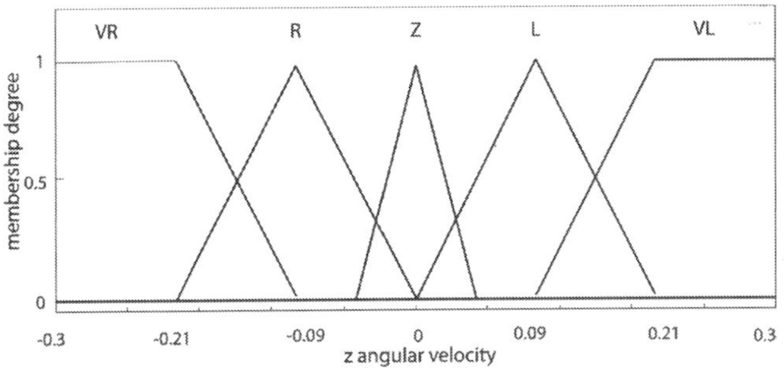

Figure 14. Membership functions of z angular velocity output for controller 2.

3. Analysis and results

Figures 15–17 depict the responses of the system in different situations. **Figure 15** shows the response when the robot makes a $\pi/2$ radians turns to the right. In this case, the robot just applies angular velocity around z-axis, while the x and y velocities stay in 0. The overshooting was of 4.09%, the settling period was achieved in 4.2 s, and the integral absolute error (IAE) was of 2.83. It is important to have a small overshooting because that is translated into less controller force and less oscillations. **Figure 16** depicts the reference of a given angle that NAO had to follow to keep a straight walking during 10 s. From that, one can analyze that without control the robot could go to its left because the effort that the controller was performed had a negative velocity in z, which is translated into turning to the right. In **Figure 17**, A straight walking is presented; the difference is that the operator changes manually the trajectory of the robot. As shown in the figure, the robot reacted and return to the given reference.

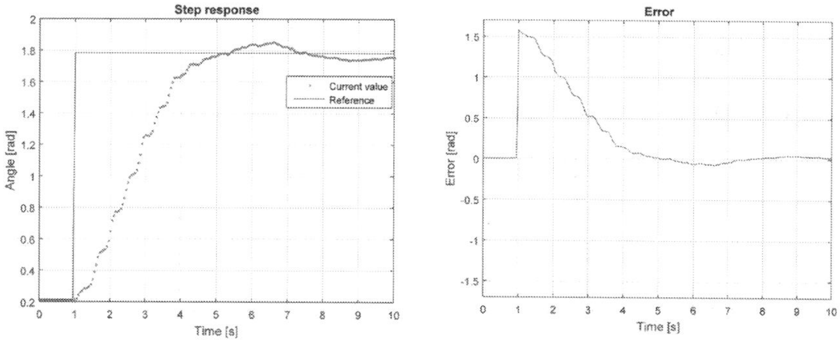

Figure 15. Step response of $\pi/2$ radians.

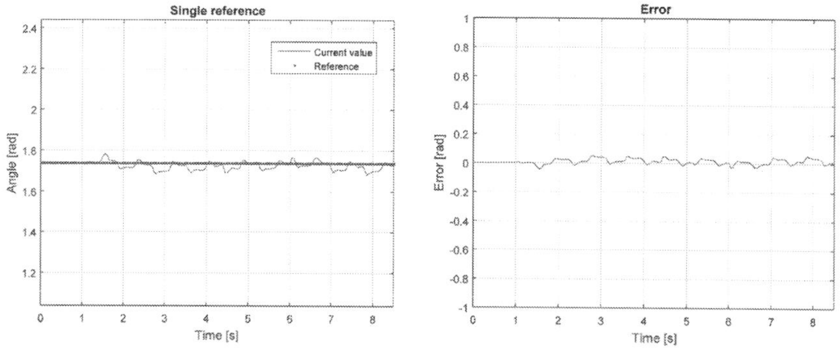

Figure 16. Following a single reference during biped walking.

http://dx.doi.org/10.5772/63979

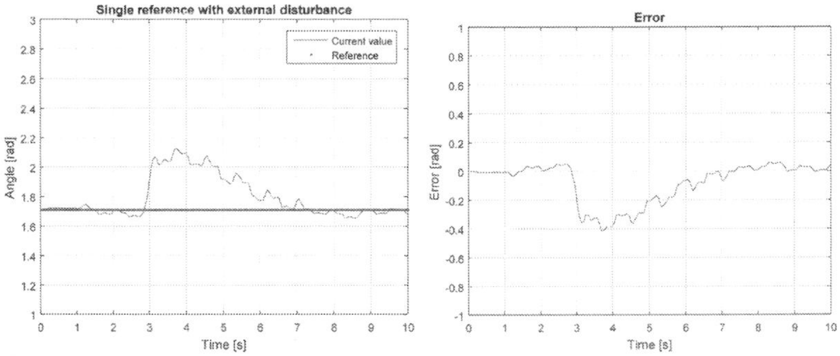

Figure 17. Disturbance response during biped walking.

Figure 18 shows the main problem of the robot during walking process. The deviation that the robot had with and without control is presented. According to the test, NAO was able to walk straight for 1.86 m and achieved the desired final position with controller 1. On the contrary, when the same target was established, taking out the control, the robot started to walk to the left and it had a displacement of 0.44 m to the left, which provoked that the robot got out from the black lines. The different deviations that the robot presents during each walking is unpredictable because it depends on the NAO's motors, the soil, and the mathematical model and that is the reason of applying a fuzzy PD controller to the plant. In Annex 1, the code is presented to build the fuzzy system controller.

The developed controller was used to take NAO to the Robotics and Artificial Intelligence National Contest 2015. In this challenge, there were different categories where the robots can

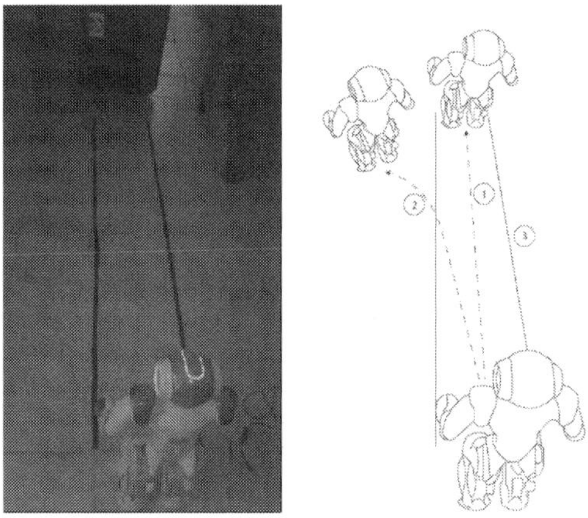

Figure 18. Comparison of biped walking with and without control.

participate. The two chosen categories were Individual Race and Resolution Maze. Individual Race consisted in walking a distance without leaving the track in the shortest time. The rules for this category are the following:

1. The robot must have an activation signal.
2. The robot must start moving within 10 s after the referee gives the whistle.
3. If the robot leaves the track, it has 3 s to return.
4. When the robot finishes the competition, the participant must deactivate it until the referee gives the signal.

In Resolution Maze, NAO had to find the exit of a given maze in which the robot was introduced. The rules for these categories are presented:

1. The robot must have an activation signal.
2. The robot must start moving within 10 s after the referee gives the whistle.
3. If the robot leaves the maze by the start entry, the robot is disqualified.
4. The robot must say the correct Naomark number when NAO finds one to accumulate points.
5. The robot has 7 min to accomplish the maze. If not, the largest displacement is registered.
6. When the robot finishes the competition, the participant must deactivate it until the referee gives the signal.

Performing straight walking and fast turns are considerations to accomplish the challenges. Therefore, the controller was tested for this contest and it allowed NAO to perform the competition. The pseudo-code for accomplish the Individual Race is the following:

Individual R ace pseudo-code

1. Touch NAO head to start routine
2. Read Z angle from IMU sensors to set the reference
3. Start walking by applying 0.8 x velocity, 0 y velocity and 0 z velocity
4. While (touch Head is FALSE)

    Get error and its derivative

    Evaluate fuzzy PD controller

    Update z velocity

5. Enter in rest mode

---

http://dx.doi.org/10.5772/63979

The pseudo-code for accomplish the Resolution Maze is the following:

Resolution Maze pseudo-code

1. Touch NAO head to start routine

2. Read Z angle from IMU sensors to set the reference

3. Thread 1:

    While (touch Head is FALSE)

    While (distance <0.35 m)

    Walk applying 0.8 x velocity

    Get error and its derivative

    Evaluate fuzzy PD controller

    Update z velocity

    While (wall in front = true)

    Calibrate reference

    If (turn right = FALSE)

    Turn right using PD fuzzy controller

    Else

    Turn left using PD fuzzy controller

4. Thread 2:

    While (touch Head is FALSE)

    If (Naomark detected = TRUE)

    Activate speech: "#number Naomark founded"

5. Enter rest mode

Figures 19–21 are evidence of NAO participation at the contest.

Figure 19. Individual race competition.

Figure 20. Maze resolution.

Figure 21. Testing the control algorithm.

4. Conclusion

The presented control approach validates that a PD fuzzy controller is enough to allow the robot following different references without having its mathematical model. Tests were executed in different environmental conditions, changing principally the soil and walking velocity that caused the robot to present different noise magnitudes during the sensor reading process. Despite that, the robot was able to achieve the trajectory, allowing to conclude that the controller was robust. Moreover, when external disturbances were applied manually, the robot also concludes its tasks. The participation of the robot in Robotics and Artificial Intelligence National Contest 2015 supports the validation of the controller.

The NAO platform is good in terms of testing different robotics algorithms. The high-level programming allows users to implement different tasks because the platform is really complete. It has different sensors such as sonar sensors, bumpers, infrared sensors, cameras, Wi-fi connectivity, DMA processes, and so on. Moreover, there are three ways of programming: Choregraphe, Python, and C++. Also provides API that includes not only very high-level functions to perform complex task such a speech recognition, simple walking task, face recognition, and so on, but also one can develop its own high complex function using Python or C++ programming.

5. Annex

The following code is written in Python Language, and it contains classes to construct Fuzzy Systems and some membership functions.

```
class FuzzyTriang:
def __init__(self,pi,pm,pf):
self.pi = pi
self.pm = pm
self.pf = pf
def alpha(self,x):
if(x>=self.pi and x<self.pm):
return (1/(self.pm-self.pi))*(x-self.pi)
elif(x>=self.pm and x<=self.pf):
return -(1/(self.pf-self.pm))*(x-self.pf)
else:
return 0
def alphaCut(self,x):
```

```
cuts = list()
cuts.append([self.pi,0])
cuts.append([x/(1/(self.pm-self.pi))+self.pi,x])
cuts.append([x/(-(1/(self.pf-self.pm)))+self.pf,x])
cuts.append([self.pf,0])
return cuts
def getCenMax(self):
return self.pm
def getPI(self):
return self.pi
def getPM(self):
return self.pm
def getPF(self):
return self.pf
def getPuntos(self):
return [self.pi,self.pm,self.pf]
class FuzzyLinSh:
def __init__(self,p1,p2,ext,side):
self.p1 = p1
self.p2 = p2
self.ext = ext
self.side = side
def alpha(self,x):
if(self.side == "l"):
if x <= self.p1:
return 1
elif (x > self.p1 and x < self.p2):
return -(1/(self.p2-self.p1))*(x-self.p2)
else:
return 0
```

```
else:
if x <= self.p1:
return 0
elif (x > self.p1 and x < self.p2):
return (1/(self.p2-self.p1))*(x-self.p1)
else:
return 1
def alphaCut(self,x):
cuts = list()
if(self.side == "l"):
cuts.append([self.ext,0])
cuts.append([self.ext,x])
cuts.append([x/(-(1/(self.p2-self.p1)))+self.p2,x])
cuts.append([self.p2,0])
else:
cuts.append([self.p1,0])
cuts.append([x/(1/(self.p2-self.p1))+self.p1,x])
cuts.append([self.ext,x])
cuts.append([self.ext,0])
return cuts
def getCenMax(self):
if(self.side == "l"):
return (self.ext + self.p1)/2
else:
return (self.ext + self.p2)/2
def getP1(self):
return self.p1
def getP2(self):
return self.p2
def getPoints(self):
```

```
return [self.p1,self.p2]
class FuzzySystem:
def __init__(self, input1, input2, outputs, rules):
self.input1 = input1 # error
self.input2 = input2 # derivada
self.output = outputs
self.rules = rules
self.vn = 0
def evaluar(self, x, y):
alphas = []
auxreglas = [[0, 0, 0, 0, 1], [0, 0, 0, 0, 1], [0, 0, 0, 0, 1],
[0, 0, 0, 1, 0], [0, 0, 0, 1, 0], [0, 0, 1, 0, 0],
[0, 0, 0, 1, 0], [0, 0, 1, 0, 0], [0, 1, 0, 0, 0],
[0, 0, 1, 0, 0], [0, 1, 0, 0, 0], [0, 1, 0, 0, 0],
[1, 0, 0, 0, 0], [1, 0, 0, 0, 0], [1, 0, 0, 0, 0]]
nr = len(auxreglas) #inputs
nc = len(auxreglas[0]) #outputs
nr = len(auxreglas) # inputs
nc = len(auxreglas[0]) # outputs
nE = len(self.input1)
nD = len(self.input2)
alphase = list()
alphasd = list()
# Evaluacion del sistema
for i in range(0, nE):
alphase.append(self.input1[i].alpha(x))
for i in range(0, nD):
alphasd.append(self.input2[i].alpha(y))
alphasin = list()
for i in range(0, nE): # error
```

http://dx.doi.org/10.5772/63979

```
for j in range(0, nD): # derivative
if alphase[i] < alphasd[j]:
alphasin.append(alphase[i])
else:
alphasin.append(alphasd[j])
# Rules evaluation
for i in range(0, nr):
for j in range(0, nc):
auxreglas[i][j] = auxreglas[i][j] * alphasin[i]
# Find maximums
alphasF = []
centrosM = []
for i in range(0,nc):
aux = 0
for j in range(0,nr):
if(auxreglas[j][i] > aux):
aux = auxreglas[j][i]
alphasF.append(aux)
centrosM.append(self.output[i].getCenMax())
num = 0
den = 0
for i in range(0,nc):
num = num + alphasF[i]*centrosM[i]
den = den + alphasF[i]
if (den!=0):
res = num/den
self.vn = res
return self.vn
else:
return 0
```

Acknowledgements

The contributions of several students from Tecnologico de Monterrey, Mexico City Campus, are gratefully acknowledged, specially Kennet García Oviedo and Enrique Jiménez Vázquez. This work has been supported by School of Engineering and Sciences from Tecnologico de Monterrey.

Author details

Edgar Omar López-Caudana* and César Daniel González Gutiérrez

*Address all correspondence to: edlopez@itesm.mx

Tecnológico de Monterrey, Campus Ciudad de México, Ciudad de México, México

References

[1] B. Siciliano, O. Khatib (Eds.), *Springer handbook of robotics*. Berlin: Springer, 2008.

[2] M. E. Rosheim, *Robot evolution: the development of anthrobotics*. New York, NY: Wiley, 1994.

[3] S. Behnke, Humanoid Robots—From Fiction to Reality, *KI-Zeitschrift*, vol. 4, pp. 5–9, Dec. 2008.

[4] V. Bruce, A. W. Young, *In the eye of the beholder: the science of face perception*. Oxford, England; New York: Oxford University Press, 1998.

[5] B. Adams, C. Breazeal, R. A. Brooks, B. Scassellati, Humanoid robots: a new kind of tool, *IEEE Intell. Syst.*, 2000, 15(4):25–31.

[6] K. Sreenath, A. K. Sanyal, The reaction mass biped: equations of motion, hybrid model for walking and trajectory tracking control, 2015 IEEE International Conference on Robotics and Automation (ICRA), Seattle, WA, 26–30 May 2015, IEEE; 2015, pp. 5741–5746.

[7] Y. Bar-Cohen, C. L. Breazeal, *Biologically inspired intelligent robots*. Bellingham, WA, USA: SPIE Press, 2003.

[8] D. Kastsian, E. Oertel, M. Monnigmann, Optimal parameters for stable walking of a compass-like biped robot, 2014 IEEE Conference on Control Applications (CCA), 8–10 October 2014, Juan Les Antibes, IEEE; 2014, pp. 814–819.

[9] M. Yilmaz, U. Seven, K. C. Fidan, T. Akbas, K. Erbatur, Circular arc-shaped walking trajectory generation for bipedal humanoid robots, 2012 12th IEEE International

Workshop on Advanced Motion Control (AMC), Sarajevo, 25–27 March 2012, IEEE; 2012, pp. 1–8.

[10] R. Kurazume, S. Tanaka, M. Yamashita, T. Hasegawa, K. Yoneda, Straight legged walking of a biped robot, 2005 IEEE/RSJ International Conference on Intelligent Robots and Systems, 2–6 Aug. 2005, IEEE; 2005, pp. 337–343.

[11] S. Kajita, K. Tani, Experimental study of biped dynamic walking in the linear inverted pendulum mode, Proceedings of the 1995 IEEE International Conference on Robotics and Automation (volume: 3), Nagoya, 21–27 May 1995, IEEE; 1995, pp. 2885–2891.

[12] P. Wieber, Trajectory free linear model predictive control for stable walking in the presence of strong perturbations, IEEE-RAS International Conference on Humanoid Robots, Genova, Italy 2006, pp. 137–142.

[13] L. A. Zadeh, R. R. Yager, Fuzzy sets and applications: selected papers. New York: Wiley, 1987.

[14] E. H. Mamdani, S. Assilian, An experiment in linguistic synthesis with a fuzzy logic controller, *Int. J. Man-Mach. Stud.*, 1975, 7(1): 1–13.

[15] J.-S. R. Jang, C.-T. Sun, E. Mizutani, Neuro-fuzzy and soft computing: a computational approach to learning and machine intelligence. Upper Saddle River, NJ: Prentice Hall, 1997.

[16] Nima Shafii, Abbas Abdolmaleki, Nuno Lau and Luis Paulo Reis. Development of an omnidirectional walk engine for soccer humanoid robots. *Int. J. Adv. Robot Syst.*, 2015, 12:193. doi:10.5772/61314.

[17] S. Wen, J. Zhu, X. Li, A.B. Rad, X. Chen. End-point contact force control with quantitative feedback theory for mobile robots. *Int. J. Adv. Robot Syst.*, 2012, 9:236. doi: 10.5772/53742.

[18] E. Al Gallaf, Transputer Neuro-Fuzzy Controlled Behaviour-Based Mobile Robotics System, Mobile Robotics, Moving Intelligence, Jonas Buchli (Ed.), InTech, 2006. doi: 10.5772/4726. Available from: http://www.intechopen.com/books/mobile_robotics_moving_intelligence/transputer_neuro-fuzzy_controlled_behaviour-based_mobile_robotics_system.

[19] W. Higgins, A comparison of complementary and Kalman filtering, *IEEE Trans. Aerosp. Electron. Syst.*, May 1975, vol. AES-11(3):321–325.

[20] Aldebaran Robotics. NAO Documentation. Retrieved from http://doc.aldebaran.com/2-1/home_nao.html.